THE
SHAAR
PRESS

THE JUDAICA IMPRINT
FOR THOUGHTFUL PEOPLE

NOT

A
SHAAR
PRESS
PUBLICATION

JUST STORIES

The Chassidic Spirit
through its Classic Stories

RABBI ABRAHAM J. TWERSKI, M.D.

Published by **SHAAR PRESS**
Distributed by MESORAH PUBLICATIONS, LTD.
4401 Second Avenue / Brooklyn, N.Y 11232 / (718) 921-9000

Distributed in Israel by SIFRIATI / A. GITLER
10 Hashomer Street / Bnei Brak 51361

Distributed in Europe by J. LEHMANN HEBREW BOOKSELLERS
20 Cambridge Terrace / Gateshead, Tyne and Wear / England NE8 1RP

Distributed in Australia and New Zealand by GOLD'S BOOK & GIFT SHOP
36 William Street / Balaclava 3183, Vic., Australia

Distributed in South Africa by KOLLEL BOOKSHOP
22 Muller Street / Yeoville 2198, Johannesburg, South Africa

ISBN: 0-89906-386-1 Hard Cover
ISBN: 0-89906-387-X

Printed in the United States of America by Noble Book Press
Custom bound by Sefercraft, Inc. / 4401 Second Avenue / Brooklyn N.Y. 11232

Table of Contents

Introduction

The Torah is a Divine gift to the world, and therefore prior to reading the Torah we recite a blessing of gratitude, that G-d has given us the Torah. This is then followed by a second blessing, "That He has implanted within us an eternal life." The written Torah as well as the Talmud, the Oral Law, is comprised of two parts: instructions on specific *mitzvos* (commandments) that we are to do and on those acts which are forbidden, and narrations of the lives of our ancestors. We are to study the latter and derive lessons on living, to emulate the patriarchs and the *tzaddikim* (righteous individuals) of Scripture. Similarly, we are to study the lives of the *tzaddikim* who composed the Talmud.

Rabbi Chaim Shmulevitz points out that all this notwithstanding, we are to learn primarily by emulating the *tzaddikim* closest to our own time (*Sichos Mussar* 5732:10). The chronological gap between ourselves and the patriarchs, the prophets, and the compilers of the Talmud is so vast that we may consider their spiritual achievements totally beyond our grasp, and give up without even trying. It is therefore important that we take as our models the *tzaddikim* who lived closer to our own time, some of whom were personally known to our grandparents and great-grandparents.

In 1927 my father visited Canada, and a man of 86, who hailed from my father's *shtetl* (village), asked him to please visit his father. Surprised, my father asked, "Your father?" "Yes," the man said, "my father is in the home for the aged. He is really 114, but he denies this, and claims he is only 112."

My father visited the aged man who told him that he had seen the great chassidic master, the *Maggid* of Chernobel, who died in 1836. There was a span of six generations between the *Maggid* of Chernobel and my father, and here was a person whose life bridged this enormous gulf, back to the time of a *tzaddik* who was a contemporary of the disciples of the Baal Shem Tov. Such a link brings these great Torah personalities out of the realm of legend and makes them real — real enough for us to touch.

We are fortunate in having many accounts of the lives of our great *tzadikkim* of the past several generations. There are, of course, countless tales of their wondrous achievements, of their blessings being fulfilled, of miraculous healing of the sick, of children born to parents who had been hopelessly barren, and of rescues from perilous dangers. But while such miraculous occurrences testify to the great virtues of these *tzadikkim,* they do not serve as lessons for us. The latter are contained in the accounts of their *middos,* their character traits, those that they toiled to develop, because it is these that we must emulate. We may never achieve the capacity to perform miraculous deeds, but we all have the capacity to become more spiritual and to refine our character traits.

The Torah relates how Eliezer, the servant of the patriarch Abraham, journeyed to choose a wife for Yitzchak (*Genesis*

24:1-52). Eliezer said that the maiden who would offer to fetch water for him and for his camels would be the appropriate wife for Yitzchak. When Rivkah came to the well, Eliezer noted that the water of the well rose miraculously for her, and he then waited to see if she would offer to fetch water for him and his camels.

Rabbi Chaskel of Kuzmir asked: Why was any further test necessary? Was it not enough of a Divine sign for Eliezer that the water rose miraculously, which indicated that Rivkah was the designated wife for Yitzchak? Rabbi Chaskel answers, "*One good deed is worth a thousand miracles.*" Eliezer was not impressed by miracles. He wanted to see *character.*

I have therefore chosen, from among the many accounts of our *tzaddikim,* those episodes from which we can learn, and apply their teachings to our own lives. Thus, while these are beautiful stories, they are not just stories, but lessons.

It is customary when speaking of great *tzaddikim* to say, "May their merits protect us." We can implement this blessing by learning from their lives, and in this way, their merits will indeed both protect and elevate us.

NOT JUST STORIES

To Feel for Others

R abbi Akiva said that the all-encompassing principle of Torah is "You shall love your neighbor as yourself" (*Jerusalem Talmud, Nedarim* 9:3). One of the masters of *mussar* (ethical teachings) said that a general principle is one that encompasses each detail, which is a derivative of the general principle. Therefore, he reasons, since loving another as oneself is the general principle of Torah, all the 613 *mitzvos* must be considered derivatives of this principle. If so, then observing the Shabbos, eating matzah on Pesach, wearing *tefillin,* avoiding prohibited foods, taking the four species on Succos, and all other *mitzvos* must somehow be related to this general principle. If eating matzah on Pesach or taking the four species on Succos does not contribute to and enhance loving one's neighbor, the *mitzvah* is incomplete!

Chassidism places great emphasis on *ahavas Yisrael,* loving one's fellow. The Baal Shem Tov said that there are two parallel *mitzvos*: (1) to love G-d, and (2) to love one's neighbor. Since G-d is an abstraction and is not perceived by the senses, it may be difficult to generate love for Him. The way to achieve this, said the Baal Shem Tov, is to love people, because this will lead to love for G-d.

My great-grandfather, the Rabbi of Hornosteipel, once said, "If any of my *chassidim* experiences pain, even in the tip of his little finger, I feel that pain myself." To truly love another person means to so empathize and identify with him that one feels his suffering.

True love precludes offending or hurting someone. Parents who love their children suffer distress when they must implement discipline that hurts their children. With the exception of the need to discipline, one who loves another person will avoid doing anything that might cause discomfort to the beloved person. To the contrary, one will go out of one's way to show respect and affection for that person and prevent any distress from occurring to him.

The Rabbi of Rozadov had a dedicated chassid who was childless, and who frequently importuned the Rabbi for a berachah (blessing) that he have a child. The Rabbi often blessed him, but the blessing did not materialize.

One time the Rabbi's brother, the Rabbi of Zhikov, a chassidic master in his own right, visited Rozadov, and the chassid unburdened himself to him, stating that nothing in his life was fulfilling since he was childless. The Rabbi of Zhikov said, "If you will come to Zhikov and spend Rosh Hashanah (New Year) with me, I promise you that you will have a child." The chassid then related this conversation to *the Rabbi of Rozadov who said, "If my brother assured you that you will be blessed with a child, you can be confident that this will come true. By all means, do as he says, and go to Zhikov for Rosh Hashanah."*

On Rosh Hashanah, the Rabbi of Rozadov noted that the chassid was in shul (synagogue). "What are you doing here?" he asked. "You were supposed to be with my brother in Zhikov."

"I know," the chassid said, "but I got to thinking that everyone knows that over the years you have been giving me a berachah for a child, but that berachah was not fulfilled. If I had gone to your brother for Rosh Hashanah and then did have a child, what would people say? 'The Rabbi of Zhikov is a greater tzaddik than the Rabbi of Rozadov, because his blessings are more potent.' That might cause you to feel slighted. Just because I have a desire to have a child is no reason to cause you any distress."

The Rabbi of Rozadov was deeply moved and said, "Well, in that case, I will promise you a child this year," and indeed that year a son was born to him.

The Rabbi of Rozadov said, "Do not think that I am a miracle worker and that my berachah brought him a child. When a person is so concerned about another person's feelings that he is willing to give up an assurance of having a child, something which is his greatest desire in life, certainly that mitzvah merits his being amply rewarded. This chassid earned the blessing of a child because of his deep concern that I might have been slighted, and it was his merits and not mine that brought him this reward."

We see this principle in the *Midrash*, which states that Moses was reluctant to accept the Divine mission to liberate the Israelites from Egypt because his older brother Aaron might feel offended that he was passed over. Imagine! The entire Jewish nation was in need of redemption, but Moses was concerned lest his assumption of the leadership could cause someone to feel slighted, and it was not until G-d assured Moses that Aaron would not feel hurt that Moses undertook the assignment (*Exodus* 4:14).

Once the Gaon of Vilna was sitting in the succah engrossed in his study of Torah when a man walked in to greet him on the festival. The Gaon was so absorbed in his study that he was unaware of the man's presence. After waiting some time and still not being acknowledged, the man left, and on a subsequent occasion asked the Gaon what he had done that caused the Gaon to ignore him.

The Gaon was deeply affected, because he had inadvertently caused a person to feel slighted. "Ignore you? My dear friend, why would I wish to ignore you?", said the Gaon. He apologized profusely, explaining that he had not been aware of his presence because of his preoccupation with his study. He tried to compensate for this dereliction. "Please forgive me," the Gaon said, "And let me bless you to live 100 years."

The man did indeed live to be 100. When he was 98, he fell ill but refused the services of a doctor. "I know I will recover," he said, "because the Gaon promised me 100 years, and I know I shall not fall short by even a single day." He died on his 100th birthday.

Sensitivity to avoid offending someone was exemplified by the Rabbi of Vizhnitz, who visited a town where his chassidim complained that the shochet (ritual slaughterer), who was growing old, refused to relinquish his job, and that perhaps the Rabbi could impress him that it was time to retire.

The Rabbi called the shochet and invited him to eat with him. He had a bottle of wine placed on the table, and after the meal the Rabbi said, "It is my custom that if there happens to be wine on the table, we say the Grace After Meals over a cup of wine." He then poured a full cup of wine and placed it in the shochet's hand, and as his hand was tremulous, the cup shook visibly. After finishing the prayer, the shochet said, "My hand is obviously shaking. I guess it is time for me to retire from being a shochet." The mission was accomplished, and the man's dignity was preserved.

We must maintain a state of alertness and develop sensitivity to other's feelings.

A Joyous Farewell

The *mitzvah* of bringing joy and happiness to a *chas-san* and *kallah* (groom and bride) is one which has few counterparts in Judaism. The Talmud is unusually lavish with praise and with rewards for those who enhance the joy of newlyweds, and is unusually harsh and critical of those who fail to do so (*Berachos* 6b). Why is this so great a *mitzvah*? Perhaps because the stresses in life that the couple are likely to encounter are so great that we should at least give them a most positive beginning. Let them have a reference point of supreme joy when they first bond together, and perhaps that can mitigate the various distresses that are likely to be encountered in the years ahead.

The Kabbalists add another dimension to this *mitzvah*. Inasmuch as the relationship between G-d and Israel is considered much like that of a husband and wife, we wish to stress the joy in this spiritual union. Every day as we recite the *Shema* prayer, declaring our faith in and loyalty to G-d, we are, as it were, renewing our marriage vows with G-d. And yes, as a devoted "husband" to Israel, He is to support us and protect us, as is incumbent upon every husband.

The Talmud tells us how the great sages would bring cheer to a new couple. Hillel would sing the praises of the bride, how charming and beautiful she was, to endear her to her husband (*Kesubos* 17a). Rav Shmuel would dance before the couple while juggling myrtle branches, and the Talmud states that when he died, a heavenly flame in the shape of a myrtle branch surrounded his bier (ibid.).

Many of the chassidic masters excelled in this *mitzvah*. In those instances where the bride and groom were poor, they would collect money to give them the resources to establish their home, and they would actively participate in the wedding preparations and festivities. If the young couple were orphaned, the chassidic masters led the community in preparing for the wedding as though it were their own children who were being married.

But even among this distinguished group there are those who are outstanding. Rabbi Moshe Leib of Sassov was the paragon of these, the greatest among the great. Rabbi Moshe Leib was widely known for his incomparable *ahavas Yisrael,* love of his fellow Jews. Although everyone is familiar with the classic story of Rabbi Moshe Leib, it is nevertheless worthwhile repeating.

D*uring the days prior to Rosh Hashanah and Yom Kippur, when Jews congregate in the predawn hours for special prayers of forgiveness, Rabbi Moshe Leib was noticeably absent. Some skeptics in the community taunted* the chassidim that their Rabbi was a late riser. The chassidim countered, "The reason the Rabbi is not at early services is because each morning he ascends to heaven," a remark which elicited ridicule from the skeptics.

One skeptic, quite sure that the Rabbi did not ascend to heaven, nevertheless found it difficult to believe that the Rabbi just slept late. It was out of character for him. He decided to satisfy his curiosity and find out for himself the reason the Rabbi did not attend early services. He therefore woke up very early one day, and in the darkness of the predawn went to spy on the Rabbi.

Peeping through the window, he saw the Rabbi don the clothes of a woodsman, take a huge ax, and set off for the woods near the village. Now his curiosity was truly aroused, and he followed the Rabbi into the woods, and watched him chop branches and tie them into bundles. With the bundles of wood on his back, the Rabbi made his way to the outskirts of town, the "spy" trailing behind.

The Rabbi knocked on the door of a little hut. "Come in," a voice said. As the door opened, the "spy" could see an elderly, frail woman lying in bed, in a house that was essentially bare. "I have brought you wood for the fire," the Rabbi said.

"I wish I could buy your wood," the woman said, "but I have no money."

"Never mind that," the Rabbi said. "I trust you. If you can't pay me now, you will pay me in the future."

"But what good is the wood to me?" the woman asked. "I am so weak that I cannot get out of bed to make a fire."

"No problem," the Rabbi said. "I can easily do that," and proceeded to kindle the flame. Standing at the window, the "spy" heard the Rabbi recite the special prayers of forgiveness as he added wood to the fire. When the blaze was strong and healthy, the Rabbi opened the bag he had brought, saying, "Here is some milk and eggs for you, and some bread and cookies my wife baked," setting the food at the bedside. The Rabbi then left the hut, returned home, changed his clothes, and went to shul, by which time the congregation had already completed the special prayers.

Later that day the skeptic met several chassidim and said, "I told you that you were mistaken when you said that your Rabbi ascends to heaven each morning. That is not true. He ascends much higher."

Rabbi Moshe Leib would say, "How fortunate are the poor who must trust in G-d. It is the rich who are to be pitied, because they think their security is in their wealth." He would also say, "*Simchah* (joy) is far superior to tears." The Talmud states that even when all the gates to heaven are closed, the gates of tears are never shut (*Berachos* 32b). Joy is more powerful than tears, because whereas tears require an open gate, joy can penetrate even the thickest gates.

There was one wedding at which Rabbi Moshe Leib was unusually ecstatic. This was the wedding of a bride and groom who had both been orphaned as children, and Rabbi Moshe Leib had been like a devoted father to the two of them. He had arranged the shidduch, and had traveled from village to village to raise money for the young couple, both for the wedding and to set up their home. The klezmer (band) at the wedding played lively tunes, and Rabbi Moshe Leib danced before the chassan and kallah as never before. At one point Rabbi Moshe Leib exclaimed, "How lovely a melody! I wish that when they lead me to my eternal resting place, I could be accompanied by this beautiful melody."

Many years passed, and on the fourth day of Shevat, 5567, a wedding party was traveling to Brody, bringing the local klezmer along with them. Approaching a fork in the road, the horses took the wrong path, and nothing the driver did could pull them back. In fact, they continued to pick up speed, and the wedding party was helplessly carried away from their destination. As they neared a cemetery, the horses slowed, and the party saw a huge crowd gathered for a funeral. On inquiring whose funeral this was, they were told that it was that of Rabbi Moshe Leib of Sassov.

Upon hearing the Rabbi's name, one of the klezmer, an older man said, "That name is familiar to me," and then he remembered that many years earlier he had played at a wedding where Rabbi Moshe Leib had officiated, and that he had expressed the wish that he be accompanied to his eternal rest by a particularly lively melody.

The musician then said, "I remember the melody well," and proceeded to lead the klezmer in playing the tune which Rabbi Moshe Leib had loved so.

To tzaddikim the sojourn on earth is a task, a heavy burden. Their goal is not this earthy existence, but a far more beautiful world. The day they leave this world for Gan Eden (Paradise) is a day of liberation, a day on which they reach the goal they worked so hard to achieve. What is perceived as a day of sadness to most people is a day of joy to tzaddikim.

Rabbi Moshe Leib wished to be accompanied to his eternal home with the same joy that he experienced in fulfilling the mitzvah of bringing cheer to a chassan and kallah.

The Essence
of Teshuvah

The Talmud says that *teshuvah* (repentance) preceded creation of the world. Just as the creation of air and
nutrients preceded the creation of man, because man
cannot live without these, similarly *teshuvah* preceded
creation because man cannot exist without *teshuvah*. As mortals we are fallible and vulnerable to sin, and without a method
to rectify and remove our sins, all mankind would be doomed to
eternal damnation. *Teshuvah* is therefore an essential for human life.

But what constitutes *teshuvah*? In the Talmud and the early ethical writings it is evident that fasting and mortification
of the flesh was practiced as penance. In the later writings,

particularly those of the Baal Shem Tov and his disciples, self-imposed fasting as a method of penance is discouraged. Rabbi Schneur Zalman states that such fasting was appropriate for people whose function was not significantly impaired by fasting, but those who are unable to pray and study Torah properly and fulfill *mitzvos* when fasting are better advised not to fast. Others say that people may mistakenly think that fasting is *the* important factor in *teshuvah,* and may neglect taking the necessary steps that would lead to corrective action of their behavior. One chassidic master said, "You have sinned primarily with your eyes, by looking at things you should not have looked at, and with your ears and tongue by listening to and speaking *lashon hara* (gossip) and untruths. Why are you penalizing your stomach, which is innocent in all these? To do proper *teshuvah,* avoid looking at things you should not see, avoid listening to *lashon hara* and lies, and guide your tongue from indulging in these. That will constitute proper *teshuvah.*"

Other chassidic masters were concerned that the discomfort experienced in fasting may lead a person to think, "See how much I have sacrificed for G-d. Just look what kind of *tzaddik* I am." In this way, fasting may lead to vanity, which is the worst of all sins. One chassidic master said, "I prefer a *rasha* (sinful person) who knows that he is a *rasha* to a *tzaddik* who knows he is a *tzaddik.*"

One chassidic master noted that one of his followers was doing penance by fasting. "I see you are doing a complete job," he said. "First you sinned to ruin your *neshamah* (soul), and now you are fasting to ruin your body."

True *teshuvah* consists of sincere regret for having done wrong and a firm commitment never to repeat the wrongful act. But even such commitment is not yet enough. One must think, "How is it that I came to do this wrongful act?" One must analyze oneself to discover the character defects that made such an act a possibility, and improve upon these defects, developing oneself to a level of spirituality at which such an act could not recur. If one achieves this, then there is no need for fasting. If one has not achieved this, the fasting is of no value.

A man once came to Rabbi Michel of Zlotchow, stating that he had inadvertently done something forbidden on Shabbos, and asked the Rabbi what he must do for his teshuvah to be accepted. Rabbi Michel explained the gravity of violating the Shabbos to him, and that Shabbos is equivalent to all the other 612 mitzvos. His sin was indeed a serious one, and he therefore prescribed a rigorous course of fasting and self-mortification as penance.

This man subsequently came to the Baal Shem Tov, who told him that the fasting prescribed by Rabbi Michel was unnecessary, and that as penance he should provide the candles for the pulpit in shul. The man proceeded to buy candles, and since in those days the candles were made of tallow from animal fat, a dog who wandered through the open door of the shul sniffed the candles and ate them. The man then replaced the candles, but whenever they were lit, the wind blew them out. He took these as being Divine signals that his teshuvah was rejected, and he reported this to the Baal Shem Tov.

The Baal Shem Tov understood that the problem was due to Rabbi Michel's interference, and that the latter believed that a more strenuous penance was necessary. The Baal Shem Tov sent a message to Rabbi Michel, asking that he come to him for Shabbos.

Rabbi Michel accepted the invitation and set out on the trip on Wednesday, giving himself ample time to arrive before Shabbos. However, the trip was plagued with one mishap after another. First the axle of the wagon broke, and this took considerable time to repair. Then a severe thunderstorm caused the roads to be muddy and hindered *their progress. Then a wheel fell off, and then they took a wrong fork in the road. In short, there were a series of misfortunes that resulted in their arrival at the Baal Shem Tov's home late Friday afternoon, shortly before sunset. Rabbi Michel, who was by this time terribly anxious that they not travel into the Shabbos, took his belongings and rushed into the Baal Shem Tov's house, where he saw the Baal Shem Tov in his Shabbos garments, standing with the goblet of wine in his hand, reciting the Kiddush. Assuming that it was already Shabbos and that he had violated the Shabbos by traveling, Rabbi Michel fainted.*

The Baal Shem Tov revived him and said to Rabbi Michel, "You did not violate Shabbos, because the sun had not yet set. I accepted the Shabbos upon myself earlier than usual, but for you it is not yet Shabbos. But tell me, Reb Michel, when you thought that you had violated the Shabbos, how distressed were you? Don't you see that if the awareness that one has sinned causes a person to feel deeply distressed at having transgressed the Divine word, this is the essence of teshuvah? Once this regret has occurred, there is no need for additional self-punitive behavior. The man who had sought a method of penance from you had already experienced the pain of the awareness of having transgressed, and all that was necessary was some token act of penance, because the true teshuvah had already taken place."

The chassidic master, Rabbi Mordechai of Lechovitz, practiced the Baal Shem Tov's teaching.

O*ne time a man confessed having committed a multiplicity of sins, and asked for instructions for* *penance. Rabbi Mordechai said, "I will give you instructions, provided that you promise me that you will not deviate from them one iota." Assuming that he would be instructed in rigorous self-mortification, the man nevertheless agreed to accept his fate.*

"Here is what you must do," Rabbi Mordechai said. "Every day you must eat a hearty breakfast, with pleasant-tasting foods. For dinner you must have roast meat or other delicacies, and condiments for dessert. Avail yourself of the finest mattress and pillows to make your bed most comfortable. Do not deny yourself any pleasurable activity. At the end of the year, return to me."

The man returned home and began to follow Rabbi Mordechai's instructions. As he ate his food, he thought, "How dare I partake of delicious food when I have been so sinful. I do not deserve this." But when he wished to set the food aside, he remembered that he had promised not to deny himself any pleasures, and he virtually had to force himself to eat, feeling as though he was choking with every bite. Indeed, rocks and sand would have been more palatable. As he retired to a soft and comfortable bed he would think, "A sinner like myself should be sleeping on a bed of nails," and he would cry himself to sleep with remorse. In short, the indulgence prescribed by Rabbi Mordechai was far more punitive than any course of self-denial would have been, and the sincere remorse the man experienced constituted true teshuvah.

My father used to cite the verse (*Psalms* 23:6) "May only goodness and kindness pursue me all the days of my life," and he would ask, "'Pursuit' connotes that someone is fleeing. Why would someone flee from goodness and kindness, making pursuit necessary?"

My father then told the story of a man who had rebelled

against the king, and one day, while the king was riding in the royal coach, the man threw a rock at the coach. He was promptly arrested, put on trial, and given a severe prison sentence. When the king heard of this he gave the man a pardon, and had him appointed to a well-paying and honorable position in the palace. The man was seized by remorse. "How could I have been so stupid and so vile to rebel against a king who is so benevolent?" From time to time the king had the man promoted, giving him ever greater honors and more money. With each promotion the man's remorse intensified, and he was consumed with regret for having acted against the king, so that he was far more distressed than he would have been with a harsh prison sentence.

This is the meaning of the verse in *Psalms*. We pray, "Dear G-d, if You must punish me, pursue me with goodness and kindness rather than with harshness, because the former can result in my correcting my ways even more than the latter."

R*abbi Zusia of Hanipoli had yet another way of bringing people to teshuvah. One time he took lodging at an inn, whose proprietor was a flagrantly sinful person, and who had been resistant to reprimands by others. Late at night, when the inn was quiet, Rabbi Zusia awoke to recite the midnight prayers. His tears and sincere grief in chanting the prayers bemoaning the destruction of the Temple and the exile of Israel penetrated the heart of the innkeeper, who had been woken by Rabbi Zusia's prayers.*

After reciting Psalms with great devotion, Rabbi Zusia then began saying, "Oh, Zusia, Zusia! What audacity you have to pray to G-d. How dare you show yourself to G-d, Zusia, when you have been so sinful. Have you no sense of shame, Zusia? Why have you done thus and so," then he began listing the sins of the innkeeper as though he

had committed them himself, directing the reprimand to-
ward himself, and saying, "G-d has been so kind to you,
Zusia, and you have been so rebellious. Where is your
sense of gratitude, Zusia?" This litany resulted in the
innkeeper breaking down in tears, and asking Reb Zusia
for instructions on how to mend his errant ways.

Two attitudes should dominate the concept of *teshuvah*. One
is that out of devotion to and love for G-d, a person should not
do anything that displeases Him, and the second is that by dis-
obeying the Divine will, we are actually harming ourselves,
which is simply a foolish thing to do.

A chassid *of Rabbi Mordechai of Lechovitz, whose*
business was dealing in lumber, once complained to
the rebbe that he had bought a huge forest for lumbering
and that the price of wood had dropped, causing him a
significant loss. Rabbi Mordechai said, "The Talmud says
that when a person is in distress, this causes the
Shechinah (the Divine presence) to also be in distress. If
you are in pain because of your financial loss, this causes
G-d to suffer along with you. Now tell me, is it worthwhile
to cause G-d to suffer because of a few pieces of wood?"

A young man who was in recovery from drug addiction decided to become a drug counselor, and in his training, he
worked with adolescents and their families. One day he said, "I
never realized before how much suffering I had caused my parents, and their greatest pain was for the harm that I was doing
to myself." I am sure he will be an excellent counselor, because
he will be better able to convey to young addicts that their behavior is causing their parents much distress, and that this

distress is primarily due to their parents' love for them, and this is why their parents are trying to prevent them from harming themselves.

The Baal Shem Tov was equally displeased with itinerant preachers who used to harshly reprimand people with their sermons. Instead, he wished to convey to people how much G-d loves them and that the Divine commandments are for their own welfare. When one deviates from the Divine rule, one not only causes distress to G-d, but also injures oneself. It is the understanding of these concepts that comprises the essence of *teshuvah*.

When Bad Things Happen to Good People

Which thinking human being has not felt himself challenged by this question? A person who believes in G-d believes that He is kind and benevolent. Why would a kind and benevolent G-d allow innocent people to suffer? One believes that G-d is all-powerful and in total control of everything. It is certainly not beyond His capacity to prevent and eliminate suffering. One believes in *hashgachah* or Divine providence, that G-d takes an interest in and has not abandoned the world. If He sees the suffering, why does He not eliminate it?

Throughout history people have dealt variously with this vexing question. Several ancient religions posited that there were two gods, one who does good and one who does evil, and that they were constantly struggling with one another, neither being able to triumph over the other. Some of the ancients believed that after creating the world, G-d retreated to His heavenly abode and abandoned the world to the forces of nature. Some try to justify G-d by saying that the innocents who suffer only appear to be innocent, but are guilty of sins that are known only to G-d.

Jews believe in one G-d, an all-powerful G-d, Who has not abandoned the world, and Who is benign and benevolent. No one in his right mind will try to say that every victim of the Crusades, the Inquisition, the pogroms, and the Holocaust was a sinner in secret. Taking all the principles of faith together, we are not privy to any reasonable explanation as to why bad things happen to good people.

We are hardly alone in being bothered by this existential question. The Talmud states that when Moses asked of G-d, "Let me know Your ways" (*Exodus* 33:18), he was essentially posing this very question: Why do the righteous suffer while flagrant sinners enjoy success? According to one opinion in the Talmud, Moses did not receive an answer (*Berachos* 7a). This would appear to be in keeping with the opinion in the Talmud (*Bava Basra* 15a) that Moses wrote the Book of *Job* wherein all the arguments to logically explain the suffering of the righteous are presented and refuted, and ultimately G-d says to Job, "Where were you when I laid the earth's foundation?" (*Job* 38:4).

G-d's answer to Job was that it is absurd to pick up a single piece of a multimillion-piece jigsaw puzzle, analyze it, and conclude that it does not make any sense. Of course it does not make any sense, and it cannot make any sense unless one sees how it fits in with the millions of other pieces, at which time its part in the entire picture makes perfect sense. Thus, no individual or series of happenings can be understood on its own, and it makes sense only when one has a perspective of infinity in space and eternity of time, a perspective belonging only to G-d.

No amount of explanation, however genius, will ever justify to our minds the horrors of the Holocaust, and we can only defer to the superiority of Divine wisdom. This is what is done whenever, G-d forbid, tragedy strikes, when one is required to recite the *Tziduk Hadin*, the acceptance of Divine justice.

The ethical works state that only G-d can mete out perfect justice, and that human administration of justice is always faulty. Suppose a man commits a crime for which he is sentenced to prison. His wife and children are deprived of their source of support, although they did not commit a crime, and they suffer too, which is unjust to them. Courts cannot calibrate a punishment which will not impinge on innocent people. Only G-d has the capacity to do that, and G-d's judgment is just to all, even if we fail to see how this is so.

Our belief in the absolute justice of G-d is often put to the test, but we must reinforce our faith and trust, as Moses said, "He is a G-d of faith without iniquity, righteous and fair is He" (*Deuteronomy* 32:4).

The Divine system of justice is not only perfect, but as it were, it binds even G-d himself. Scripture says "Through justice a king establishes the land" (*Proverbs* 29:4), and in our prayers we refer to G-d as the King of justice. The ethical works state that G-d always operates within the system of justice, and never overrides the principles of justice. This is why the Talmud states that one may not say "G-d will overlook it" (*Bava Kamma* 50a). G-d never overlooks anything, and the slightest action will be weighed in the balances of justice. G-d may forgive, when the conditions meriting forgiveness are satisfied, and such forgiveness is within the Divine system of justice. But to overlook, never. There is an exquisitely exact system of accountability.

Our human field of vision is so restricted that we cannot appreciate the precision of the Divine system of justice, and we must therefore accept it as a principle of faith. It is not irrational but rather suprarational. If we knew all there is to know, we would understand.

Now and then we are privileged to have a glimpse, just a brief sampling, a mere taste of the Divine system of justice, and if we are wise, this sampling should strengthen our faith. A taste of a tiny spoonful is an accurate indication of what is contained in the entire pot.

W hen the fame of the Baal Shem Tov spread far and wide, one man who had heard of his greatness was determined to see this phenomenon for himself. He made his way to Mezhibozh where the Baal Shem Tov resided, and was warmly received.

"And how can I be of help to you?" The Baal Shem Tov asked him.

"I have no need of help," the man replied. "Thank G-d, I and my family are well. I have a thriving business, and all my needs are met. I did not come to ask for anything, just to have the opportunity to meet you."

"Well, if you feel you have no needs," the Baal Shem Tov said, "perhaps you will listen to a story I have for you. But you must listen attentively."

The Baal Shem Tov continued, "There were once two young boys who grew up together and became close friends. They attended the same cheder, and always played together. Baruch and Chaim were inseparable, and every-one knew that wherever Baruch was, there you would find Chaim as well. Their friendship continued through their adolescence and well into their early adulthood, and they were about as inseparable as Siamese twins.

"When they married, Chaim married a young woman from a distant town to the east, and Baruch married a woman from a distant town to the west. As was the cus-tom, they moved to live with the wife's family, and for the first time in their lives, they were separated. They pledged to remain in close contact and continue their friendship *unto eternity. Initially, they exchanged letters frequently, but as time passed and their families grew and there were so many distractions, the communication began to wane until it ultimately stopped completely.*

"Chaim and Baruch each went into business and prospered, but life is often a cycle, and as the wheel turns, what was once at the top is later at the bottom, and this is what happened to Baruch. His business failed and he was penniless. Remembering that he had a devoted childhood friend, he felt that perhaps Chaim would come to his aid, and borrowing money for the trip, he traveled to Chaim's town. Upon seeing Baruch, Chaim embraced him with tears of love, and the two sat and reminisced for hours. Baruch finally told Chaim of the misfortune that had befallen him, whereupon Chaim called in his bookkeeper and asked him to calculate the value of all his assets. Once he received the figure, he promptly wrote out a check, giving half of everything he owned to Baruch, who thanked him profusely and returned home.

"With the capital to invest, Baruch started a new business and prospered. But lo and behold! As Baruch's mazal ascended, Chaim's mazal descended, so that now Baruch was wealthy and Chaim was impoverished. Remembering their devotion to one another, Chaim came to Baruch for help. How utterly disappointed he was when Baruch said, "Chaim, I would love to help you, but the pattern is clear. It is not destined for both of us to prosper at one time. If one of us succeeds, the other will fail. If I put you back into business and you prosper, I know that I will lose everything. I realize that out of our deep friendship I should make this sacrifice, but while I may waive my own welfare, I do not have the right to sacrifice the welfare of my large family, my children and grandchildren who are dependent on me for their livelihood." Chaim returned home empty handed and broken hearted.

"Years passed by, and both Baruch and Chaim went to the eternal world. When they appeared before the Heavenly Tribunal, Chaim was awarded Paradise for his loyalty and generosity to Baruch, whereas Baruch was condemned to Gehinnom for turning his back on his friend at his time of need. Chaim then said, "How can I enjoy Paradise when I know that the friend of my youth is suffering the torments of Gehinnom? True, Baruch was unable to withstand the test to which he was put, and he put his self-interest first, but that is no reason to condemn him to Gehinnom. I will not enter Paradise unless Chaim can accompany me."

"The Heavenly Tribunal said that this was out of the question, that behavior as outrageous as Baruch's rejection of Chaim's plea for help cannot go unpunished, but Chaim was adamant. He will not enter Paradise if Baruch is doomed to Gehinnom."

At this point the Baal Shem Tov said to the man, "Now listen carefully, and look me in the eye."

The Baal Shem Tov continued, "The Heavenly Tribunal debated over the situation and came up with a solution for this dilemma. Both Chaim and Baruch will be sent down to Earth for another life span. Baruch will be wealthy and Chaim will be poor. If Baruch will help Chaim in this renewed existence, Baruch will have rectified his wrongdoing and redeemed himself, and will be permitted to join Chaim in Paradise.

"And so it came to be," the Baal Shem Tov said. "The souls of the two came down to Earth again, and the person having Baruch's soul became wealthy, while the person bearing Chaim's soul was poor, a beggar who survived on alms. The beggar would keep only pennies for himself, and gave everything he collected to his wife and small children.

"One day the beggar, making his rounds from village to village, came to the town where the wealthy man lived.

He was weary and hungry, and did not feel that he had the strength to continue. Perhaps someone would be generous enough to give him an adequate sum, so that he could rest a bit and restore his failing strength. Winter was approaching, the children would need shoes and warm clothes, and they would need firewood to keep their house warm and dry. If he could only speak to a wealthy man in person and explain his plight, perhaps he could prevail upon him for a sum which would meet his family's many needs.

"The beggar knocked on the door of the wealthy man, and was met by the butler, who gave him the usual dole of a few pennies. 'Please let me talk for just a few moments with your master,' he said. The butler explained that this was impossible, since his master was occupied with important business dealings. The beggar began to cry, 'Ask your master to have mercy and spare me just a few minutes of his time to listen to me.'

"The wealthy man, hearing the commotion, asked the butler what the problem was, and he explained that there was a stubborn beggar who would not accept the alms he gave him and was insisting on meeting with the master personally. The wealthy man became angry. 'These beggars are a thankless lot! The audacity they have. If he refuses to leave, throw him out!' The butler did as he was told, and threw the beggar down the stairs. Exhausted, hungry, and depressed, the beggar breathed his last and expired."

As the Baal Shem Tov said these last words, the visitor took hold of his head with his hands and exclaimed, "Ribono Shel Olam! That is what happened to me! Just last week a pesky beggar refused to take what my butler gave him, and I had him thrown out, and he died right in front of my house! But how was I to know that I was being put to the test? It is common for many beggars to be dissatisfied *with what they receive and they ask for more. I did not mean to be the cause of his death! What can I do to redeem myself now?"*

The Baal Shem Tov said, "The Divine system of justice is perfect. You were given the opportunity to rectify what you had done wrong in a previous existence. Had your riches not hardened your heart, you would have listened to the beggar, and perhaps the relationship of your two souls would have resulted in him impressing you with his needs, and you would have responded appropriately, thus correcting the previous mistake.

"Now," the Baal Shem Tov said, "you still have an opportunity to redeem yourself. You must leave for yourself only enough to meet the necessities of life for yourself and your family, and you must take all the rest of your wealth and give it to the widow and orphans of the beggar. I know that this is a major sacrifice, but this is the only way you will know peace both in this world and in the World to Come."

Today we do not have a Baal Shem Tov who can see both the past and into the future, but we must know that the Divine system of justice prevails, and that nothing happens by chance. If we will live our lives as the Torah requires of us and trust in G-d, we will achieve that which is true and just.

The Spirit
of Tzeddakah

Tzeddakah is generally translated as "charity." It is clear, however, that the Torah concept of *tzeddakah* is quite different than that of charity, which signifies a favor from the donor to the recipient. The word *tzeddakah* is derived from the word *tzedek* which means "justice," connoting that it is only just and fair that the "haves" share their assets with the "have-nots." The Talmud says that in the transaction of *tzeddakah* the recipient benefits the donor more than the donor does the recipient (*Vayikra Rabbah* 34:10). The value and reward of the *mitzvah* which the donor accrues far exceeds the value of the gift to the recipient.

Whereas the essence of every other *mitzvah* is in the *kavannah* (intent) associated with it, and *mitzvos* that are lacking in *kavannah* are considered defective, this is not true of *tzeddakah*. The purpose of *tzeddakah* is that the poor should be spared from hunger and cold, and as long as this is accomplished, the *kavannah* of the donor is secondary. Indeed, although it is improper to ask for reward for other *mitzvos*, *tzedakah* is an exception (*Pesachim* 8a). Rashi states that even if a person loses money and it is found by a needy person, the former has acquired a *mitzvah* of *tzeddakah* (*Deuteronomy* 24:19).

There are, however, various degrees of *tzeddakah*, and although all are commendable, the finer the *kavannah*, the greater is the *mitzvah*. Inasmuch as the recipient of *tzeddakah* may be embarrassed by having to rely on the graces of others, it is a finer version of *tzeddakah* to spare him such embarrassment, and to give the *tzeddakah* in secret, so that the donor remains anonymous and the identity of the recipient is protected.

My aunt told me that in their village in Russia there was a man who would give much *tzeddakah* and whose home was always open to wayfarers. When he fell upon bad times and could no longer afford such benevolence, my grandfather, the Rabbi of Hornosteipel, would give him huge sums of money so that he could continue to give *tzeddakah* and have an open house. My aunt related that after midnight, when almost all were asleep, she would carry the money to this man in secret.

There is a story about a butcher who was known in town to be a tightwad, and who gave little to *tzeddakah*. The week he died, when the poor in town came to the agent in the community who distributed money and provisions to the needy for Shabbos, they were told that he had but a pittance to give them. In the past, the butcher was the secret benefactor, who had provided meat and money to be given to the poor for Shabbos, but had done so anonymously, concealing his benevolence so that he not be praised for it. Now that the butcher had passed away, the community coffers were empty.

The *Midrash* states that when G-d told Moses that the Israelites were to donate for the building of the Sanctuary, and that their contributions would merit forgiveness for their sins (*Exodus* 30:12), Moses was bewildered. How can a gift of money eradicate a sin? Thereupon G-d showed Moses a fiery coin, saying, "This is how" (*Rashi* ibid. 13). The Chasam Sofer explains that the Divine answer to Moses' question was that if the donation is made with fiery enthusiasm, with an intense passion to glorify the Name of G-d, it can indeed serve as a forgiveness. Thus, the *kavannah* of *tzeddakah* can accentuate the *mitzvah* greatly .

There are many instances of people who made great sacrifices for *tzeddakah*.

R abbi Mordechai of Neshchiz saved his pennies all year around in order to have enough money to buy an esrog (citron) for the mitzvah of the four species on Succos. On the way to buy the esrog, he encountered a man who was weeping bitterly, and his inquiry revealed that this man had made his meager living as a porter, hauling things by horse and wagon. That day his horse had perished, and he was now without a means of livelihood. Rabbi Mordechai promptly gave the man the entire of sum of money he had saved throughout the year, in order that he might buy another horse. The man rushed off overjoyed, and Rabbi Mordechai turned his eyes to heaven saying, "Dear G-d, all other Jews will fulfill the mitzvah of the four species with an esrog, but I will do so with a horse."

≈)≈

N ot far from Lizhensk, the home of the chassidic master Rabbi Elimelech, there lived a man whose household staff, included a young man named Benzi. Benzi had been taken into this man's home as a young orphan, and the man had provided for his education and other needs until he was old enough to work for him. Benzi heard from some of the townsfolk that there was a great tzaddik in the nearby town of Lizhensk, and he went to see Rabbi Elimelech, who received him warmly. Rabbi Elimelech told Benzi to ask his employer whether he might be in need of someone to help with the cooking, because there was a young woman named Blima, also orphaned at an early age, who needed a job. Benzi carried the tzaddik's message and the employer did indeed hire Blima.

Benzi and Blima became friends and eventually decided to marry, but delayed their marriage until they would save up enough money to set up a home. Benzi and Blima both gave whatever they earned to their employer for safekeeping. But alas! One day a fire broke out, totally destroying the property with all that was in it, including their savings. Their employer now found himself impoverished, and Benzi and Blima had to seek work elsewhere. They eventually found work in different places, and continued to save their money so that they would have enough to make a start in their married life.

A little more than a year went by, and one day Benzi noted, among a troupe of beggars who had come to town for alms, his former employer. He was devastated to see his previous benefactor in so sorry a state, and he embraced him tearfully. The man told Benzi that after the fire his business had failed, and he was now destitute. "The world is but a cycle, Benzi," he said. "As the wheel turns, those who were once on top find themselves on the bottom. I have sunk so low that I think my fortunes may now begin to rise again. I have to beg for alms, and I am saving pennies to try my luck again. I will buy some merchandise and peddle it, and hopefully gradually increase my earnings, and perhaps one day be of some means again."

Benzi's heart went out to the man who had been so kind to him. He rushed off to Blima and told her that he had met their former employer, and how he had fallen to being a beggar. "Blima," he said, "I believe he can do well again if he has the opportunity, but it may take him forever to save enough money from the alms he receives. I want to take the money I have saved and give it to him. It will mean that we may have to postpone our marriage a bit longer until I can save more money, but I cannot see this man who did so much for me in my childhood go with a troupe of beggars from door to door."

Blima wiped away her tears and said, "If you can give him your money, Benzi, then I will give him mine too." She fetched the money she had saved, and Benzi ran off to find his friend, and gave him all their money. The man wept profusely at the young couple's sacrifice for him, at first refusing to take their life savings, but as Benzi insisted, he said, "I know G-d will bless you for this, and I have great hope that this will be the beginning of my salvation."

Shortly afterward, Benzi again visited Rabbi Elimelech, and related what had happened to him and Blima. Rabbi Elimelech said, "It is time for you to marry. We will arrange for your wedding, and as for money, G-d will bless you."

Rabbi Elimelech and his disciples made all arrangements for the wedding, and it was a most joyous event, attended by all the townsfolk. The tzaddikim attending the wedding danced with ecstatic simchah, and Rabbi Elimelech then instructed his young disciple Reb Naftali, who later was known as the Rabbi of Ropschitz, to announce the wedding gifts as was customary. Rabbi Elimelech was the first to declare, "I give the young couple one of the mansions of the poritz (the feudal lord)." Reb Mendel, who was later the Rabbi of Rimanov, declared, "I give the couple the flour mill of the poritz," and Reb Naftali said, "And I will give them 1,000 ducats." The guests at the wedding laughed politely, taking these declarations of gifts as just part of the merrymaking.

After the wedding, the young couple made their way to the hut in the nearby woods which was to be their home. As they entered the woods, they heard a cry for help, and following the voice, they came upon a pond of quicksand, wherein a young man was struggling to stay afloat. Benzi quickly removed his jacket, and tearing it into strips, fashioned a rope which he threw to the young man, and he and Blima pulled the young man from the quicksand.

The young man thanked them profusely, and told them that he was the son of the poritz, and had been out horseback riding. He had imbibed a bit too much and had lost his way in the woods, and then his horse threw him into the quicksand. "Had you not come upon me just then, I would have died." Benzi took the young man into his hut, allowed him to wash up, and gave him some clean clothes. He and Blima then escorted the young man out of the woods, back to his father's estate.

The poritz and his wife, who had been worried and anxious because of their son's failure to return from his ride, were overjoyed to see him, and when he told them that this newlywed couple had saved him from certain death, the poritz said, "I will give these newlyweds a home they deserve. They can have one of my mansions." The wife of the poritz said, "And for a livelihood, I will give them our flour mill." The young prince then added, "And I will give them, as a token of my gratitude, a thousand ducats."

Benzi and Blima later visited Rabbi Elimelech, who told them, "Your sacrifice of giving everything you had saved as tzeddakah to your former employer, and your doing so with a sincere desire to help him, was so meritorious *that you deserved a great reward. When we announced our gifts, we did so as blessings that we knew would be fulfilled."*

There is no greater *mitzvah* than *tzeddakah*, and as mentioned earlier, it is most meritorious regardless of how it is done. But there are some types of *tzeddakah* that are very special, particularly when one truly empathizes with the recipient, and tries to help him in a way that elevates his spirits and encourages him to a better life.

The Healing Pearl

W hereas one cannot vouch for the authenticity of each and every tale told about the chassidic masters, they all *could* have been true. But the following story is especially dear to me, since I know it to be authentic, having heard it from a reliable source close to an eyewitness.

R eb Menachem was a young chassidic scholar who was anxious to receive semichah (rabbinic ordination) from the renowned sage, Rabbi Chaim Soloveitchik of Brisk. He obtained an audience with Rabbi Chaim and asked to be tested.

"Have you received semichah from any other rabbis?" Rabbi Chaim asked.

Reb Menachem answered affirmatively, and showed Rabbi Chaim a letter of commendation from a rabbi who had ordained him. Rabbi Chaim reviewed the letter and remarked, "This ordination is not too impressive."

Reb Menachem, impetuous in his youth, said, "After all, he is a misnaged (adverse to chassidim)."

Rabbi Chaim raised his eyebrows. "And what do you think I am?" he asked.

"At least partially a chassid," Reb Menachem answered.

"What makes you say that?" Rabbi Chaim asked.

"Because of what the Torah says in Genesis (18:8), 'He stands near them,'" Reb Menachem said.

Rabbi Chaim was excited. "Then you know the story!" he said, and beckoned several bystanders to come close. "Tell them what you know," he said to the young man.

Reb Menachem began, "Rabbi Chaim's father, Rabbi Yoshe Ber, was the son-in-law of a chassid of the chassidic master Rabbi Moshe of Kobrin. Rabbi Moshe once traveled through the town, and had his lodging at the home of his chassid. Rabbi Yoshe Ber was then living with his father-in-law, and Rabbi Chaim, who was then a small child, had fallen gravely ill. The doctors said there was nothing they could do for him, and did not expect the child to live. The chassid appealed to Rabbi Moshe to pray for his grandchild.

"Rabbi Moshe asked to be taken to the child's room, and standing at the crib said to his chassid, 'The patriarch Abraham excelled in the mitzvah of hachnasas orchim, hospitality to travelers. The Torah relates that he was visited by three angels in the form of humans, and that he provided them with food. Then the Torah states, "and he stands near them as they ate." Is it not strange that the Torah uses the present tense rather than the past tense? Obviously it should have read, "and he stood near them as they ate." '

" 'What the Torah means to tell us,' Rabbi Moshe continued, 'is that the mitzvah of hachnasas orchim was so dear to the patriarch that whenever one of his descendants fulfills that mitzvah, the patriarch Abraham personally comes down from heaven to witness it. Therefore, the Torah states that Abraham stands there, at all times. It is an eternal presence.'

" 'Since I am lodging here, you are fulfilling the mitzvah of hachnasas orchim, and the patriarch is therefore in our very presence now. The Midrash relates that Abraham had a pearl suspended from his neck, which had the unique property that any sick person who looked at it would recover. So let the child look at this pearl of the patriarch, and he will certainly recover,' Rabbi Moshe concluded."

When Reb Menachem finished his narration, Rabbi Chaim then proceeded to test him rigorously, and he answered all the questions satisfactorily. Rabbi Chaim then wrote out a certificate of ordination for Reb Menachem, one of the very few Rabbi Chaim issued throughout his entire lifetime.

In Pursuit of Truth

"The seal of the Almighty is truth" (*Shabbos* 55a). This led chassidic masters to say that everything in the world can be imitated, and we can make an exact replica of everything, except truth. Why? Because if it is not genuine, it is not truth.

In our daily prayers we say that G-d *is* truth, and indeed, some pious Jews do not use the Hebrew word *emes* (truth) in conversation, because it is one of the Divine Names, and should be accorded the same reverence as the other Names ascribed to G-d. The Talmud states that truth is the foundation of the world (*Ethics of the Fathers* 1:17). Torah commentaries point out that the first three words of the Torah, which begin the account of Creation, end with the letters that spell *emes*. Similarly, the last three words of the account of Creation also end with the letters that spell *emes*. This is to teach us that truth is the beginning and the end, the basis for Creation.

Many people consider themselves truthful, although they may have little difficulty in justifying "white lies." But one does not necessarily have to verbalize falsehood to be lying. If a person perceives reality other than it is, that is a deviation from truth. If someone perceives himself other than he really is, that too is a deviation from truth. Since distortions of reality and self-deception are so widespread, the existence of absolute truth anywhere is a rarity.

Many ethicists and chassidic masters expounded on the importance of truth. Few, however, were as vigorous and as fierce in their insistence upon truth as Rabbi Mendel of Kotzk. Modern technology has developed apparatuses that are so sensitive that they can detect impurities in as minute quantities as one part in several million. The Rabbi of Kotzk was able to detect traces of falsehood as minute as one in several trillions, and he rejected whatever had the faintest hint of falsehood. There was simply no compromising on truth. In contrast to some chassidic masters who welcomed large numbers of followers, the Rabbi of Kotzk drove them away, and only those few who could meet his exacting standards of truth were welcome. For the last twenty years of his life, he withdrew into total solitude, complaining that the very air of the world was polluted with falsehood.

Rabbi Mendel was born in Tomashov, and when he was but a youth, the Seer of Lublin dispatched two emissaries to Tomashov to bring young Mendel to him, because he desired to have him as a disciple. Arriving in Tomashov, the emissaries inquired about a Reb Mendel, but none of the men bearing that name appeared to them to be the one the Seer had requested. One night they remained *late in the shul, and toward midnight a young man came in and began reciting Tehillim (Psalms) with intense devotion. At one point he opened the Ark and exclaimed, "Master of the Universe! Show me just a grain of truth!" The emissaries came out of hiding and said to him, "If it is truth you are seeking, then come with us to Lublin."*

Arriving in Lublin, young Mendel bought a pocketknife from a street vendor. When Mendel came to the Seer, the latter greeted him with, "Is that what you came to Lublin for, to buy a pocketknife?" Young Mendel, exhibiting the boldness which characterized him throughout his life, said to the venerable master, "I am here to find truth. Your omniscience does not impress me."

And what is truth? It is hardly that which we know by sense experience. People who hallucinate sights and sounds are as certain of the veracity of their experience as we are of the things we see and hear, and perhaps even more so. The Rabbi of Kotzk did not concur with the philosophical conclusion of *cogito ergo sum*, that one's existence is the absolute truth, but rather that the only truth is the word of G-d. Everything else may be false and deceptive.

The Rabbi of Kotzk asked, "Why were the spies sent by Moses punished for their account of the Holy Land (*Numbers* 13:25-29)? After all, they gave an accurate report about what they had seen." And the Rabbi answered that seeing something does not mean it is real. Truth and reality are what G-d says they are, and since G-d had said the land was good and that the Israelites would inherit it, that was the absolute truth, one's sense perceptions notwithstanding. When the spies deviated from the word of G-d, they were lying.

One time he was told that one of the chassidic masters said that he actually saw the patriarchs in the *succah*, to which the Rabbi of Kotzk responded, "I did not see them, but I believed they were there, and believing is a greater certainty than seeing."

When the Rabbi of Kotzk remarried, he sent a message to his betrothed, "A marriage that is entered into under fraudulent assumptions is not a valid contract. You may be mistakenly assuming that I am a *tzaddik* because some people think that of me. You must know the truth about me." To which she cleverly replied, "I am not assuming anything about you. I am marrying a man whom people consider to be a *tzaddik*, and that is certainly true."

The Rabbi of Kotzk demanded that his disciples demolish their personalities and rebuild them in the spirit of truth. This would result in a feeling of nothingness, which the Rabbi felt was essential to building a personality of truth. All concepts that one had of oneself were tainted, and he felt that building "from the ground up" should be taken literally. "The Psalmist says that truth will sprout from the earth (*Psalms* 85:12). The reason that so few people have truth is that they are not humble enough, not lowly enough to reach down to the ground to pick it up."

*A*nother *champion of truth was Rabbi Pinchas of Koritz. Rabbi Pinchas was a contemporary of the Baal Shem Tov, and the two were close friends; nonetheless, Rabbi Pinchas did not become a disciple. Although Rabbi Pinchas was a great scholar, relatively few of his teachings were preserved. He would say, "Other scholars expound copiously on Torah, giving forth so much truth that if by chance a tiny bit of untruth should happen, it is negligible. I, on the other hand, hesitate to say anything, for fear that I may utter a less than truthful word."*

Rabbi Pinchas had a magnetic personality, and was loved by all. Every day people besieged him with requests for his blessings, so much so that he felt his time for prayer and Torah study were drastically compromised. One day he prayed, "Dear G-d, let me have my peace and privacy so that I may pray and study Torah properly. Make it so that people shun me instead of clinging to me."

The following morning Rabbi Pinchas stood at his window, and as people passed by, not a single person turned to greet him as they had always done. He sat down to meditate in undisturbed quiet, and when he entered the Beis Midrash for prayer, it was empty. None of the usual worshipers had come, and he had to pray in solitude. Every day Rabbi Pinchas would have many guests at his table, but today there was no one, and he ate alone.

Later that day Rabbi Pinchas' wife told him that she could not understand what had happened. When she went shopping, all the people seemed to ignore her. In the past everyone greeted her and chatted with her, but suddenly they were shunning her. She was certain that she had not offended anyone.

"This is undoubtedly due to G-d's response to my prayer to be shunned by everyone, so that I would not be bothered by people and could devote my time to Torah study," Rabbi Pinchas said, "and you are included in this with me."

His wife shed a tear. "It hurts me to be so isolated, but if this will enhance your Torah study, I am for it."

Soon Succos approached, and whereas Rabbi Pinchas always had adequate help in building the succah, this time he had to do it alone.

Succos night Rabbi Pinchas awaited the spirits of the patriarchs, but the patriarch Abraham stood outside the door, refusing to enter the succah. "I will not enter a succah where none of my children is welcome as a guest."

That was the last straw. Rabbi Pinchas realized that as precious as Torah study and prayerful meditation are, they only have value when this is done in the company of fellow Jews. He then prayed for return of his charm, and soon his home was again buzzing with people who sought his counsel and blessing, and who burdened him with their everyday problems.

Rabbi Pinchas' principal disciple was Rabbi Raphael of Bershad, who followed in his teacher's footsteps, and did not impart many of Rabbi Pinchas' teachings for fear he might not be repeating them accurately. Rabbi Raphael was extremely reticent, because remaining silent was the only foolproof method to avoid uttering a falsehood.

One day Rabbi Raphael was asked to be a character witness for a person involved in litigation. He would have been glad to be of help, but he was devastated by the thought that as a witness he would have to swear to tell the truth. How can a person ever take a solemn oath that everything he said was the truth? Mere mortals cannot have such certainty. Sometimes we may accidentally make an inaccurate statement, and at other times our memories are faulty and we may assert that something is factual because we think it was so. The Talmud states that when G-d uttered the third of the Ten Commandments, "You shall not take the Name of G-d in vain," i.e., do not swear falsely, the entire universe trembled. How could he submit to taking an oath? Yet, if he refused to testify, it would lead the judge to conclude that there was nothing he could say in the litigants favor, and he would thereby be harming the person.

Rabbi Raphael was in a dilemma, and he prayed fervently to G-d to extricate him from this terrible situation. He wept before G-d all night, and chassidic lore has it that he died before dawn that day.

Perhaps next time we are tempted to say, "I swear it's the truth," we will pause and think twice.

It's Not What You Do but How You Do It

From Scriptures down to contemporary ethicists, the trait of humility is cited as the foundation of character development. The greatest of our teachers, Moses, is not commended in the Torah for any of his many noble attributes, other than humility (*Numbers* 12:3). The opposite trait, vanity, is considered an abomination, so much so that whereas G-d states that He provides atonement for even the worst sinner (*Leviticus* 16:16), He cannot be in the presence of a vain person (*Psalms* 101:5, *Arachin* 15b).

The chassidic master, Rabbi Mendel of Vitebsk, would sign his letters, "The one who is truthfully humble." When asked how could someone say about himself that he is humble, and is not it actually vanity to claim humility, Rabbi Mendel cited a passage from the Talmud. The *Mishnah* says that Rabbi Yehudah HaNasi was the last truly humble person, upon which Rabbi Yosef commented, "Not so, there is me." Here, too, we may ask, how could Rabbi Yosef boast about being humble? Isn't that an inherent contradiction?

Rabbi Mendel continued, "There are two types of humility. One is a person who has achieved much and has a wealth of Torah and *mitzvos* to his credit, yet does not let this go to his head, and is humble. The second type of person is one who has achieved nothing, and there is no way he could be vain. Even though his humility may not be as praiseworthy as the first type, it is nevertheless commendable.

"What Rabbi Yosef was saying is that although he does not have the humility of Rabbi Yehudah HaNasi, who was humble in spite of his greatness, he does have the second type of humility. Feeling that he had not achieved anything, he said, 'I have no option but to be humble, for what is there for me to be vain about?'

"That is why I can state that I am truthfully humble," said Rabbi Mendel. "If I wanted to be vain, I cannot find anything concerning myself about which to be vain."

Rabbi Elimelech of Lizhensk would say, "I know I will be permitted to enter *Gan Eden* (Paradise). The heavenly tribunal will ask me, 'Elimelech, did you pray properly?' and I will say, 'No.' 'Did you learn Torah adequately?' I will say, 'No.' 'Did you do enough *mitzvos*?' I will say, 'No.' Then the tribunal will say 'He tells the truth, and for that he deserves to enter *Gan Eden.*' "

The virtue of humility hardly needs much emphasis. We know from personal experience how pleasant it is to relate to a humble person, and how unpleasant it is to be in the company of a vain, bombastic, arrogant person. What we may not realize is how far reaching these traits may be in their effects upon everything we do. And for that reason, it is well to tell this story.

Munish was a tailor in the town of Moglinitz, and was an accomplished craftsman. His skill at tailoring was appreciated by all, and even some of the local nobility had their clothes sewn by Munish. He was well paid for his services, and gave liberally to tzeddakah.

One day a handsome coach drawn by four white horses stopped before his shop, and no less a personage than the poritz (feudal lord), accompanied by his attendants, entered Munish's tiny shop. "Look here, Jew," the poritz said. "I hear you sew well. I have brought you some expensive imported wool from England and silk from the Far East. If you sew them well, you will become the tailor for my court, but if you ruin them, I swear you will do nothing but patchwork for the rest of your life."

Munish responded humbly, "I will do my best to please your lordship." Munish proceeded to sew the clothes, and the poritz was thrilled with his work. Not only was Munish well paid, but he was also permitted to keep the remnants of the material, which were quite valuable. He was indeed appointed tailor to the court of the poritz, and as his wealth increased and his work was admired, Munish began to think, "I am the finest tailor in the country." With his increased wealth, he was accorded various honors in the community, which he began to believe were his due.

One day the poritz told Munish that he was throwing a gala banquet and dance for all the nobility of the nearby fiefdoms, and he wished Munish to sew clothes for his entire family and staff. "But they must be outstanding, Munish," the poritz said. "Some of my guests have their clothes fashioned in France and Italy, and I am not about to be embarrassed. Do you hear?" Munish assured the poritz that his clothes would compare admirably with those of the finest French and Italian tailors.

Munish completed his work, and delivered the clothes to the poritz, but when they were tried on, heavens! What had gone wrong? They had never seen such ill-fitting clothes in their entire lives. The poritz was livid with rage. "You wish to humiliate me before the other nobility, Jew? I'll have you hung for this!" He piled up the garments and threw them at Munish. "Take these back and make them fit, or you will be hung from the highest tree."

Munish was crushed and broken hearted. What could have possibly gone wrong? In all his years as a tailor he had never produced such ill-fitting garments. He could not understand it, and what was worse, he did not have the slightest idea what he could do to make the garments fit better. In desperation, he sought the counsel of the chassidic master, who was known as the "the Seraph" of Moglinitz.

The Seraph listened sympathetically to Munish's tearful tale of woe. "I am pleading for my very life," Munish said. "That poritz does not make empty threats. He is a madman when he is enraged, and he will surely kill me. I don't know what to do."

The Seraph then said, "I will tell you what to do, Munish, but you must follow my instructions without the slightest deviation. Go back to your shop, undo the seams on all the garments, then sew them back exactly as they were, on the original seams. Do not deviate even a fraction of a millimeter."

"But what good will that do?" Munish protested. "They will be unchanged, and they do not fit at all."

"Do as I say," the Seraph said, and dismissed him.

Bewildered and broken hearted, Munish returned to his shop. The Seraph's suggestion made no sense at all. But what else was he to do? He had no inkling as to what sort of alterations he could possibly make to improve the fit. Munish laboriously undid the seams, taking care that his *profuse tears did not fall on the delicate materials and stain them. Having undone the seams, he sewed them back again just as the Seraph had said. When he had done that with all the garments, he brought them back to the poritz, trembling with fear that he would be sentenced to death.*

But when the poritz put on the clothes, his eyes gleamed with joy. Never before had he seen clothes fit so perfectly! Munish had outdone himself! "Let those pompous fools come with their French and Italian fashions! I will show them who has the finest garments in the world," the poritz exclaimed with glee. He gave Munish a handsome bonus, and sent him on his way.

Overjoyed but completely bewildered, Munish returned to the Seraph with the story of his success. The Seraph smiled and said, "You had always been a humble person, Munish, and the pleasantness of your humility influenced the outcome of your work. But when your success and your wealth went to your head, you became proud and vain. Vanity is an abomination, Munish, and it actually permeated the clothes you fashioned. When you redid the garments, this time with an attitude of being broken hearted, your vanity had disappeared and your humility made the very same clothes into beautiful garments.

"People think that character traits are mere abstractions. That is not so. They are real, and they can be conveyed in various ways. The clothes you originally sewed were ugly because you sewed them with the abominable attitude of vanity. The very same clothes, sewn with humility, had a charm that made them beautiful."

Our ethical works tell us that everything that Torah requires of us is ultimately for our own advantage. This story reinforces that principle. Everything we do is influenced by what we are.

Faith in Righteous People — Emunas Tzaddikim

This is a subject which requires understanding and clarification. Every person has a direct line with G-d, and we are not permitted to pray to intermediaries. Indeed, the propriety of prayers where we appear to be asking for blessings from angels or for their intervention on our behalf is the subject of debate, and must be interpreted in such a way that does not violate our basic belief that we relate only to G-d as the One from Whom everything emanates.

Yet, there is also a concept of faith in a *tzaddik*, which is derived from the verse in *Exodus* (14:31) "They had faith in G-d and in Moses, His servant" i.e., they believed that Moses was G-d's faithful servant and prophet. The sages derived from this verse that believing in the leader of Israel is equivalent to believing in the Creator (*Mechilta*). What does it mean to believe in a leader? In addition, the Talmud states that if there is a sick person in one's household, let him go to a *chacham* (a wise man) to pray for his recovery (*Bava Basra* 116a). Inasmuch as everyone has a direct contact with G-d and we do not work through intermediaries, why is the prayer of a *tzaddik* more potent than one's own prayer?

There as several ways in which we can understand the concept of faith in a *tzaddik*. First and foremost is that the opinion of a wise man, a *tzaddik*, as a Torah authority, must be accepted and followed even if we are in disagreement with it (*Sifri, Deuteronomy* 17:11). The principle of deference to the accepted Torah authority is emphasized by the account in the Talmud of the disagreement between Rabbi Gamliel and Rabbi Yehoshua, in regard to the proclamation of the first day of the month of Tishrei, where there was a difference of one day between the two opinions. Inasmuch as Yom Kippur is the tenth day of Tishrei, there was a disagreement as to which day would be Yom Kippur. Rabbi Gamliel, who was the formal Torah authority, ordered Rabbi Yehoshua, who was assumed to be a greater scholar, to come before him with his purse and walking staff on the day which, according to Rabbi Yehoshua's calendar, should be Yom Kippur. Rabbi Yehoshua deferred to Rabbi Gamliel's authority, even though he believed that day was in fact Yom Kippur.

Rabbi Schneur Zalman once said to his young grandson, who later became the *Tzemach Tzedek*, that the degree of *emunas tzaddikim* that had prevailed in the previous generation no longer existed.

"O ne time," he said, "I was returning from a trip to my master in Mezeritch, and it was a bitterly cold winter day. I suffered frostbite, and we stopped at an inn on the way and the driver had to carry me in because I could not walk.

"The innkeeper, an elderly man and obviously a pious Jew, cared for me tenderly. I asked him how long he had been living in this rural area, and he said 50 years. 'What do you do for prayer with a minyan (quorum of 10)?' I asked. 'I pray by myself,' the innkeeper answered, 'except for Rosh Hashanah and Yom Kippur, when I go into the nearest village to pray in a shul.'

"Is that the proper way for a Jew to live," I asked, "not to pray with a minyan all year around?"

"But I make my living here," the innkeeper said.

"How many Jews live in the village?" I asked.

"About 100," the innkeeper answered.

"And do you think that for 100 Jews G-d could provide a livelihood in the village, but not for 101?" I asked.

"We then continued in conversation, during which I related that I was returning from Mezeritch, and that I was a student of the Maggid.

"The following morning, when I awoke, I noted that the innkeeper had loaded all his belongings on a wagon. On inquiring, he told me that he was moving to the village as I had indicated was proper.

"The innkeeper did not know anything about me, except that I was a student of the Maggid, but for him that was sufficient to uproot himself from a place in which he had lived and earned his livelihood for 50 years, to move into a village where he had no idea how he was going to support himself. That is what is meant by emunas tzaddikim, his trust in the counsel of a Torah authority."

There is also a concept of receiving a blessing from a *tzaddik*, and this has its basis in a statement from G-d to the patriarch Abraham "And you will be a blessing" (*Genesis* 12:2), which the *Midrash* interprets to mean that G-d gave Abraham the power to bless people, and that gift has been given to other *tzaddikim* as well. Nevertheless, a person must understand that even though the *tzaddik* conveys the blessing, the origin of the blessing is G-d.

A woman once came to Rabbi Mordechai of Chernobel, pleading for a blessing to have a child. To the amazement of the bystanders, the Rabbi, who was exceptionally kind and benevolent, said brusquely to her, "I'm sorry, I cannot help you." The woman left the room tearful and broken hearted.

Noting the bewilderment of his chassidim, Rabbi Mordechai said, "Just wait a few moments, then go find the woman and bring her back here." The chassidim did as they were told, and when the woman came back, the Rabbi asked her, "What did you do when you left here?"

The woman replied, "I turned my eyes to heaven and I said, 'Dear G-d, the Rabbi refuses to help me. Now You are my only hope. Bless me that I have a child.'"

Rabbi Mordechai said to the chassidim, "This woman believed that I had magical powers, and she was trusting in me rather than in G-d. When I refused her request, she placed her trust in G-d where it belongs. She will now be blessed with a child."

The primary function of a *tzaddik* is to assist people in the proper service of G-d, to help them recognize their character defects and show them how to do *teshuvah*. The Rabbi of Chernobel was once asked by a *misnaged* (opponent of *chassidim*), "Why do you have people come to you for blessings? What makes you think that you have the power to bless people?"

The Rabbi answered, "The Talmud says that the sin offering

was sacrificed in the exact place in the Sanctuary where voluntary offerings were sacrificed, because if a special place had been assigned for the sin offering, then anyone bringing a sin offering could easily be identified. To make the penitent person less conspicuous and shield his identity, the Torah provided that the sin offering not have a separate place (*Jerusalem Talmud, Yevamos* 8:3).

"My function," the Rabbi continued, "is to teach people about *teshuvah*, to help them become aware of improvements that they must make in themselves. But if that was all I did, then anyone coming to me would be conspicuous and would immediately be identified as a penitent in need of *teshuvah*, and people would be reluctant to expose themselves as such. Therefore, I give blessings, so that when people come to me, no one can suspect that they are coming for *teshuvah*, and instead will assume that they are coming for blessings."

But as we have seen, the Talmud does indicate that the prayer of a *tzaddik* can be more effective. Why is this so?

There is another question that many theologians discuss. Why is prayer effective at all? Does one cause G-d to change His mind by praying?

Among the various answers that are given is that there are constantly emanations from G-d to provide for all peoples' necessities. These emanations flow along channels which can be affected by peoples' actions. Thus, there are things that people do that can cause obstruction of or diversion from these channels, so that the Divine emanations do not reach their intended targets. Prayer may correct these defects in the channels, thereby allowing the nurturing Divine emanations to proceed to the persons in need. *Tzaddikim* may have special knowledge just where the existing defects or obstructions may be, and they are therefore in a better position to rectify them.

But, we may ask, what is all this about channels and diversion of flow? Why does G-d not simply respond to people directly and give us our needs?

The answer is provided by an understanding of Divine truth and justice. Rabbi Moshe Chaim Luzzatto in his works, *Derech Hashem* (The Way of G-d) and *Daas Tevunos* (Wisdom of Understanding), makes it clear that G-d created the world with a system to which He adheres. While there is room for forgiveness of sins in the system of justice, there is no overlooking of transgressions, great or small.

The Talmud is sharply critical of anyone who says that G-d "overlooks" any transgressions (*Bava Kamma* 50a).

The Talmud relates a miraculous incident of a man whose wife died, leaving him with a tiny nursing infant. The man was too poor to hire a wet nurse, and miraculously he grew breasts and nursed the child. One of the Talmudic sages comments, "This indicates this person's lowly status, that he caused G-d to change nature for him" (*Shabbos* 53b). Rather than considering the man meritorious because he warranted a miracle, this sage considers this to be a degradation. Why?

G-d did not create an imperfect world. All eventualities were taken into Divine consideration at the time of Creation. For example, the *Midrash* states that at the time of Creation G-d provided that the sea should divide for the Israelites when they leave Egypt. What appears to us to be miraculous alterations in nature were actually all foreseen and included in the Divine plan of Creation. This particular incident, the sage believed, was not provided for, and necessitated an intervention by G-d to alter nature, which might be interpreted as an inadequacy in Creation. Causing G-d to intervene and override His own plans is not considered a merit.

It is thus not really a testimony to anyone's greatness that he is a beneficiary of an unplanned-for miracle. When prayers are answered, and the results appear to be miraculous, it is because, as we just explained, there were defects in the conduits for the Divine emanations, and these were rectified by the prayers, allowing the Divine emanations to reach their original target. Thus, this is not actually an alteration of nature. The greater skill of *tzaddikim* in restoring these channels accounts for the special efficacy of their prayers. The faith in the *tzaddik* is not in any magical powers he possesses, but in his knowledge of how to direct his prayers so that they are more effective.

The chassidic master, Rabbi Mordechai of Neshchiz, provided this insight into *emunas tzaddikim*. The *tzaddik* of Apt comments on Rashi's remark that Noah did not fully believe that there would be a flood (*Genesis* 7:7), because believing in something strongly enough can actually cause it to happen. He states that the word *emunah* is related to the word *omen*, which means to bring up (cf. *Esther* 2:7). Noah therefore tried to maintain an element of doubt about the deluge in the hope that it could be averted, and was afraid that his belief in it might bring it into reality.

The power of a *tzaddik*, said Rabbi Mordechai, is in his strong belief in G-d, and anyone who had that strong a belief could bring about similar results. When the *tzaddik* prays for a sick person, for example, and says that G-d is the healer of the sick, his belief is so strong that it actually brings down the Divine healing upon the person. In fact, said Rabbi Mordechai, the prime reason for having a relationship with a *tzaddik* is to learn how to perfect one's belief in G-d.

The Talmud compares the relationship to a *tzaddik* to one's relationship with G-d, as, for example, when Rabbi Akiva interprets the extra word in the Hebrew verse "You shall have reverence for G-d," to be inclusive, and that one must also have reverence for a Torah scholar (*Pesachim* 22b).

Someone asked the Rabbi of Rizhin: "Why did the Israelites not sing the praises of G-d until the splitting of the sea? Why did they not compose songs of praise when they saw the miracles of the ten plagues in Egypt?"

The Rabbi of Rizhin answered, "The Israelites were so convinced of the omnipotence of G-d that they were not impressed by miracles. The song of praise is preceded by the words 'They had faith in G-d and in Moses, His servant' (*Exodus* 14:31). The stimulus for the song of triumph was not the miracle they beheld of the dividing of the Reed Sea but rather the joy of having achieved a level of belief in G-d and in Moses that they had not had heretofore. This was what they celebrated in song."

The World As a Mirror

Denial is a psychological term referring to a person's inability to see reality. Denial is a frequently occurring phenomenon, and is one of the many psychological defense mechanisms, whose function is to shield a person from an awareness that would cause him distress. Denial has its counterpart in the behavior of a person who is confronted by a sight which causes him great anxiety or revulsion, and the person covers his eyes with his hands to block his vision. This is a conscious maneuver to block the visual perception. Denial is an *unconscious* maneuver to block a psychological perception.

We encounter denial in many forms. A person may ignore a symptom and may not seek medical help because he is terrified that he will be told he has cancer. A person who has lost a loved one may be unable to accept the fact of death. An alcoholic refuses to accept that his life has become unmanageable due to his drinking. A compulsive eater may swear that he consumes no more than 500 calories a day, and is unable to explain his weight gain. In all these situations there is a reality which a person, for one reason or another, cannot accept. In such situations, the psyche may turn off the awareness, so that the person simply cannot perceive that which would cause him much distress. It is not that he is consciously concealing or lying, but that he simply does not perceive reality. While everyone else who is in his environment does perceive reality and may confront the person with the facts, he simply does not hear them, and their words do not register in his mind.

Denial can often be dangerous, because a proper adjustment to reality requires an accurate awareness of reality. The person who denies the existence of a symptom may be allowing an early, treatable cancer to progress to a lethal stage. This is true of many other varieties of denial as well. You cannot successfully cope with a situation or correct a problem if you are unaware of its existence.

A very common form of denial is a person's inability to see his own character defects. The reason is obvious: Awareness of the presence of this defect in oneself is too much for a person to bear. Yet unawareness of these defects will result in one's doing nothing to improve upon them. Even a dedicated soul-searching may fail to reveal one's shortcomings, since denial obscures their existence from him.

The Baal Shem Tov was well aware of the mechanism of denial and its dangers in thwarting a thorough self-awareness. He said that G-d provided a way to circumvent this denial. "The world is a mirror," said the Baal Shem Tov. "The defects you see in others are really your own."

While denial prevents a person from seeing his own character defects, it does not prevent him from seeing defects in other people. Quite the contrary. We seem to be quite perspicacious in detecting faults in others. All we need to do, then, said the Baal Shem Tov, is to realize that these are but a reflection of our own shortcomings. We do not see defects in others that are nonexistent in ourselves.

The Baal Shem Tov once saw a person violating the Shabbos. In keeping with his teaching, he did a thorough soul-searching to discover when and how he had violated the Shabbos, because he was convinced that otherwise he would not have noticed this. When a thorough soul-searching failed to reveal any Shabbos violation, he prayed for Divine assistance to help him discover when he had been derelict in observance of the Shabbos. It was revealed to him that he had once heard someone speaking disparagingly of a Torah scholar, and he had failed to defend the scholar's honor.

Inasmuch as the Zohar says that a Torah scholar has the sanctity of Shabbos, this dereliction in defending the scholar's honor was tantamount to a violation of Shabbos. There is, of course, a vast difference between an active desecration of Shabbos by doing a forbidden act, and the passive failure to defend a scholar's honor, yet there is sufficient similarity between the two to allow one to represent the other.

How are we to understand this? Suppose that I walk along the street on Shabbos and I happen to notice a car being driven by a Jew. Why does this indicate a dereliction on my part? How was I not to notice it?

There are two answers to this. Firstly, it may be that this person's action was put before me by Divine providence in order to alert me to the fact that I had been derelict. But there is also a valid psychological explanation.

If you place 10 people on a busy street corner and tell them to observe what is going on, and later ask them what they observed, you are likely to get 10 different reports. Although all 10 were exposed to the same scene and stimuli, each one's attention was drawn to something else. One may report having noticed the repairs being made on a building, while another may describe the traffic jam, and yet another noticed something in the store window, and so on. It is clear that a person's perceptions are influenced by his interests.

The Scriptural statement, "Love covers all offenses" (*Proverbs* 10:12), has filtered down to the colloquial aphorism that "Love is blind." It is common knowledge that we may be oblivious to defects in someone we love, although they may be blatant to other observers. Just as we may not see that which we do not wish to see, so is a converse true, that we may see only that which, for some reason, attracts our attention. The Baal Shem Tov states that when we see defects in others, the reason for this recognition is that, in one way or another, they represent our own defects.

This principle is a major dynamic in the effectiveness of group therapy. In treatment of some types of emotional disorders, group therapy may be far more effective than individual therapy. A therapist's interpretation or his pointing out a particular character defect to a client may be rejected, with the latter's denial preventing the necessary insight. In a group session, the client is very likely to note this very defect in another group member, and the group may then help him realize that he too has this particular characteristic, and this is extremely effective in overcoming one's denial. It is the persistence of denial that constitutes a major obstacle to therapy and corrective action.

R abbi Dov Ber of Lubavitch was receiving his chassidim, when he abruptly told his gabbai (assistant) to close the door and not allow anyone entry. Some of the chassidim, eager to understand the Rabbi's sudden desire for solitude, put their ears to the door and heard the Rabbi reciting Tehillin (Psalms) with heartrending tones.

The Rabbi later explained that whenever a chassid asks him for guidance to do teshuvah for a transgression, he immediately searches for that transgression within himself, according to the Baal Shem Tov's teaching that the world is a mirror, and had he not been guilty of the same thing, even in a much more diluted form, it would never have come to his attention. The discovery of an analogous defect within himself then allows him to make the necessary amends.

"When one chassid told me about something he had done wrong, I promptly began searching for a similar shortcoming in myself. However, I was unable to find it. This meant that I was deceiving myself, and that somewhere there was a dereliction of which I was unaware. Being oblivious of this would preclude my taking any corrective action, and I therefore had to pray intensely for Divine guidance to help me discover this defect in myself."

Chassidic teachings are so beautiful! Just think what a wonderful world it would be if every time we saw some defect in another person, we would do some soul-searching and take corrective actions for self-improvement, rather than being critical of others and denouncing them. Observing and practicing this single teaching of the Baal Shem Tov could convert the entire world to utopia.

Just a Bit of Light

There are two somewhat conflicting approaches in *mussar,* both based on interpretations of the same verse, "Desist from evil and do good" (*Psalms* 34:15). One interpretation is that one must first avoid all objectionable behavior before embarking on the path of positive achievements. The metaphor used in support of this approach is that it makes little sense to put on fine clothes and use fragrant perfumes as long as one is wallowing in mud. Only after one has emerged from the mud and has thoroughly cleansed himself is one ready to improve one's appearance. This approach appears to be supported by another verse, "And unto the wicked, G-d said, 'To what purpose do you recount My decrees?'" (*Psalms* 50:16), which appears to indicate that one must first do *teshuvah* to remove one's sins before engaging in the study of Torah.

The opposite approach interprets the Scriptural verse as "Desist from evil *by* doing good," and as a metaphor uses the fact that just a tiny bit of light can disperse a vast amount of a great deal of darkness. Just as the flame of a single candle can eliminate an entire room full of darkness, so can a single positive act disperse a vast amount of negativity. The Rabbi of Kotzk used to say, "I don't want my *chassidim* to avoid sin only because it is wrong. I want them to be so totally occupied with doing *mitzvos* that they simply have no time to sin."

Chassidic teaching appears to favor the second approach. Delaying doing *mitzvos* until one has not yet adequately cleansed oneself of sin may be used as a tactic by the *yetzer hara* who may say, "Who do you think you are to be learning Torah?" The *yetzer hara* may use the verse — which indicates that a wicked person should not study Torah — to deter people from the study of Torah, claiming that one has not yet done adequate *teshuvah*. Masquerading under the guise of piety, the *yetzer hara* may thereby deter a person from the Divine service. The *yetzer hara* is cunning, in that he can convert the commendable trait of humility to his own nefarious purposes, saying, "You are too unworthy to participate in the Divine service."

M*y father told me of an incident of which he had personal knowledge. In Kiev there was an ambitious young man, who found that all avenues for success were closed to Jews in the anti-Semitic society of Czarist Russia. He therefore shed all vestiges of his Judaism, and adopted a non-Jewish identity, including working and eating on Yom Kippur. He was then able to advance to a prestigious position in the government.*

One day a body of a man was washed ashore, and there was no way of identifying him. Inasmuch as he wore a talis kattan (a four-cornered undergarment with tzitzis), he was identified as a Jew and was given a Jewish burial. The young man who had rejected everything Jewish heard of this, and although he did not wish his Jewish identity to be an obstruction to his fortunes, he nevertheless wanted to be buried among his own. After all, once he was dead, he did not stand to lose anything by being Jewish. He therefore began to wear a talis kattan, which would not reveal his identity during his lifetime, but when he would die, it would be evident that he was Jewish and he would be accorded a Jewish burial.

Once he began wearing the talis kattan, subtle changes began to take place. He fasted on Yom Kippur, and found an excuse to explain his absence from work. He began to avoid treifah (non-kosher) foods, and gradually became observant of those mitzvos which he could do without revealing his Jewish identity. Eventually he quit his position in the government and became a total baal teshuvah. The performance of a single mitzvah set an entirely new lifestyle into motion.

There is also a story of a man who lived in a town near Lublin, and who was bitterly despised by everyone in the community because he was an informer. The taxes imposed on Jews by the anti-Semitic poritzim (feudal lords) were ruthless and confiscatory, and Jews had no option other than to conceal their belongings from the tax assessor. The informer would tell the assessors about anyone's undisclosed earnings, leading to his total impoverishment. Some of the chassidim of the Seer of Lublin appealed to the tzaddik to bring down the wrath of G-d on this evil person who threatened their very survival.

When the chassidim handed the petition to the Seer, he exclaimed, "What a tzaddik! His brilliance illuminates the heavens. Please bring him to me!" The bewildered chassidim carried the message to the informer, who agreed to visit the Seer simply out of curiosity as to why anyone would consider him to be a tzaddik.

The Seer warmly welcomed the man, and said to him, "There have been many terrible accusations against you, yet on that particular day, I saw that your light penetrated all the celestial spheres. Tell me, what good deed did you do on that day to merit such holiness?" The man then recalled that on that day he had celebrated the bris (circumcision) of his newborn son. "That was it!" the Seer declared. "I saw you in the presence of the patriarch Abraham and the prophet Elijah, who come to share in this great mitzvah." The awareness of the kedushah (holiness) which he could attain had a profound impact upon the man, and he never again returned to his previous practices of being an informer.

❧

A person who was a scoffer once told Rabbi Levi Yitzchak of Berditchev that he could prove the Torah to be wrong. "It says in the Shema that if we sin, G-d will be angry at us and punish us. I am a profligate sinner, yet I am wealthy and happy." Rabbi Levi Yitzchak replied, "My son, the only way you could know this would be because you must have read the Shema. You should know that the reward for reciting the Shema even a single time is so great that all the wealth in the world may not be enough to compensate one for it!"

❧

Rabbi Moshe Leib of Sassov would wander from village to village, explaining, "If a person had a brother *in a distant place, wouldn't he travel far to visit him? All Jews are my brothers, and I want to get to know them." In one community his chassidim objected to his visiting an outspoken sinner. "The rabbi should not enter the home of such a rasha (wicked person)," they said. Rabbi Moshe Leib looked at them with bewilderment. "How dare you say about a tzaddik that he is a rasha?" he said. "Look, he has a mezuzah on his door!"*

≈)⌒

R abbi Elimelech of Lizhensk composed a beautiful introductory prayer to the morning services, in which he says, "Please help me to see the good in everyone, and not their faults."

The emphasis on seeing what is right in someone instead of what is wrong is an important ingredient, not only in achieving amicable social relations and unity among Jews, but also in effective parenting. In several books, I have emphasized the crucial role of self-esteem (*Let Us Make Man*, CIS 1987; *I am I*, Shaar Press 1993; *Life's Too Short*, St. Martin's Press 1995; *Positive Parenting*, Mesorah 1996). It is not unusual for parents to "catch" a child doing something wrong and reprimand him for it, but how often do we "catch" our children doing what is right and commend them for it? We take it for granted when they make a *berachah* (recite a blessing) over food, and we may not point out how pleased we are that they understand that everything emanates from G-d and that we must express our gratitude toward Him via *berachos*. Yet if one were to see a child eating without a *berachah*, one would likely exclaim "What! Eating without a *berachah*?" How can we expect to elevate a child's self-esteem if we focus only on the negative and fail to appreciate the positive?

It is important, both in child rearing and self-development, to do *mitzvos* and help children do *mitzvos*, based on the principle that the performance of one *mitzvah* leads to the performance of many others. Improper behavior cannot continue for long in the presence of *mitzvos*. It is just as if one has purchased a new piece of furniture for the living room. If the carpet clashes with the new item, then one will likely get a carpet that harmonizes with the furniture. This new carpet may not blend well with the wallpaper; hence, the latter must be replaced to be compatible. Eventually everything in the room is changed, all as a result of the introduction of a single piece of furniture.

So it is with a person's character. It is generally uncomfortable to maintain traits and practices which are mutually contradictory. Therefore, doing one *mitzvah* may give a person a mindset that makes it more difficult for him to violate Torah principles, and as with the room decor, one is likely to gradually make adjustments until the entire lifestyle becomes consistent and one is totally observant of Torah. This may be why the wearing of the *talis kattan* by a person who otherwise blatantly rejected Judaism was able to eventually revolutionize his character.

The Talmud appears to be in support of the second interpretation of "Desist from evil by doing good." The Talmud quotes G-d as saying, "Give Me an opening as tiny as the point of a needle, and I will enlarge it to admit passage of huge wagons" (*Shir HaShirim Rabbah* 5:3). Just a tiny opening, a single ray of light, can banish much darkness and usher in an abundance of *teshuvah*.

The Rabbi of Kotzk, in his inimitable and uncompromising demand for truth, qualified the *Midrash* by saying, "Yes, a pinhole of *teshuvah* may suffice, but this tiny opening of *teshuvah* must be sincere, and penetrate the personality from one end to the other." A superficial glow, such as that of a luminescent clock in a dark room, is not the kind of light that banishes any darkness.

All one must do is make a start, and take a first step, but that step must be firm and unfaltering.

Return of a Favor

I noted earlier that chassidic stories have value even if their factual validity is questionable. When I hear a story whose authenticity is not questionable, it has even greater value. One such story was told to me by my father, who was a first-person participant.

My father lived near Kiev prior to the communist revolution, under czarist rule. At age 18, young men were conscripted into the Russian army, which, for observant Jews, was nothing less than disastrous. The czarist army was not the United States Army, where one's religious practices are given considerations. Furthermore, anti-Semitism was rampant even among the civilian population, and to be a Jew in the military was virtually to risk one's very life. There was no deferment for Divinity students, and the only way to avoid conscription was through personal contact, which often meant buying one's freedom via a bribe to an official.

When my father became of draft age, my grandfather, the Rabbi of Hornosteipel, tried to contact influential people who might arrange a deferment for him, but all efforts were futile. He then thought of trying to explain to the medical officer who was authorized to reject recruits on the basis of health considerations that my father's rigorous religious observance and his refusal to eat non-kosher food would soon result in physical deterioration which would render him unfit for military service. My grandfather was told that this medical officer, Dr. Primakow, was an assimilated Jew, who had little sympathy for religion, and there was no reason to expect that he would be willing to help. Nevertheless, since there was nothing else to do, my grandfather felt that it was worth a try, and accompanied by his shamas (sexton) and my father, they went to Kiev to see Dr. Primakow.

When the secretary told the doctor who the people were that wished to see him, he came to the waiting room, looked at my grandfather, and said, "That is not the Rabbi of Hornosteipel. He is a much shorter person." The shamas explained that the doctor must be referring to the previous rabbi of Hornosteipel who had died, and that my grandfather was his son, who had succeeded to his position. Dr. Primakow escorted the three into his office, and my grandfather set forth his request.

To their astonishment, Dr. Primakow listened attentively and appeared to be genuinely interested. When my grandfather finished his explanation, Dr. Primakow said, "I understand. Normally, I would not give a second thought to such considerations, but I do feel that I am indebted to your father, and I should return a favor." My grandfather was bewildered, being unable to imagine what kind of indebtedness Dr. Primakow could possibly have to his father.

"When I was a young doctor," Primakow continued, "I was assigned to physically examine on the draftees, and I traveled from town to town to the various draft boards. On one such trip I stayed at an inn in Hornosteipel, and all I heard people talking about was the greatness and the saintliness of their Rabbi.

"I had no interest whatever in religion and no use for a rabbi, but the exalted praise he received aroused my curiosity, and I simply wanted to see for myself who this person was. I was ushered into the Rabbi's study, and he greeted me very warmly. I had the strange feeling that he was looking right through me, yet his eyes were so soft and comforting that I did not feel uneasy about this. It was indeed a pleasant experience.

"As I rose to leave, the Rabbi said to me, 'I hope that you will never cause harm to any Jew, and I give you my blessing that a non-Jew should never cause you any harm.' I thanked the Rabbi for his kind words, and as I left, we walked down a long corridor and he escorted me all the way to the door. As I was about to step out he said, 'Remember, you must not do any harm to a Jew, and a non-Jew will never do any harm to you.' The repetition of this remark irritated me. What need was there to say it twice, and to urge me to remember it?

"As you well know, we were often approached by men who wished to buy their freedom from military service. All of us were on the take, but we were concerned that if we were caught accepting a bribe, that could result in severe punishment. I therefore had concluded that I would keep the number of bribes to a minimum, accepting only a few very substantial bribes.

"In one town I was approached by a young Jewish boy who explained to me how difficult it would be for him to serve in the military because of his religious observance. '300 rubles,' I said. The young boy was taken aback. '300 rubles? My family could never raise anywhere near that amount. Perhaps we could manage 25 rubles.' I stood firm. '300 rubles,' I said, 'and when you have that amount you may return. Otherwise don't bother me.'

"A while later another young man, a non-Jew, asked to be deferred. I told him my price was 300 rubles, and he said that was satisfactory. His father had a number of local merchants with whom he did business, and he would return in a few hours with the money.

"Just opposite my office was that of another military medical examiner, who was an ardent anti-Semite, and although I was not a practicing Jew, he hated me nonetheless. When the second young man returned with the money, the Jewish boy was still standing in the corridor, somehow hoping that perhaps I would reconsider. He saw the non-Jew mistakenly knock on the door of the other doctor's office, and when he entered and saw that he was in the wrong office, he excused himself and stepped back, whereupon the doctor said, 'Don't go away. Just come here.'

'You probably were looking for Dr. Primakow, weren't you?' he said. 'I can take care of that for you. We are all in this together. How much did he ask you for?' The young man told him that he had brought 300 rubles. 'Let me see the money,' the doctor said.

"The Jewish boy observed all this through the open door, and saw that the doctor counted the money, then made some markings on the money and returned it to the young man saying, 'Yes, it is the right amount. You can go across the hall and give it to Dr. Primakow.' This was clearly done in order to trap me as having accepted a bribe.

"After the young man brought me the money and left, the Jewish boy knocked on my door. 'Do you have the necessary amount?' I asked. 'No,' he said, 'but I did not come this time on my behalf. I came on your behalf,' and he proceeded to tell me what he had observed.

"I took out the money and noted that there were indeed identifiable markings on it. I then said to the Jewish boy, 'Don't worry. You will be deferred.'

"Several days later, when the young men appeared for their medical examinations, I noted that the other doctor was in high spirits. I knew that he was gleefully anticipating the opportunity to expose me for having accepted a bribe. When I examined the Jewish boy, I put the stethoscope on his chest and exclaimed, 'This is no specimen for our army. I'm surprised you're even alive,' and I dismissed him.

"Soon afterward the non-Jew came for his exam. I noticed the sneer on the other doctor's face as I began my examination. I listened carefully to the young man's heart and said, 'Very healthy. You will make a fine soldier.'

"The other doctor was taken aback. 'Are you sure he is healthy?' he asked. 'Perhaps you should listen to his heart again. He looks somewhat asthenic to me.'

"I said, 'No. He is fine. Let me tell you something. This young man had the audacity to try to bribe me to defer him, and he offered me 300 rubles.' I then took the 300 rubles out of my pocket and threw it on the desk in front of the members of the draft board. 'There you have the bribe. Let no one dare say that the czar's offices are corrupt.'

"I then understood what the rabbi had meant. 'I was to avoid harming any Jew, and I would be blessed that no non-Jew would harm me.' His words and blessings had come true, and I had narrowly escaped being trapped and convicted of bribery. I owe the Rabbi a favor in return for his blessing." Then turning to my father, the doctor said, "This young man is hardly the kind that would serve well in the army," and with that he dismissed him.

I asked my father, "Didn't the fulfillment of grandfather's blessing have any impact upon him to become more religious?" My father explained that the Midrash states that when the Israelites saw the Reed Sea split before their eyes and when they crossed the divided waters on dry land, they nevertheless carried an idol along with them. "That is the cunning and the power of the yetzer hara. A person can be confronted with incontrovertible evidence of G-d's presence and might, and nevertheless deny Him."

This story has always captivated me, but perhaps its most important teaching is that if a person has a need to deny the truth of Judaism, even obvious miracles may not be convincing. This is a most sobering thought.

The Joy of Being Upstaged

Most often people are not pleased when they are on the losing side of a dispute, but there are times when losing can be enjoyable. We have precedent for this in the Talmud, which relates a *halachic* dispute wherein Rabbi Eliezer argued with all of the other authors of the *Mishnah*. To prove that he was right, Rabbi Eliezer called for a sign from heaven.

"Let that carob tree prove I am right," he said. The carob tree uprooted and moved 100 cubits. "Carob trees do not dictate *halachah*," the rabbis said. "Let the stream of water prove my point," Rabbi Eliezer said. The stream reversed its direction and began flowing uphill. "Streams of water do not dictate *halachah*," the rabbis said. "Let the walls of the academy prove my point," Rabbi Eliezer said. The walls began to cave in, whereupon Rabbi Yehoshua shouted to the walls, "What right do you have to intervene when the rabbis engage in *halachic* dispute?" The walls did not return to their upright position in deference to Rabbi Eliezer, nor did they cave in, in deference to the rabbis, and they remained fixed at an angle.

In desperation, Rabbi Eliezer exclaimed, "Let the heavens proclaim that I am right." A voice rang out from the sky, "Why do you disagree with Rabbi Eliezer, whom the *halachah* follows in all places?" Rabbi Yehoshua responded, "The Torah is no longer in heaven. G-d gave the Torah to us, and the Torah states that the opinion of the majority shall prevail."

The Talmud goes on to relate that Rabbi Nassan met the prophet Elijah and asked him, "How did G-d react to this dispute?" Elijah responded, "G-d was jubilant and said, 'My children have triumphed over Me'" (*Bava Metzia* 59b).

The message, of course, is that Torah law is absolutely unalterable. Not even the Almighty has the right to override Torah law. This principle is so important that G-d rejoiced in its observance, even if His will in the rabbinic dispute was not heeded.

R abbi Levi Yitzchak of Berditchev once overheard a person in shul reciting the prayers so rapidly that the words were unintelligible. He approached the worshiper and mumbled some meaningless sounds. The worshiper was puzzled and asked him to repeat what he said. Again Rabbi Levi Yitzchak mumbled some nonsensical syllables.

"I'm sorry," the man said, "but I have no idea what it is you are trying to tell me."

Rabbi Levi Yitzchak said, "But that is exactly how you

are reciting the prayers. You run the words together so rapidly that they are unintelligible. You should speak clearly to G-d just as you wish me to speak clearly to you."

The man responded, "But that is not really necessary. Before an infant learns how to speak, he makes sounds which are unintelligible to anyone else except his parents. The father and mother, however, do understand him. They know which sound means he wants milk, which sound means he wants a cookie, which sound means he wishes to be taken for a walk, and so on.

"G-d is our Father," the man continued, "and as a Father He understands exactly what I am saying even though it may be unintelligible to you." Rabbi Levi Yitzchak was ecstatic. He embraced the man and kissed him.

Rabbi Levi Yitzchak has come down in history as the greatest advocate of his people, always looking for ways to interpret people's actions favorably, regardless of their obvious negativity. It was Rabbi Levi Yitzchak who managed to obtain contraband Turkish goods when their possession in Russia was punishable by death, and he then sent out messengers to find a piece of bread in a Jewish home on Pesach. When the messengers returned empty handed, Rabbi Levi Yitzchok said, "Dear G-d! The emperor has his police armed with guns, and they can shoot anyone who violates his edicts, yet I had little difficulty in obtaining forbidden Turkish goods. You have no soldiers or police who shoot violators, yet because You forbade possession of *chametz* on Pesach, there is not a crumb of bread in any Jewish home. People with such devotion and loyalty deserve to be treated better than You are treating them."

Nevertheless, Rabbi Levi Yitzchak found it necessary to reprimand a person who appeared to be treating his prayers with a lack of proper respect. When his reprimand was rebutted by a favorable interpretation of the mumbled prayer, Rabbi Levi Yitzchak was overjoyed. He was pleased to be the loser in this encounter.

The tzaddik of Sanz was asked by a woman for his blessing that she be relieved of her distressful circumstances. The tzaddik replied, "Have faith in G-d, and He will certainly help you," whereupon the woman said, "That is not what the siddur (prayer book) says. In our prayers we say that G-d saved the Israelites in their exodus from Egypt, and when they saw the great miracles, they believed in Him. So first G-d must help us, and then we believe."

The tzaddik smiled and said, "You are right. What the siddur says must be practiced. First G-d will help you, and then you will grow in your faith."

≈≈

The Rabbi of Rizhin rebuked some of his chassidim for their laxity in not praying within the time limits prescribed by the Shulchan Aruch. "You may have heard that some tzaddikim do delay their prayers, but this does not give you license to do so," he said, and then he related the following parable.

"A man was accustomed to his wife serving him a simple meal every night, consisting of cooked beans. One day he returned home from work, but his meal was not on the table as usual. 'Ah,' he thought, 'tonight's meal must be something special, and its preparation is taking a bit longer.' He waited with anticipation for better than the usual fare.

"When more time elapsed and the meal was not yet served, he grew even more excited. 'My wife must be preparing roast meat, and that it why it is taking so long.' He anxiously awaited the gourmet delight he would enjoy.

"After a long delay the wife served his meal: cooked beans. The husband became angry. 'I would gladly have waited for something special, but if all I am getting is the usual cooked beans, why did you make me wait?'

"The Rizhiner continued, 'When a tzaddik delays his prayers, it is because he meditates on teshuvah and elevates himself spiritually so that his prayers are recited with intense kavannah (concentration) and the quality of his prayers is so special that G-d gladly accepts the delay. But if the prayer consists of the usual recitation without any special kavannah, what justification is there for delaying it?'"

On their way home, the chassidim stopped at an inn and reviewed what they had heard from the Rabbi. As they repeated his rebuke about the delay of prayers and the parable of the husband who became angry with his wife for making him wait and serving him nothing more than the usual daily fare, one of the guests at the inn who overheard the discussion remarked, "I don't know about that. It seems to me that if the husband truly loved his wife, he would not get angry with her even if after a long delay she served him only cooked beans."

The next time the chassidim came to the Rizhiner, they told him of this man's comment. The Rizhiner was ecstatic with joy. "He is right! G-d's love for us is so great that he will accept our prayers even after a long delay, although they may not really be special in quality." How thrilled he was to rescind his rebuke! After a few moments of meditation, the Rizhiner said, "That person at the inn was sent down to Earth with the specific assignment of defending those who are lax in praying at the proper time, and finding a zechus (merit) for them. Nevertheless," the Rizhiner continued, "one is obligated to observe the time limits specified in the Shulchan Aruch."

⁓⌒

The tzaddik of Apt once responded to a supplicant, "Have no worry. G-d will help you."

"What am I to do until such time as G-d helps me?" the man said. "I need help right now!"

The tzaddik smiled and said, "You are right. But G-d will sustain you until He gives you definitive help. This is what He promised to our forefather Jacob, 'I will not forsake you until I have fulfilled what I have promised you' (Genesis 28:15)."

⁓⌒

The Baal Shem Tov was once approached by a man who appealed for help. He had bought merchandise and while he had stopped briefly at an inn, someone absconded with his wagon, and this theft impoverished him. The Baal Shem Tov directed the man to go to a certain village and find a particular person, and tell him that he must return the stolen goods. "If he denies the theft, tell him that Yisrael Baal Shem Tov was an eyewitness to it, and that if he does not return it he will deeply regret it."

The man did as he was told, and the thief confessed, but said, "I want to meet this Baal Shem Tov." Upon meeting the Baal Shem Tov the thief said to him, "If G-d has given you prophetic vision, do you not have anything better to do with it other than to spy on thieves?"

The Baal Shem Tov apologized and said, "At the particular moment when I had this vision I was in a place where
I was not permitted to think of anything holy."

Imagine what previous generations were like! Here we have a
thief who reprimands the Baal Shem Tov for misusing his
prophetic vision. If this was the quality of the sinful of previous
generations, we can just imagine what the *tzaddikim* of those
times must have been like.

We Shall Do and We Shall Listen — Naaseh VeNishma

We have already noted that the Baal Shem Tov taught that the world is a mirror, and that any defects we see in other people are merely reflections of our own shortcomings. He also taught that we should listen carefully to comments people make, because they may contain important messages.

The spoken word is given great weight in Judaism. Idle talk is by no means innocent, and making a disparaging remark about another person is a grievous sin. The Chofetz Chaim dedicated his life to eliminating *lashon hara* (gossip) and emphasized that it is the worst of all sins. The distinctive feature that separates man from beasts is the capacity to speak, and this Divine gift should not be abused. By the same token, the Baal Shem Tov taught that a person's speech can be revealing.

⁓⁓

The Baal Shem Tov and some of his disciples were once at an inn, and the Baal Shem Tov remarked, "That man should be reprimanded for not observing the rituals of family purity." "How do you know that?" the disciples asked. "Just listen," the Baal Shem Tov answered.

Moments later the man helped himself to a glass from the cupboard, whereupon the innkeeper said, "Don't use that glass. It is new and has not yet been immersed in the mikveh." The man replied, "What difference does it make whether or not it has been immersed in the mikveh?" — thus proving the Baal Shem Tov's observation.

⁓⁓

Rabbi Zusia of Hanipoli was once hurrying along his way when someone shouted to him, "Help me get my wagon upright." Rabbi Zusia, who felt that he could not delay the mission he was on, replied, "I'm sorry, I can't." The man shouted back to him, "Yes you can. You just don't want to!" Rabbi Zusia said to himself, "Zusia, Zusia, you have just received a rebuke from Heaven. There are many things you should be doing and you are simply too indolent, and you excuse yourself by saying that you can't do them. You can indeed do them, Zusia, but you just don't want to."

⁓⁓

One of the chassidic masters was traveling and the driver stopped off to feed and water the horses. He laughingly remarked to the master, "Just look at those horses eat and drink. They must think that I am giving them hay and water to provide for their pleasure, while in fact I'm doing so only so that they get me to where I want to go."

The master took the driver's message as a reprimand. "When I eat and drink, I may sometimes think that I was given this food to gratify my appetite. I must remember that it is there only that I should have the energy to fulfill the Divine will, and to bring myself to the ultimate goal in life. If I forget this, I share the mentality of a horse."

One time a driver remarked to his passengers, "Have you ever noticed that when the horse runs faster, the wheels of the wagon revolve more rapidly in the same amount of time?" A chassid who heard this took it as a message that when one is more diligent and avoids delay, one can do more mitzvos in the same amount of time.

❧

Then there is the famous story of Rabbi Moshe Leib of Sassov, who said that he learned the meaning of ahavas Yisrael (love of fellow Jews) from a drunkard. When passing a tavern, Rabbi Moshe Leib overheard a conversation where an obviously inebriated man said, "Ivan, I am your best friend. I love you, Ivan." The other man, equally tipsy, said, "Not true, Stepan. You do not love me." Stepan began crying, "Don't say that, Ivan. I truly love you." "Well, then," Ivan responded, "if you really love me, tell me where I hurt. Tell me what I am lacking." Rabbi Moshe Leib said, "One cannot claim to love another person unless one can feel his pain and know what he is lacking."

❧

One of the masters of Lubavitch was once served a bowl of soup, and as he took the first spoonful, the waiter said to him, "There are noodles at the bottom. If you dip a bit lower, you can get them."

The rabbi was overjoyed by the waiter's comment. "The human being is a composite of an animal body and a spiritual soul," he said. "The former tends to pull him down, while the latter tends to elevate him.

"When Adam was punished for his sin, he cried to G-d, 'Am I and my mule to eat from the same trough?' When we eat for pleasure we descend to an animal level. A human being must be spiritual, and his eating should serve to provide the necessary nourishment that will give him the strength to fulfill his mission on earth. The gustatory aspects of eating are irrelevant to this purpose.

"We may often forget this, and let ourselves be swayed by the pleasant taste of food. I am grateful that the waiter reminded me that to enjoy the noodles I must dip a bit lower. It is a descent from a spiritual level to strive for better-tasting food. "

◠◠

One of the chassidic masters passed a jail just as a thief was being released. The officer said to him, "I hope that the thrashing you received taught you a lesson, never to steal again." The thief responded, "I may try again. Perhaps next time I can be more careful or I will be luckier."

The master took this as a teaching. "When we have a goal we wish to achieve, we should never be discouraged by failure. Just because one failed in the past is no reason to resign oneself. One should try to study the failed attempt and see what might be done better next time. If no mistake can be discovered, one should nevertheless try

again. The time and circumstances might be more propi-
tious, and one can indeed succeed."

≈⌒

A chassid was present when a soldier who was on
guard duty was being flogged for having briefly left
his post to warm up from the bitter cold. He pleaded, "It
was so cold that I was getting frostbite." His superior re-
sponded, "You took a pledge of allegiance to the czar, and
that should have kept you warm enough."

The chassid heard, "My prayers and Divine service have
turned frigid. If my allegiance to G-d was sincere, this
should have given them greater warmth and fervor."

A friend told me that he was at a very busy airport and there
was so much commotion and conversation among the passengers in the waiting area that the announcement of the
public-address system was drowned out. One of the passengers
commented, "There is so much noise here that I couldn't make
out what was said. They might have announced something
important about the flight, but I don't know what it was. I'll have
to ask the agent at the desk what that was all about."

My friend said, "The Talmud says that every day there is a
voice that emanates from Sinai, urging us to return to the study
and observance of Torah. I have often wondered, 'Of what use
is this voice if we cannot hear it?' This incident made me think
that perhaps the reason we do not hear the voice is because we
are drowning it out with the hustle and bustle of our daily activities. Perhaps we too have to turn to the 'agents,' our spiritual
leaders, to tell us what the voice is saying. Someone who does
not get a clarification of the announcement may miss the flight
and never reach his destination. If we do not get clarification of
the voice from Sinai, we may not reach our goal in life."

When a missile is sent off to outer space, it is given a trajectory to follow to its destination. There may often be slight deviations from the prescribed path, and midcourse corrections may be necessary to assure that the missile reaches its target.

Perhaps this was the meaning of the declaration of our ancestors at Sinai, *Naaseh VeNishma*, we will do what G-d instructs us, and we will continue to listen. We will keep our ears open for cues that can help us remain on the correct path to our goal.

Not Just Pranksters

Every culture has a legendary folk hero, a witty
prankster whose mischievous jokes are most entertaining. Jewish lore has Herschel of Ostropl, to whom
many merry antics are attributed.

How many of these antics actually occurred and whether
Herschel was the protagonist in any of them is questionable,
but Herschel himself is not a legendary figure. He was a real,
flesh and blood human being who served in the court of the
chassidic master, Rabbi Baruch of Mezhibozh. Like other famous chassidic wits, Herschel was a pious, serious, scholarly
person who used humor to bring people — even leaders — out

of their dejection. By infecting them with joy, he enabled them to engage in fruitful spiritual activity.

Several of the chassidic masters were known to have had severe depressive moods, and the source of these moods is no mystery. Not only were they deeply distressed by the plight of the Jews of their time, most of whom lived in the anti-Semitic environment of Eastern Europe, with an abundance of oppressive, virulent edicts against both body and soul, but the masters also lived in dread of the fulfillment of the Talmudic prophecies and the sufferings that Jews would have to undergo before the ultimate Redemption. Many of them devoted their lives to prayer, in the hope of averting these terrible forebodings.

T he Rabbi of Rizhin once visited the tzaddik of Apt and found him to be in tears. He inquired as to the reason for his sadness, and the tzaddik of Apt said that he foresaw terrible times awaiting Jews. The Rizhiner tried to comfort him. "We know," he said, "that G-d will never give us greater suffering than we can tolerate." This caused the tzaddik to cry even more profusely. "That is precisely the problem," he said. "The level of tolerance that Jews have is exceedingly great, and they are thus vulnerable to unimaginable suffering." How true the tzaddik's perceptions proved to be!

Before his death, the Rizhiner predicted, "There will come a time when Jews will have a homeland because they will be expelled from other countries and will have no other place of refuge. This homeland will thus be accompanied by the humiliation of expulsion. But I prefer a homeland with humiliation to a diaspora with pride and honor."

Inasmuch as the Talmud says that the Divine Presence does not rest with one who is dejected (Shabbos 30b), the chassidic masters would have people of wit about them who could extricate them from their morose moods. The Seer of Lublin had Reb Mordechai of Rakov who served in this capacity.

O*ne time there was an epidemic in Lublin with many fatalities. The Seer was broken hearted over this, and although it was believed that his prayers could elicit Divine mercy, his extreme sadness precluded effective prayer. The chassidim prevailed on Reb Mordechai to do something to lift the Seer's spirits. Reb Mordechai entered the Seer's study. "Good news!" he said. "The epidemic is over."*

"What are you talking about, Mordechai?" the Seer said. He pulled aside the curtains and there was a funeral procession in the street. "Look, they are carrying another body to burial."

"Oh, no!" Reb Mordechai said. "Resurrection has just occurred, and what you see is them bringing people back from the cemetery." The Seer cracked a smile, and was able to begin his fervent prayers that brought an end to the plague.

Another time Reb Mordechai was sent in to arouse the Seer. It was on Tishah B'Av, and the Seer's lamentations on the destruction of the Temple were so profound that the chassidim were concerned that he might die of grief.

Reb Mordechai said to the Seer, "The Rebbe is so sad because the holy Temple was burnt? Never mind! The land it stood on is still worth the money."

⊰⊱

R*eb Mordechai was once entertaining at a wedding at which the Seer and the venerated tzaddik of Apt were in attendance. In his merrymaking, Reb Mordechai* *mimicked some of the mannerisms of the tzaddik of Apt. The next day he fell gravely ill.*

The Seer assumed that Mordechai was being punished for having offended the tzaddik of Apt, and sent the latter a message. "Please forgive Mordechai. He was carried away by the merrymaking and meant no offense." The tzaddik of Apt responded, "I hold no grudges against him."

When Reb Mordechai's condition deteriorated and it was feared that his end was near, the Seer again appealed to the tzaddik of Apt for mercy, assuring him that Reb Mordechai had been acting in the line of duty, to bring cheer to the wedding party.

"Is that so?" said the tzaddik of Apt. "Then let him show his skill at making witty remarks now, and then he will recover." The messenger returned to find the members of the chevra kadisha (burial society) in attendance, expecting Reb Mordechai to breathe his last. When he was told what the tzaddik said, Reb Mordechai called the chevra kadisha to his bedside and whispered to them, "Do not bury me near a small child. I don't want to be awakened by his crying." He then recovered and lived to a ripe old age.

Herschel of Ostropl served the same function for Rabbi Baruch of Mezhibozh. Countless witticisms have been attributed to him as a mischievous prankster. There are some stories that have a ring of truth.

A man came to seek Rabbi Baruch's blessing for his *daughter, who was in prolonged labor. The midwives did not have any means of delivering her and they feared for her life. Rabbi Baruch was away at the time, so Herschel advised him to gather a minyan into the* daughter's room and recite Yizkor (the memorial prayer). The man did as he was told and the woman soon delivered a healthy baby.

When Rabbi Baruch learned of this he summoned Herschel. "What made you give such advice?"

"It was simple," Herschel said. "When we say Yizkor in shul, the shamas announces, 'Let all the little children exit.' I knew that if they would say yizkor, the child would come out."

⊃⊂

On another occasion, when Rabbi Baruch was away, a man came with a question about his prayers. Herschel sat behind the Rabbi's desk, pretending to be Rabbi Baruch, and listened to the man's question.

"I say the assigned chapters of Tehillim (Psalms) for each day of the month. There is also a specific chapter for each day of the week. If one chapter appears both for the day of the week and for that day of the month, must I say this chapter twice?" he asked.

Herschel took on a meditative attitude. "What do you do for a living?" he asked.

"I am a porter," the man said. "I haul loads with my horse and wagon."

"And do you lubricate the wagon wheels with pitch?" Herschel asked.

"Of course," the man answered.

"Now suppose you were hauling a load of pitch," Herschel said. "Would you still lubricate the wheels with pitch?"

"Of course," the man answered.

"There you have it," Herschel said. "The chapter for the day is the 'lubricant' for that day. If you have a load of Tehillim which happens to contain the particular chapter

*for that day, you still have to say that chapter again to lu-
bricate that day."*

↬

Some of the stories about Herschel of Ostropl carry a
moral; for example, one time he was desperate because there was no food in the house for the children. He
went into the marketplace and called out. "Who wants to
go to Zhitomir for half-fare?" Soon a group of people gathered about him rather than take the coach, and after
collecting the money, he began walking with them to
the countryside. After they had walked a bit, one asked,
"Well, Herschel, where are the horses?", to which
Herschel replied, "Horses? I never said anything about
horses, just that I could take you to Zhitomir for half-
fare."

Later Herschel said to his wife, "All I did was announce
a ridiculous bargain, and you should have seen how
many 'horses' gathered about me!"

↬

Herschel exploited his intimacy with Rabbi Baruch to
deliver a witticism directed against the master, something which others to accomplished chassidic masters —
would never have dreamt of doing. My father used to relate
this story.

One day Herschel told Rabbi Baruch, "I have asked you
several times for a salary increase, but you have never giv-
en it to me. Well, I must tell you what has transpired.

"One Thursday I was very despondent. Shabbos was
approaching, and the meager wage you were paying me

was long since gone, and I had no way of buying provisions for Shabbos.

"As I was walking down the street, the yetzer hara met me. 'What's wrong with you, Herschel?' the yetzer hara asked. 'Why are you so glum?' I told him about not having any money to buy wine and fish for Shabbos.

" 'Listen to me, Herschel,' the yetzer hara said. 'The Rebbe has many more silver kiddush cups than he uses. Take one of these cups and pawn it, and you'll have more than enough money for Shabbos provisions.'

" 'But that would be stealing,' I said.

" 'No way,' the yetzer hara said. 'You are only borrowing the cup until you have enough money to redeem and return it.'

"I did as the yetzer hara said, and I had a great Shabbos. But next week the same thing occurred, and by Thursday I was penniless. This time I met the yetzer tov, who asked me why I was so despondent. When I told him he said, 'Herschel, you must have faith and trust in G-d. Things will get better.'

" 'Your adversary gave me better advice,' I said, "and I proceeded to tell him what the yetzer hara had advised me. 'But that was stealing, Herschel,' the yetzer tov said. 'You don't dare do that. Just have faith.'

"Well, I listened to the yetzer tov, and I don't wish the Shabbos I had on my worst enemy. No challah, no wine, no fish, but just an abundance of complaints from my disgruntled wife.

"Next week I again met the yetzer tov, and I told him how disappointed I was with his advice. He said, 'Herschel, go into the Rabbi, and tell him that you simply must have an increase in salary.'

" 'I have done that many times,' I said to the yetzer tov, 'but it is of no use. Why don't you intercede for me?' I suggested.

*"The yetzer tov said, 'Me? Go to your Rabbi? Impossible.
I have never been with him before.' "*

Only Herschel could deliver such a stinging remark, that the
great master had never before been visited by the *yetzer tov*.
But this poignant witticism served the purpose of bringing the
tzaddik out of his dejected mood.

16

Don't Look for Excuses

A chassid of Rabbi Yehudah Leib of Radzovil, who had been an innkeeper for many years, told the Rabbi that he had decided to retire and move into the village, where he could have greater opportunity to be in the *beis midrash* (house of study), to recite *Tehillim* (Psalms), study the *Mishnah*, and *Ein Yaakov* (the non-halachic portions of the Talmud).

During his many years as proprietor of the inn, this *chassid* had provided a warm welcome for travelers, giving them nutritious meals and comfortable accommodations. He would inquire about their families and business dealings, which eased their burdens of being on the road. For those who did not have money to pay, he extended liberal credit, and to the poor who traveled from village to village for alms, he gave food and bread gratis. When he retired, his son ran the inn in a much more businesslike manner, and the homey touch was lacking, as were the liberal credit and the *tzeddakah* to the poor.

The Rabbi told the *chassid* the following story.

R ecruits who were drafted into the army would be put through the rigors of boot camp, and were subjected to grueling exercises. Those who volunteered were treated much better, and if they showed promise, were given preference for officers' training.

One young man, the son of a poritz (feudal lord), waited until he was drafted, and was exposed to the rigors of boot camp. This was not at all to his liking, so he deserted the army and went to another city. He then took on a different identity, and obtained a false birth certificate, making himself several years younger than his true age, and volunteered for the army. As a volunteer he was treated much better, and since he was very bright, he was soon admitted to officers' training. He received a commission and several promotions.

One time, in the company of a general, he had a bit too much to drink, and told the general about the son of a poritz who had deserted the army and outsmarted them by volunteering under a new identity. The general quickly grasped that this was an autobiographical account, and became very angry. He ripped off the young man's insignia which indicated his officer's rank, and demoted him to a common soldier.

"The army's need for soldiers is as great as its need for officers," he said. "You did not volunteer because of your loyalty to the emperor, but simply to further your own career and achieve your selfish interests. If you were *sincerely devoted to the emperor, you would have looked out for his needs rather than your own."*

The Rabbi then said, "G-d's needs were for you to provide the comfort and consideration of wayfarers as you did. You could study the Mishnah and say Tehillim right where you were. Your retirement was intended to make things easier for yourself, rather than to do the Divine will.

"Every person can find excuses why he is not praying or learning Torah to the utmost. 'If only I were somewhere other than where I am, I would be able to do more.' These are self-deceptive excuses. You can stay right where you are and make the time and effort to improve your service to G-d."

In my practice I often come across people who try the "geographic cure." Instead of making the necessary changes within themselves, they try to make a change in external circumstances, which is generally of little value.

The Fall of the Prodigy

I t is of interest that among the great number of chassidic masters, all of whom were spiritual giants, there are only two who have been given the title of *HaKadosh* (the Holy). The first is the Baal Shem Tov *HaKadosh*, and the other is the *Yehudi HaKadosh*. This latter master was Rabbi Yaakov Yitzchak of Pschis'che, who was the founding father of many chassidic courts in Poland, including Kotzk, Gur, Izhbitza, Aleksander, and others.

Why was Rabbi Yaakov Yitzchak singled out to merit this distinction of *HaKadosh*? Many theories have been set forth, none of which really satisfies our curiosity. While we are hardly in a position to make an appraisal of the Torah scholarship and spiritual heights of these great masters, we are nevertheless on safe territory if we assume that there were other chassidic masters who equaled Rabbi Yaakov Yitzchak in scholarship and devotion. Perhaps his uniqueness which merited this unusual distinction may be found in an episode of his youth.

R abbi Yaakov Yitzchak's father was an eminent Torah scholar who resigned his position as rabbi of his community because it required him to reprimand community members who were lacking in their Torah observance. "Who am I," asked Rabbi Asher, "to discipline others? Have I eradicated all my faults and overcome all my personal deficiencies that I should reprimand others?" He therefore resigned his position, moved to another community, where he became the shamas (sexton) in a shul, which resulted in his income being much less than the salary of a rabbi, which had not been that great either. However, Rabbi Asher and his wife adjusted to the substandard income, and lived in peace.

After a number of years of a childless marriage, their prayers were answered with the birth of a son. The child showed exceptional intellectual brilliance, learning to read the siddur (prayer book) before the age of two. When he was three, Reb Asher took the child to the cheder (Hebrew school), but several months later the teacher brought him to his parents, saying that he had already surpassed the five and six-year-old students who were learning Chumash (the Five Books of Moses), and suggested that the parents enroll him in a more advanced school.

The mother suggested to Reb Asher that he teach the child at home. "Why subject him to the risk of an ayin hara (evil eye)?"

In Judaism there is a widespread belief of the harm of an ayin hara. While this may be understood in the sense of a malevolent power of an evil eye, there is also a more logical explanation. Flaunting one's greater assets, whether intellectual or material, may cause others to feel deprived and therefore hurt. Causing any other person to feel hurt may have punitive consequences, and it is therefore recommended that people avoid arousing the envy of others.

Be that as it may, Rabbi Asher felt that the study of Torah would protect against the harm of an ayin hara, and he took young Yaakov Yitzchak to the Talmud class. Here the young prodigy flourished, soon surpassing all the other students. At age eight he entered into complex and intricate halachic discussions with his teacher, and was then sent to the higher Talmudic classes of the local rabbi, the famous scholar Rabbi Leib Charif (the Brilliant). Here too he soon made his mark, and entered into a close relationship with a senior student, Yeshaya, who was later in life to become the noted scholar, Rabbi Yeshaya of Pshedborzh.

One time Rabbi Leib delivered a highly complex lecture, which seemed to be over the heads of all other students, and only young Yaakov Yitzchak appeared to grasp it well. Rabbi Leib then suggested that Yaakov Yitzchak explain it to his classmates, which the youngster did in a most lucid way. Rabbi Leib was beside himself with admiration of this prodigy, and exclaimed, "Why can't all of you be as bright as Yaakov Yitzchak!" Unfortunately this comment offended the feelings of many other students, and Yeshaya, who was unusually sensitive, burst into tears.

From that day on, there was a notable change in Yaakov Yitzchak. He seemed to have lost his keen understanding, and his prodigious characteristics evaporated, until he became just an average student. His parents were deeply affected by this, and his mother felt that her worst fears about his being the victim of an ayin hara had come true. They would ask him what had happened, but he seemed to have no explanation for the change in his academic level. Their only consolation was that Yeshaya, who was now the most advanced student of Rabbi Leib, maintained his close friendship with Yaakov Yitzchak, and the two were inseparable.

Reb Asher's practice was that he would retire at 10 p.m., then arise at midnight, when he would go to shul to recite the tikun chatzos services of lamentation for the destruction of the Temple. Shortly before dawn he would return home for a brief sleep before morning services.

One night, Rabbi Asher began to feel sickly during the midnight services and returned home. As he passed Yaakov Yitzchak's room, he noted that the bed was empty. Curious, he kept vigil, and saw that before dawn, the youngster came home, undressed, and went to bed.

The following night Rabbi Asher decided to learn the mystery of his son's nocturnal activities, and found that after midnight the young boy got dressed and went in stealth to one of the small shuls. Rabbi Asher stood outside the shul, eavesdropping by a window, and heard his son begin recitation of the Psalms. Never before had he heard the Psalms chanted with such purity of heart and devotion. When he heard the sweet tones of his son's pleading to G-d, "My soul thirsts for You, my flesh craves for You (Psalms 63:2) "and "Like a hart pines for a stream of fresh water, that is how my soul thirsts for G-d" (ibid. 42:2), Rabbi Asher felt that he was listening to angelic hymns, and that not since King David had composed these Psalms had anyone ever recited them with such devotion.

Rabbi Asher had discovered that young Yaakov Yitzchak was leading a secret life. He thanked G-d profusely for having given him such a holy child, but had decided not to tell his wife about it, respecting Yaakov Yitzchak's wish for secrecy. He now knew that every night after he left for midnight service, young Yaakov Yitzchak would go to this place of worship to recite the entire Book of Psalms, returning before his father came home, so that his unusual devotion in service to G-d would remain undetected.

One day Rabbi Leib delivered a highly complex lecture on Talmud, which he asked the class to review. When he tested the class on their grasp of the material, the only one who had understood it properly was Yeshaya, whereupon Rabbi Leib complimented him and said, "All of you would do well to emulate Yeshaya and his diligence in his study of the Talmud." At this point Yeshaya could not contain himself any further, and he exclaimed, "I can no longer continue this deception and accept praises which are not my due. The only reason I understood this material was because Yaakov Yitzchak explained it to me. He has been the leader in our relationship for the past several years, and it is to him that I owe whatever knowledge I have."

The subterfuge was now exposed. Yaakov Yitzchak's genius had not suffered in the least, but following that fateful day when he became aware how deeply Yeshaya had been hurt by his prodigious brilliance, Yaakov Yitzchak had decided to retreat into the shadows, and keep his genius under wraps, so that never again would anyone be hurt by his outstanding intellectual capacities. Thus, for years he had assumed the role of being simply an average student, placing his colleague, Yeshaya, in the forefront at all times.

Perhaps it was this attitude of self-effacement, which continued during the years that he advanced as a disciple of the great chassidic master, the Seer of Lublin, that earned him the unusual distinction of being the Yehudi HaKadosh.

18
Two Paths to the Same Goal

Throughout generations there were people who wished to avoid anything that would distract them from contemplating G-dliness. They sought a close communion with G-d, and inasmuch as G-d has placed Himself in the Torah, as the Talmud says, "In My writing I have given Myself to you" (*Shabbos* 105a), the only way to embrace G-d is through the study of Torah. These *tzaddikim* therefore isolated themselves from the affairs of the world and spent their entire days absorbed in the study of Torah.

Closer to our own times, this approach was portrayed by the great Gaon of Vilna, who did not separate himself from the study of Torah even momentarily. It is related that when his sister visited him after a long separation, the Gaon rose and recited the prescribed *berachah* on seeing someone dear after an extended absence, then said, "My dear sister, we will have abundant time to converse in *Gan Eden* (Paradise). Here we must use every available moment for Torah," and promptly returned to his studies.

The Gaon would seek discipline from others, and once asked the *Maggid* of Dubno to reprimand him, but there was nothing in the Gaon's life that warranted any rebuke. The *Maggid* then said, "It is no trick to be a *tzaddik* when you seclude yourself in your study, totally engrossed in Torah. Let me see you go out among people and interact with them, and then be a perfect *tzaddik.* That would be some trick." The Gaon smiled and said, "I am not a performing magician, and I do not have to do tricks."

Many of the chassidic masters, however, chose another path. While they would spend some time in seclusion and meditation, they felt it was essential to mingle with people and bring them closer to observance of Torah. As a prototype, they had the high priest Aaron, whom the Talmud describes as someone who loved people and brought them closer to Torah (*Ethics of the Fathers* 1:12). Commentaries explain that Aaron's closeness with people would stimulate them to *teshuvah*, as they would think, "If Aaron only knew the truth about me, he would avoid me. I must correct my ways so that I do not lose Aaron's friendship."

Rabbi Elimelech of Lizhensk once expounded on the overriding importance of truth, and in extolling its virtues said, "If a person were cautious not to utter a single false word for 24 hours, he would be assured of being admitted to *Gan Eden* even if he had many sins."

S hmuel, an innkeeper who was in the audience, decided to take advantage of this guarantee for Gan

Eden. He reasoned that avoiding a lie for a 24 hour period should not be all that difficult a feat. One night he told his wife that he wished her to serve the customers in the inn the following day, because he was going into seclusion.

Shmuel isolated himself in his room, and began reciting Tehillim (Psalms). He fought off sleep, because he was afraid that he might talk in his sleep and say something false. He did everything possible to keep himself awake that night and throughout the following day. The next night, when he was just about one hour shy of 24 hours of absolute silence, there was a knock at the door. Since the inn was closed for the night, he tried to ignore the knock, but it became ever louder, and he finally decided to answer the door, but to exercise great caution not to say anything that was not true.

At the door was a peasant who said, "I've come for my shovel. Please give it to me."

Shmuel had never set eyes on the man before, and knew nothing about a shovel, so he felt confident in saying, "You must be mistaken. I do not have your shovel."

"Yes you do," the peasant said. "I came here for a drink earlier today, and I did not have any money to pay for it. I therefore left my shovel as a pledge with the lady at the bar until I brought the money. Here is your money, and give me back my shovel."

Shmuel then realized that he had inadvertently told an untruth. His nearly 24 hours of total silence had been futile. He found the shovel and returned it to the peasant.

The next time Shmuel went to Rabbi Elimelech, the master smiled and said, "Shmuel, avoiding falsehood by isolating oneself from the world was not what I intended. One must learn to be truthful while interacting with people, because that is when truth is meritorious. There is little virtue in not lying when one is not in contact with people.

"You tried to do it the easy way, and your efforts were thwarted. If you really wish to deserve Gan Eden, see that all your communications with people be free of falsehood."

There are those select few for whom total seclusion is appropriate. The Talmud says, however, that there were some who tried to emulate Rabbi Shimon bar Yochai, but they did not succeed. For most of us, it is necessary that we do interact with people, but be on the alert to be honest and truthful in all our dealings.

Love for the Holy Land

The love of the chassidic masters for Eretz Yisrael knew no bounds. The Baal Shem Tov began his journey to the Holy Land, but traveled only as far as Istanbul when, as a result of a number of happenings that indicated to him that it was not the Divine will for him to be there, he turned back. A similar fate occurred to his oldest disciple, Rabbi Yaakov Yosef of Polnoah. His younger disciples, lead by Rabbi Menachem Mendel of Vitebsk, eventually reached Eretz Yisrael and established the chassidic settlement in Tiberias. Rabbi Nachman of Breslov visited Eretz Yisrael for a brief period, and said that there were levels of spirituality that are not attainable outside of Israel.

Travel in those days was fraught with great danger, and the trip from the Land of Israel to Europe took many weeks. When a visitor from the Holy Land came to any of the chassidic masters, he received a royal welcome. All the chassidic masters raised money to support the Jewish settlements in the Holy Land, especially collecting for the various charities under the name of Rabbi Meir Baal HaNess.

Rabbi Avraham Dov of Ovrutch, who was a disciple of the tzaddik of Chernobel had a burning passion to move to Eretz Yisrael, which he finally satisfied in his later years. One time a traveler from Eretz Yisrael visited him, and he questioned him thoroughly about every aspect of the Holy Land. The visitor was lavish in his praise, describing various sacred sites, where the patriarchs had lived, and where so much of Jewish history had taken place. The visitor exclaimed ecstatically, "Even the rocks of Eretz Yisrael are precious jewels."

Rabbi Avraham Dov ultimately reached Eretz Yisrael and settled in Tzefas (Safed). He was euphoric about being in the Holy Land even though he lived there in poverty.. One time the visitor who had so extolled the land came to see him in Tzefas, and Rabbi Avraham Dov confirmed that everything the visitor had said in the praise of the land was true, except that he did not see that the rocks were precious jewels. "They seem like ordinary rocks to me," he said. The visitor replied, "If one merits, one can see them as jewels."

Several years went by, and one day Rabbi Avraham Dov called a group of people together for a festive celebration. He explained, "When I was told that I had not been deserving of seeing the rocks of Israel as precious jewels, I devoted myself to intense teshuvah. It was clear to me that human beings have two perceptions, physical and *spiritual, and that one can see spiritually even with one's physical vision. When the Torah was given at Sinai, the Israelites 'saw ... the sounds' (Exodus 20:15). They reached a level of spirituality where the physical body became angelic, and the physical senses perceived spirituality.*

"When Moses sent the spies to scout the land of Canaan, he chose men of great spirituality, because he thought they would see the land through spiritual lenses. The Midrash states that these men were poisoned by vanity, and that they feared that upon entering the Holy Land they might lose their positions of leadership, and this ego drive toppled them from their spiritual heights, so that they looked at the land only with a physical vision.

"Since coming to Israel, I have not been able to see the rocks as anything but rocks. Today I have finally been able to see them as precious jewels, and for me this is a most festive day."

Rabbi Avraham Dov had a small *shul* (synagogue) in Safed, which is still in existence and can be visited. In 1838 much of Safed was destroyed by an earthquake. It is related that moments before the quake struck, Rabbi Avraham Dov suddenly called all the worshipers to stand near him. When the quake hit, part of the ceiling collapsed, but the place where Rabbi Avraham Dov and the worshipers were standing was miraculously spared. The building was later reconstructed, and one can clearly differentiate the original part of the ceiling toward the front of the *shul*, where Rabbi Avraham Dov stood, from the newer part.

Rabbi Avraham Dov wrote a chassidic commentary on Torah, *Bas Ayin*, which is full of love for Eretz Yisrael. He cites the *Midrash* which describes how Moses pleaded with G-d to permit him to enter the Promised Land, and he states that

Moses persevered so because there are levels of spirituality that are unattainable unless one is nourished by the fruits of the Holy Land, eaten in the Holy Land, and it was to these spiritual heights that Moses aspired.

If we only reflect that Moses ascended to the celestial spheres three times for forty days each, and was in the company of the heavenly angels, "Bread I did not eat, and water I did not drink" (*Deuteronomy* 9:9), and yet was unable to achieve the levels of spirituality that one can attain by eating of the produce of the Holy Land, then we might understand what Eretz Yisrael is, what it should mean to Jews, and why each grain of its earth is sacred.

Songs of
the Heart

There are many chassidic stories that emphasize the principle "G-d prefers the devotion of the heart" (*Sanhedrin* 106b). This is not to be misconstrued as meaning that one may be "a Jew at heart" as may be said by those who would like to free themselves of the obligation to perform *mitzvos*. Of what use is a heart without a body, without the brain, lungs, liver, digestive system, eyes, ears, arms, and legs? A "good-hearted" person who is devoid of *mitzvos* is as spiritually lifeless as an isolated, disembodied heart.

There may be times, however, when a person tries his utmost to perform a *mitzvah*, but circumstances beyond his control preclude his doing so. In such instances, the sincerity of the desire to do the *mitzvah* is equivalent to actually having performed it (*Berachos* 6a).

There were cases where a person could not do *mitzvos* because he never had the opportunity to learn how to do them.

The Baal Shem Tov once dreamed that there was a shepherd whose service to G-d surpassed his own. Always eager to learn how he could improve his devotion to G-d, the Baal Shem Tov, accompanied by several of his disciples, traveled to the locale where he had been told the shepherd could be found.

The Baal Shem Tov and his disciples noted how the shepherd blew his horn to gather the flock. Then he looked up to the sky and said, "Master of the Universe! I know You created the sky and the earth and all the peoples of the earth. I know that You chose the Jews to be Your people, but I was orphaned of my parents and was raised among non-Jews. I don't know what You want me to do for You, but I know that You wish people to blow a horn (the shofar) and I know how to do that. So now, I am going to blow this horn for You, G-d." The shepherd then proceeded to blow his horn with all his might.

Then he said, "I know that people pray to You, G-d, but I never learned how to pray. All I know is how to sing shepherd songs, so I will sing them for You." He then proceeded to sing several of his songs.

Then the shepherd said, "But just blowing the horn and singing songs is not enough to serve so great a God Who created the whole world. I must do something else for You!" He then proceeded to turn somersaults until he was exhausted.

"Now I have blown the horn and sung for You, and I have turned somersaults for You. I would like to give You *a gift, but all I have is this coin." The shepherd then took his coin and threw it toward the sky.*

The Baal Shem Tov said to his disciples, "You will not see that coin fall to the ground, because it will be taken up to Heaven, where it will be treasured."

This shepherd, the Baal Shem Tov said, truly fulfilled the mitzvah to love G-d with all one's heart, all one's soul, and all one's belongings.

There was another shepherd who became a chassidic master, the Rabbi of Kalev. He was "discovered" by Rabbi Leib Sarah's, a disciple of the Baal Shem Tov and the Maggid of Mezeritch.

R abbi Leib has come down in chassidic history as Leib, the son of Sarah. Why this strange appellation? That is a story in itself.

Rabbi Leib's father, Reb Yosef, was one of the hidden tzaddikim, who made his living tutoring children in Torah. There were some Jews who operated inns on the roads connecting cities, where travelers would stop for food and lodging. Being in the countryside, they did not have access to a cheder (Hebrew school) where their children could learn, and Reb Yosef would be hired for several months at a time to teach the children how to read and understand Hebrew so that they could pray and read the Torah. The innkeeper's family loved Reb Yosef, looking at him as a godly person. Reb Yosef was a widower, his entire family having been wiped out in a pogrom.

The poritz (feudal lord), from whom the inn was rented, periodically visited to inspect his property, and on one occasion, noted the innkeeper's daughter, Sarah, who was stunningly beautiful.

"I am going to have that young woman as my wife," the poritz said, and he said it in a tone that indicated he was not in jest. In czarist Russia, the feudal lords were supreme rulers over their fiefdoms, and they had the authority to sentence one to be executed at their whim. To throw an entire family into the dungeon was not an unusual occurrence. "I will be back in three days with my priest, and I will marry her right here," he thundered, and then, emitting a fiendish laugh, he said, "Unless, of course, she happens to be married already."

The family was crushed. How does one deal with such an evil fiend? There was no one to whom they could appeal. They turned to Reb Yosef — who shared in the family's anguish — who said, "All I can do is pray to G-d for a miraculous salvation."

The young Sarah then said, "We are not to depend on miracles. I know what I will do. I will marry Reb Yosef, and the evil poritz will not be able to touch me."

"What are you saying, my child?" Reb Yosef said. "I am old enough to be your grandfather. You need a young, handsome husband."

"There is no way a husband can be found for me in three days, and I will rather die than be taken by the poritz. Reb Yosef, you are the answer to my prayers, you are my only hope, and you will marry me," Sarah said, as she looked at Reb Yosef with pleading eyes.

The father gathered together a minyan (quorum of 10) and a wedding was held. Shortly before the chupah (marriage ceremony) Sarah said, "Reb Yosef, you must promise me that we will have an outstanding child."

Reb Yosef responded, "We know that G-d acts toward people accordingly to how they act. You are doing something extraordinary, marrying a man so much older than you, and G-d will therefore reward you with an extraordinary child."

Aryeh Leib was born a year after their marriage, and Reb Yosef did not live to see young Leib's bar mitzvah.

Prior to his death, Reb Yosef said to his son, " You were born as a result of your mother's determination to free herself from the clutches of an evil poritz. Your mission in life will be to travel from village to village, seek out helpless Jews who are being persecuted by their poritzim, and do whatever you can to help them. G-d will bless your efforts with success. And you, my child, will always bear the name of the noble woman who bore you, Leib the son of Sarah."

Rabbi Leib Sarah's did indeed fulfill his father's directive, and chassidic lore has many stories about how he appeared at propitious moments to save Jews from the dungeons of the *poritzim*. He is reported to have appeared before princes and monarchs, having entered heavily guarded palaces without being noticed by the guards.

Duc*uring one of his many travels, Rabbi Leib Sarah's was inspired by the fact that in a nearby village there was a young shepherd who had an especially holy neshamah, and that he should introduce this young man to the study of Torah. Rabbi Leib made his way to the countryside and found himself being attracted, as if by a magnet, to a field where a young boy was tending a flock of sheep.*

"What is your name, my child?" Rabbi Leib asked.

"My name is Yitzchak, but they call me Izik," the boy answered. "And what is your father's name?" Rabbi Leib asked.

"My father is dead," the boy answered, "and I work as a shepherd to support my mother."

"And what do you do out here all day long?" Rabbi Leib asked.

"I sing songs," young Yitzchak Izik answered, "or I hum tunes. I love to sing."

"Can you sing for me?" Rabbi Leib asked.

"Yes, I can sing you a love song," Yitzchok answered, and the young boy began to sing with a sweet, crystal-clear voice.

Rabbi's Leib's tears poured profusely down his cheeks, and he kissed young Yitzchak Izik. He accompanied the young boy home, and told his mother that he would take him to study Torah, and that he would regularly send her some money to support herself. The woman thanked him for giving her child a chance to know what it means to be a Jew, since she lacked the means to do so. She blessed her child and sent him off with Rabbi Leib, who took him to the yeshivah of the renowned Talmudist and chassidic master, Rabbi Shmelke of Nikolsburg.

Young Yitzchak Izik was a brilliant student, and progressed rapidly in his proficiency in Torah study. He later returned to his homeland, and became the rabbi in Kalev, introducing the chassidic teachings of the Baal Shem Tov to Hungary.

Rabbi Yitzchak Izik of Kalev is known in chassidic lore as the "Sweet Minstrel of Israel." He never forgot the songs of his days as a shepherd, but he changed the lyrics so that now he sang:

> "Galus, galus (the exile), how huge you are.
> Shechinah, Shechinah (the Divine Presence), how distant You are.
> Dear G-d, why did You make it so?
> Make the galus smaller, and bring the Shechinah closer to me,
> And we will spend our days together."

Chassidim sitting in the darkness of the dusk late Shabbos afternoon at *shalosh seudos* (the third meal of Shabbos) often sing this revised song of the shepherd. The melody is a penetrating one, arousing a craving for closeness to G-d, and a prayer that G-d bring our bitter exile to an end, so that we can rejoin the Divine Presence in the Sanctuary in Jerusalem.

Another song of his shepherd days underwent a change too:

"The rooster crows as the dawn breaks.
The forest is green, the fields white with grain
And a bird flies freely under the sky.
Wait for me, wait for me, bird, I will fly with you.
The holy Sanctuary will be rebuilt, and Zion will be fulfilled
And we will sing a new hymn to G-d.
I can hear it in the song of the bird."

One cannot hear a melody of the Rabbi of Kalev and not be touched. Among *chassidim,* the melodies of the Rabbi of Kalev have become the vehicle for many of the sacred prayers of Rosh Hashanah and Yom Kippur.

On these holy days, when we wish to cleanse our hearts and souls, we seek methods to remove our earthiness, and lift our spirits to come closer to G-d. The melodies of the young shepherd, transformed into sacred hymns by the Rabbi of Kalev, are powerful missiles which can penetrate the thick barriers that encircle our hearts.

"G-d prefers the heart," the heart of a young shepherd, the heart of a young woman who defends her honor and sanctity. Is it any wonder that the Rabbi of Kalev was discovered by none other than Rabbi Leib the son of Sarah? How true is the aphorism, "One heart is sensitive to another."

It Can Be Done

Rabbi Schneur Zalman's epochal work *Tanya* is based on the verses in *Deuteronomy* (30:11-14), where Moses said that the Torah is not remote and that it is not difficult to observe it, rather "The matter is very near to you — in your mouth and in your heart — to perform it." To those who might think that observance of the Torah, with its many requirements and many prohibitions, is extremely difficult, Moses says that it is not so. To the contrary, it is "very near to you," or quite easy to fulfill. All one needs to do is to make up one's mind that one will do it, and once the determination is there, the rest is easy. It is only difficult as long as one is considering "Should I or shouldn't I?"

The Torah tells us that when Pharaoh's daughter saw the basket (into which Moses had been placed) floating in the Nile, she sent her maidservant to fetch it (*Exodus* 2:5). The Midrash interprets this verse to read that she stretched her arm to retrieve it, and that although the basket was indeed beyond her reach, her arm miraculously did reach it. The message is that if there is something you feel you must do, even if you think you cannot do it, try anyway.

There is a principle in Torah that G-d does not ask anything of us that is beyond our ability to accomplish (*Avodah Zarah* 3a). A person need only decide, "Is this what G-d wants of me?" If the answer is positive, there should not be any question whether it is feasible. Because of our tendency to rationalize, we should seek guidance from a competent person to help us determine what it is that G-d asks of us when it is not clearly evident to us, for otherwise we may come to an incorrect conclusion in order to spare ourselves the hardships involved.

Rabbi Levi Yitzchak and his colleague Rabbi Menachem Mendel were busily engaged in preparation for a wedding. In fact, all the townspeople were engaged in the preparations, because the bride and groom were orphans and had been raised by the kind people of the community. Everyone felt as though it was his own child who was getting married, and the town was buzzing with activity.

Suddenly the news spread through the town that a team of kidnapers had come to the community. These were scoundrels who would kidnap a young man and haul him off to be conscripted into the czarist army for a period of 25 years. Upon hearing the news, all young men of military age took cover, but the bridegroom, who was apparently so preoccupied that he did not hear the news or had just

*not heeded it, did not go into hiding and was seized by
kidnapers.*

*When the community became aware of the kidnaping,
gloom descended upon it, and the day of anticipated joy
turned into a day of bitter mourning. The young bride was
in tears, and there was no consoling her. Once the young
man had been handed over to the military authority there
was no way of gaining his release. Any attempt to bribe
the official was fraught with the risk of being convicted of
a capital crime and executed.*

*Rabbi Menachem Mendel, who had been instrumental
in bringing the young couple together, said to the dis-
traught bride, "Have no fear, my child. G-d will help us.
Your bridegroom will be returned to you this very day."
When the young woman continued to weep, Rabbi
Menachem Mendel said, "Did you hear? This very day he
will be returned to you. I swear it!" Upon hearing that the
Rabbi swore to it, the bride felt somewhat relieved. Clearly
the Rabbi must know something, otherwise he would not
have dared to swear to it.*

*Rabbi Menachem Mendel hurried off to the local mili-
tary attache, and made his way past the guards who tried
to stop him, into the inner room where the officer resided.
He found the officer to be drunk, staggering across the
floor. He looked at the Rabbi with contempt and anger
flaring from his eyes. "Dirty Jew! How did you get in
here? What do you want here?" And followed this with
several choice expletives.*

*Rabbi Menachem Mendel began to plead the case of the
orphaned young man who was to be married that day,
and could his lordship not find the mercy in his heart to release him?*

*"Release him? Dirty dog! Never will I release him. Why
do you think you can bribe me? I can have you shot for
this, Jew. Do you think I will take 3,000 rubles to free*

someone from serving the czar?" And the officer lifted the bottle of vodka to his mouth again.

Rabbi Menachem Mendel felt a twinge of hope. At least the officer had quoted a figure. An enormous amount, yet there appeared a slim ray of hope.

"You think I will take 3,000 rubles for a bribe? Never! 5,000 rubles it must be! You Jews have all the money. 5,000 rubles before this day is over, and get out of here before I have you shot."

Rabbi Menachem Mendel ran to Rabbi Levi Yitzchak, whom he found immersed in prayer. "Levi Yitzchak," he shouted, "Now is not the time for prayer. We must take action. Before the day is over we must have 5,000 rubles."

Rabbi Levi Yitzchak looked at him with bewilderment and said, "How can the townspeople ever raise this enormous sum in one day? All the people together do not have 5,000 rubles." "Then we will take their gold watches and silverware," Rabbi Menachem Mendel said, "But we must begin promptly and go from door to door to save this young man's life."

Rabbi Levi Yitzchak concurred, but said, "Let us get Schneur Zalman to go with us. Perhaps he may be able to help us convince the people to part with their valuables."

Rabbi Schneur Zalman readily agreed to join his friends, but with two stipulations. First, they must make a list of whom they wished to solicit, and secondly, the decision as to how much to tax each person must be his and his alone. Unless they agreed with these two conditions, he would not join them.

"Who has time to make lists?" Rabbi Menachem Mendel said. "Time is of the essence; we will go from door to door."

Rabbi Schneur Zalman was adamant. Unless there was a list he would not join them. Rabbi Menachem Mendel and Rabbi Levi Yitzchak had no choice but to make a list, *which they showed to Rabbi Schneur Zalman, who then added one name to the top of the list. Rabbi Menachem Mendel looked at the added name and exclaimed, "What? Votezk, the miser? You expect us to waste our precious time to solicit from a person who cannot part with a single cent?" Rabbi Schneur Zalman said that his stipulation remained, and that they must see Votezk first rather than last.*

Votezk, as he was now called, was once known as Velvel. When he became wealthy, he withdrew from the Jewish community, left the Jewish neighborhood, assimilated with the non-Jewish population, and changed his name from Velvel to Votezk. All attempts at gaining his participation in the realm of tzeddakah had been futile. Once there had been a desperate need for emergency funds, and the local rabbi felt that perhaps this might soften the miser's heart, but the latter gave him only a copper coin, which the angry rabbi threw back in his face.

Without understanding why, but with unwavering trust in Rabbi Schneur Zalman's judgment, the trio made its way out of the Jewish quarter to Votezk's estate. They were permitted to enter, and Rabbi Menachem Mendel described the desperate plight of the young man and the anguish of the community. "This time," Rabbi Menachem Mendel said, "you have the opportunity of saving a life, which is equivalent to saving the whole world."

Votezk sighed and nodded. "Yes," he said, "I will help you," and he proceeded to open his wall safe, retrieving from there a single copper coin, green with mold, which he gave to Rabbi Menachem Mendel.

Rabbi Schneur Zalman saw the rage in his comrade's eyes, and before Rabbi Menachem Mendel could throw the coin in the Votezk's face, he grabbed it from his hand and exclaimed, "Thank you, Reb Velvel. May you have many more opportunities to do mitzvos." He seized his two comrades by their hands and headed for the exit.

Although the two had previously trusted Rabbi Schneur Zalman, they now lost their faith in him. Thanking the miser for a penny when they had expected several hundred rubles! But as they were about to leave the house, they heard Votezk's voice, "Please don't leave." They turned around and Votezk beckoned to them to come back.

"I'm sorry for being so thoughtless," he said, and he proceeded to give them two handfuls of copper coins. "I want to have a share in this mitzvah."

Rabbi Schneur Zalman put the coins into a bag, saying, "G-d bless you, Reb Velvel," and again the trio headed for the door. Rabbi Menachem Mendel mumbled angrily under his breath, "Now we have 50 pennies, a whole half-ruble."

Again as they were at the door, they heard Votezk's voice, "Don't go yet!" He approached them with a handful of coins, this time containing a few silver and gold pieces. "I'm sorry I did not grasp the full gravity of this situation earlier."

I will not bore you with the repetition of all the details of 10 more recalls, with Votezk increasing his contribution each time, until at the last time, they had the full 5,000 rubles, with Votezk constantly apologizing for his previous behavior.

The trio left in high spirits, and Rabbi Menachem Mendel ran to the office of the military attache. That official had consented to accept a bribe because he was under investigation, having been suspected of corruption and stealing government funds. He desperately needed the 5,000 rubles to cover his embezzlement.

Rabbi Menachem Mendel approached the officer, who was still quite drunk. "Here is 5,000 rubles, just as your lordship had requested."

The official counted the money, and put it in his strongbox. "Now you will see that an officer of the czar keeps his word," he said. He rang for his assistant, "Bring the crippled Jew here! The nerve of those scoundrels, cheating the czar out of five rubles and bringing this invalid to me. The czar's army is composed of heroes, not of cripples. Take him and leave." Joyous and triumphant, Rabbi Menachem Mendel took the young bridegroom, and was greeted enthusiastically by Rabbi Levi Yitzchak and Rabbi Schneur Zalman. They rested a bit, and then began their walk back home.

They had just crossed a narrow bridge when they heard the thundering sound of horses' hooves and an approaching wagon. As the sounds grew louder and closer, they heard a screaming "Faster, faster, you horses," and the ferocious cracking of a whip. Rabbi Menachem Mendel recognized the voice of the officer, who was driving his horses in a drunken frenzy. As he drove over the bridge in the darkness, he crashed through the railing and the wagon plunged into the river. There was a loud wail and then utter silence. The trio ran down to the riverbank to see whether they could rescue the officer, but in the light of the full moon they saw nothing and heard nothing other than the soft flow of the river. As they left, the bridegroom's foot struck a hard object. It was the officer's strongbox! In the moonlight they could see it contained not only the 5,000 rubles, but other valuables.

The group made its way to the Jewish quarter, where the word of the miraculous salvation spread rapidly and the populace gathered to celebrate. That evening the joyous wedding surpassed in simchah anything the community had ever experienced, and the three tzaddikim were the heroes of the celebration.

Later Rabbi Schneur Zalman told his comrades, "Do not suspect me of having Divine foresight. My reasoning was simple.

"I knew that it was impossible for us to raise 5,000 rubles from the meager donations the townsfolk could give. Yet, not only were we obligated to try and save the young man, but having heard that Rabbi Menachem Mendel had sworn that he would return, I knew that his promise must come true. There was only one logical source for that huge amount of money, and that was Velvel-Votezk.

"You must understand what had happened to him. As he grew rich and deviated from the practice of Judaism, he began to literally worship money. To him money was as sacred as an idol to a pagan.

"Many years ago, a man who was collecting tzeddakah to marry off his daughter came to town, and needing several hundred rubles, he approached Velvel with the hope of getting a generous donation, if not 100 rubles, perhaps 50. Even 30 would have been acceptable. Imagine the rage of this desperate man when Velvel gave him a copper penny. He threw the coin in Velvel's face and left in disgust.

"To Velvel this was an unforgivable insult. He could forgive the personal offense to him, but this man had insulted money, which had become his god. Velvel was irate. 'I'll teach these beggars to respect money! They are parasites and don't work for a living, and that is why they can degrade money.' Following this incident, everyone who came to ask for alms was given the copper coin, and everyone's response was the same. Velvel had the coin thrown in his face.

"That copper coin lay in Velvel's wall safe for 20 years, and when I graciously accepted it, Velvel's vengeance for the honor of his idol was appeased. The Talmud quotes G-d as saying, 'Give Me an opening as tiny as the point of a needle, and I will enlarge it to admit passage of huge wagons for you' (Shir HaShirim Rabbah 5:3). The tiny *opening in Velvel's heart had been made, and the rest you know."*

The Talmud says "A wise man is superior to a prophet" (*Bava Basra* 12a). Rabbi Schneur Zalman may not have been operating with prophetic foresight, but his wisdom was an even greater feat.

Rabbi Schneur Zalman practiced that which he preached in the *Tanya*. Nothing that is obligatory upon a person is impossible to achieve, because G-d does not give us assignments that exceed our abilities. Things may seem difficult; nay, they may *appear* impossible, but we must know that if something is incumbent upon us, we must try. The Torah assures us, "G-d will bless you in all that you do" (*Deuteronomy* 15:18). We must do, and our sincere efforts will merit the Divine blessing.

Wherever You
Happen to Be

There is a principle in the Talmud that wherever a person is meant to be, that is where he will find himself (*Succah* 53a). If you left for the airport in plenty of time, and a multivehicle accident obstructed the highway for hours so that you missed your flight, do not fret. Nothing happens by chance, and you are where you are supposed to be. What about the crucial meeting that you missed? Had it really been to your advantage, you would have been there.

You are on a flight to Chicago and the pilot informs you that the weather in the area precludes a safe landing, and that the nearest available airport is Minneapolis, where you will be landing. You have no desire whatever to be in Minneapolis, but rest assured, you are there for a reason. What possible good is there in your being in Minneapolis? You may not know, and maybe you will one day find out, maybe not. Many people can testify to such "chance" occurrences, where they ended up someplace other than their intended destination, and later discovered why they had to be there.

This happened to the chassidic master, Rabbi Aryeh Leib, who is known in chassidic lore as the "Shpoler Zeide" (the grandfather from Shpole). Why this strange title?

I n the town of Uman, there lived a well-to-do man, Reb Baruch. Although not very learned, he was extremely good hearted, and fulfilled the mitzvah of hachnasas orchim (hospitality to travelers) to its utmost. He set aside several rooms in his large home for wayfarers, and provided them with nutritious meals. If he noticed that one of the poor was traveling with a horse that was on its last legs, he would provide him with one of the horses from his stable. He was loved and revered by the poor.

In the event that a couple came, Reb Baruch would assign them separate rooms, for how could he be certain that they were indeed married? Couples with children, however, were given a small suite.

The Baal Shem Tov, whose identity remained a secret until he was 36, used to eke out a meager living by hauling lime. Eventually his horse grew so old and feeble that it could hardly pull an empty wagon, let alone a laden one. He had heard from one of the traveling poor that in Uman there was someone who provided horses for the needy, and he and his wife made their way to Reb Baruch's place.

Reb Baruch welcomed the Baal Shem Tov, and, not knowing who he was, assigned him and his wife to rooms in separate cottages. He provided the Baal Shem Tov with a horse from his stall, which the Baal Shem Tov greatly appreciated, and he remained with Reb Baruch for Shabbos.

Having napped during the day, Reb Baruch could not fall asleep Shabbos night, and about midnight he saw some rays of light outside his window. At first he thought this was moonlight, but he then recalled that this was the end of the month and there was no moonlight. Curious, he went to the window, and saw that there were rays of light emanating from one of the guest's rooms. Thinking that perhaps something had caught fire, he ran to the window and saw the Baal Shem Tov sitting on the floor, his hands spread to Heaven in supplication, shedding profuse tears as he recited tikun chatzos, the lamentations for the destruction of the Temple. The room was filled with a heavenly glow, and standing near the Baal Shem Tov he saw a tall angelic figure. This marvelous sight was more than he could bear, and he emitted a loud cry and fell into a swoon.

Hearing the noise outside, the Baal Shem Tov ran over and revived him. Reb Baruch understood that he was in the presence of a G-dly person, and the Baal Shem Tov pleaded with him not to expose him.

"But who was the person at your side?" Reb Boruch asked.

"You saw him?" the Baal Shem Tov asked. "Then you must be deserving of seeing him. That was your ancestor, the great Maharal of Prague. His neshamah is due to return to earth again, and I give you my blessing that you will have a son who will bear this holy neshamah."

Reb Baruch asked the Baal Shem Tov to tell him who he was and where he lived, and said that he was ready to support him for the rest of his life. The Baal Shem Tov responded that his identity must remain secret until an appointed time. He extracted a promise from Reb Baruch that he would not expose his secret, and instructed him to *treat him no differently than all the other wayfarers.*

One year later Reb Baruch and his wife were blessed with a son, and Reb Baruch made a huge feast for the bris (circumcision), spreading the word that all the poor were invited to the feast. A huge throng of beggars came, and Reb Baruch searched through the huge crowd in the hope of seeing the tzaddik who had blessed him. Eventually he saw the Baal Shem Tov, who came in shabby clothes, indistinguishable from all the other beggars, and Reb Baruch ran to greet him. The Baal Shem Tov gestured to him that he should not show him any recognition. The child was named Leib after his great ancestor, the Maharal.

The local custom was that after the bris, all those attending would bless the infant, and Reb Baruch, desiring that his son be blessed by the tzaddik, said that he would circulate the child among all the attendees so that they could place their hands on him and bless him. When the child was brought before the Baal Shem Tov, he said, "I am a simple man and I don't know any formal blessings. I remember my teacher in cheder (Hebrew school) saying that G-d blessed Abraham to be the grandfather (zeide) of all Jews to come, so I am blessing this child that he too be a zeide of his people." Everyone laughed at this crude blessing, and thereafter people would ask Reb Boruch, "How is the little zeide?" As Reb Leib grew, his title Zeide remained with him, and when he became known as a chassidic master who lived in Shpole, he acquired the title "The Shpoler Zeide."

Actually, this was not his first encounter with the Baal Shem Tov. The Shpoler Zeide said that when his *neshamah* was told that it had to come down to earth, he resisted, saying that he had already been down to the physical world several times and could not tolerate its grossness. One day a man approached him in *Gan Eden,* carrying a heavy shovel on his shoulder, and shouted at him, "I have to dig in the earth to elevate Jewish spirits, while you enjoy yourself in *Gan Eden!*" The Shpoler Zeide said, "He frightened me so that I agreed to come down to the world again. Years later, when my master, Rabbi Pinchas of Koritz, took me to the Baal Shem Tov, I exclaimed upon seeing him, 'That's the man with the shovel!' and I fainted."

A man once cried to the Shpoler Zeide that he had been falsely accused of theft. The Zeide responded, "I too was once falsely accused of theft and was thrown into prison for two months. I did not bear any resentments against G-d, because I knew that He must have a purpose for my being there.

"What happened was that I lodged at an inn, and another guest and I left together. I noticed that he frequently looked over his shoulder, but I did not ask him why. After we had walked some distance, we saw a wagon approaching, whereupon my companion asked me to watch his bags for him, saying that he would return momentarily. When the wagon approached, two men alighted and one of them pointed at me and said, 'There is the thief!' They grabbed my companion's bag, and upon opening it, found several silver items he had stolen from the inn. I protested that I had not taken anything and that there was another person to whom this bag belonged, but they did not believe me. They tied me up and brought me to town, and I was thrown into jail.

"The other prisoners began tormenting me, pulling at my beard and payos (earlocks). They said that if I did not pay the initiation fee as a prisoner, they would beat me. When I told them that I had no money, they forced me to lie down and began beating me. When the first person hit me, he began to scream with pain, and his hand swelled to three times its size. The other prisoners were afraid to touch me, and I was left in peace.

"One of the prisoners was called 'the gypsy,' but I learned that he was really of Jewish origin. He had been kidnaped as a young boy by a band of gypsies. He remembered, however, that his parents were Jews and that his name was Yaakov. He had been imprisoned for stealing horses.

"I gradually impressed upon the man what it meant to be a Jew, and that he was obligated to observe the Torah and mitzvos. I taught him how to say the Shema and how to pray. Soon he began to avoid the treifah (non-kosher) food he was given and ate only fresh vegetables as I did. He accepted upon himself that if he would be freed he would become an honest person and return to Judaism.

"One night I dreamt that the prophet Elijah told me to have no fear and to leave the prison. I took Yaakov by the hand, and when we came to the cell door we found it ajar. All the guards were in a deep sleep, and we left the prison unnoticed. I went to a nearby town and became the shamas (sexton) in a shul. Yaakov kept his promise and became an honest, sincere, and devout Jew.

"It was then that I understood why the chain of events had led to my imprisonment. I had to bring the neshamah of Yaakov back to Judaism. I consider it a privilege to have been given this mission, and I am glad of it, even though it necessitated my being in a jail for two months. Sometimes a person is sent to this earth for an entire lifetime, just to bring one neshamah back to its source."

The Shpoler Zeide related this episode so that we would know that nothing happens by chance. Everything is Divinely ordained for a purpose which may be known only to G-d, the only One Who can see the entire panorama in time and space.

His Mercy
Is to All

I n the prayer of *Ashrei,* which is recited three times daily, we
say, "G-d is good to all, and His mercy is upon all His creatures" (*Psalms* 145:9). Inasmuch as we are required to
emulate the Divine attributes, we are required to show kindness to all living things. The Talmud relates that Rabbi Yehudah
HaNasi, the redactor of the *Mishnah,* the only one of all the authors of the Talmud to receive the title *Rabbeinu HaKadosh,*
"our holy teacher," was subjected to suffering because he was
callous to the plight of an animal. A butcher was leading a calf
to slaughter, and the calf fled and hid under Rabbi Yehudah's
cloak, whereupon the Rabbi said, "Go! This was the reason you

were created." The heavenly tribunal then decreed, "Since he showed no mercy, none will be shown to him." Rabbi Yehudah's misery lasted until the time his servant was sweeping the house and came upon a nest of little weasels and was about to sweep them out, when Rabbi Yehudah stopped him, saying, "G-d's mercy is on all His creatures" (*Bava Metzia* 85a).

Mercy and kindness toward people was a trait possessed by many people, and certainly many of the chassidic masters were outstanding in this respect. Prominent among these was Rabbi Dovid of Lelov, who used to say, "How can people even think I am a *tzaddik*, when I feel more love for my own children than for other people's children?"

> One time Rabbi Dovid's son, Moshe, fell gravely ill, and the doctors did not believe he would survive. The townsfolk, who loved the Rabbi's child dearly, gathered in the shul (synagogue) and prayed fervently for Divine healing, donating tzeddakah for his recovery. When the lad began showing signs of improvement, they ran and told Rabbi Dovid the good news, whereupon he began to cry. "Why are you crying?" they asked. "The child is so much better."
>
> Rabbi Dovid said, "Yes, my child is better because people gathered together and offered special prayers for him, donating tzeddakah for his recovery. But what about other people's children? When they fall ill, the shul is not filled with people praying for their recovery. Why should I not cry?"

Rabbi Dovid would travel from village to village, visiting his "brothers," as he referred to all Jews. "Why are you traveling to that village?" someone would ask him. "Because my brother lives there," he would say. He would go from house to house, greeting people, getting into a conversation with them, inquiring into their needs, and whether there was any way he could be of help.

"The Talmud says that wherever 10 Jews assemble (a minyan) the Divine Presence is there" (Sanhedrin 39a). Nine tzaddikim, the greatest Torah scholars, cannot bring down the Divine Presence, whereas 10 simple people can! Can you estimate the value of even a simple, unlearned person?

Rabbi Dovid supported himself with income from a small store. One morning, as he was about to open his shop, he noticed that his competitor's store was still closed, and several customers were waiting outside. He knew that if he opened his store, they would come to him. He ran to his competitor's house and called him. "Hurry! There are customers waiting outside your store." Rabbi Dovid knew that whatever amount was preordained for him to earn would come his way, and he was not going to take advantage of his competitor oversleeping.

Some Torah scholars could become so absorbed in their Torah study that they were oblivious to everything else in the world.

Rabbi Schneur Zalman lived on the floor above his son, Rabbi Dov Ber. One time Rabbi Schneur Zalman heard a baby crying, and upon going downstairs he observed his son to be so totally engrossed in his Torah study that he was not aware of the baby crying. Rabbi Shneur Zalman reprimanded his son, that whereas profound Torah study is commendable, it should never render one oblivious to the needs of others.

Rabbi Dovid of Lelov carried this one step further, being concerned about the needs of animals as well. One time when he saw a driver whip his horse he said to him, "If you only knew how to communicate with your horse, you would have no need to whip him. Is it fair and just to whip the horse because of your ignorance?

"Just think," Rabbi Dovid said, "that one day this horse will call you before the Heavenly Tribunal for having whipped him. Will you not be embarrassed to have to go to trial with a horse?"

O ne Rosh Hashanah, when Rabbi Dovid was at the court of the Seer of Lublin, he was noted to be absent from shul. The Seer did not want the shofar sounded until Rabbi Dovid was present, and sent people out to look for him. They found him with a sack of oats, feeding the horses, whose owners had all gone to shul for the services, and neglected their responsibilities to care for their animals.

Rabbi Dovid used to say, "The Talmud says that anyone who is pleasing to creatures is pleasing to G-d" (*Ethics of the Fathers* 3:13). Note that the Talmud does not say "people," but rather "creatures." Just as G-d's mercy is on all living things, so must ours be.

24

Tough Love

I n counseling people with problems, it is occasionally necessary to advise an approach of "tough love"; i.e., taking
measures which are difficult because they inflict pain on a
loved one. Yet, there may be no other option.

Tough love is actually practiced quite frequently, and is un-
avoidable in the rearing of children. The mother who refuses to
give her child ice cream a half-hour before mealtime and turns
a deaf ear to the child's wailing is practicing tough love. She
would certainly wish to have the child enjoy an ice-cream cone,
but to allow him this pleasure shortly before mealtime, which
would interfere with proper nutrition, is not in the child's interest, and she must therefore be "mean" to him for his own good.

Mothers who take their infants to the pediatrician for immunization and allow the doctor to administer a painful injection which will cause the child to suffer discomfort for 48 hours are practicing tough love. They must subject the child to this suffering to avoid his contracting dreaded diseases later in life.

Parents have little problem practicing this type of tough love because it is univerally accepted as the right thing to do. It is somewhat different when they are confronted with the problem of an adolescent son or daughter who is using drugs, defying the parents, neglecting school, behaving recklessly, and refusing to accept help and guidance. In such situations it may be necessary for the parents to take the drastic step of evicting their own child from their home, and stating firmly that they will not be an accomplice to his/her self-destructive behavior. Parents may need much support in implementing such tough love.

The principle of tough love is stated explicitly in the Talmud. "Whoever is merciful when firmness is called for will ultimately be cruel when kindness is called for" (*Koheles Rabbah* 7:33). It is only natural to be kind to someone you love, but there are times when what appears to be kindness is actually adverse to that person's welfare, and firmness or strictness, which appear to be cruel, are in fact true kindness.

The *tzaddik* of Apt is one of the most interesting of the great chassidic masters. Although he was an accomplished Torah scholar and lived a life of holiness, he instructed that no complimentary adjectives be written on his tombstone other than "Oheiv Yisrael," that he loved his fellow Jews. (This is indeed the title of his commentary on Torah.) How could one allow oneself to be called a *tzaddik* when one feels himself derelict in the service of G-d? How could one allow himself to be called a *gaon* when one has barely scratched the surface of the infinite knowledge of Torah? But to state that he loved his fellow Jews with every fiber of his body, that he felt was true, and the tombstone of the *tzaddik* of Apt contains only the appellation "Oheiv Yisrael."

We can well imagine how careful the *tzaddik* of Apt was to never cause the slightest distress to anyone. He was totally self-effacing and frequently set his own needs aside in order to be kind to others. It is from someone like the *Oheiv Yisrael* that we may learn that true love may at times require being tough.

The *tzaddik* of Apt used to say that he knew that in a previous existence, his *neshamah* was that of a *Kohen Gadol,* a High Priest in the Temple in Jerusalem. When he recited the Yom Kippur prayers, where the service of the *Kohen Gadol* is described and we say, "This is what he (the *Kohen Gadol*) would say," the *tzaddik* of Apt would say, "This is what I used to say."

The *tzaddik was once approached by a man who sought to do teshuvah for having sinned, and he expressed his remorse as he related his errant behavior to the tzaddik, awaiting instruction as to what would constitute proper penance for him. But instead of guiding him to teshuvah, the tzaddik only smiled with what appeared to be a derisive sneer. The penitent man began to cry. Why was the tzaddik mocking him? But his tears did not seem to impress the tzaddik, whose attitude seemed to be one of callousness. The onlookers could not understand why the tzaddik was not more sympathetic to this man, who appeared to be so sincere in his desire to do teshuvah. Seeing he was getting no response from the tzaddik, the man retreated to a corner in the beis hamidrash (house of study) and wept.*

The tzaddik, noting that the onlookers were bewildered by this unusual behavior of someone who was a passionate Oheiv Yisrael, said to them:

"Let me tell you why I acted the way I did.

"Many generations ago, when I was a Kohen Gadol, there was a man who had committed a transgression, and had to bring a sin-offering in expiation. When he went to

buy a she-goat for his offering, the livestock dealer said, 'Oh, you sinned, didn't you?' The man was deeply embarrassed, feeling remorse for having acted so foolishly.

"*As he led the goat to the Temple, some children saw him and cried, 'Look, there goes a man with a she-goat for a sin-offering.' They ran after him, shouting, 'What did you do, huh? Tell us!' Again, the poor man felt humiliated.*

"*As the man entered the Sanctuary, he heard the music of the Levites, and the melodies were heart rending, penetrating deep into his soul and arousing profound feelings of penitence. When he brought the she-goat to me to prepare the offering, his regret for having sinned was deep, almost to the point where it constituted a degree of teshuvah that would have totally eradicated his sin. He was so broken hearted, and I felt his pain so deeply, that I said some words of comfort to try and console him. I told him that humans are, after all, only mere mortals, and that no one, even the greatest tzaddik, can be totally free of sin. I tried to alleviate his pain, but alas! I thereby deprived him of reaching that final degree of repentance that would have totally washed away his sin. My sympathy for him was misguided and his teshuvah was incomplete. A remnant of the sin remained as a stain upon his neshamah. When this man died, he could never achieve true peace in Gan Eden (Paradise) and he appealed to the Heavenly Tribunal to allow him to do complete teshuvah, to remove the residual stain from his neshamah.*

"*But there is no way one can do teshuvah in Heaven, so the Tribunal offered him the option of returning to earth again, and as a mortal, he would have the opportunity to do complete teshuvah.*

"*This man who was just here before you is the bearer of this neshamah. He indeed was remorseful for his misdeed, and as I felt his regret to be sincere and saw the pain he was in, it was all I could do to restrain myself from embracing him and kissing him and telling him that he is a beloved child of G-d. That would have satisfied my desire to be kind, but it would have truncated his teshuvah. Instead, I acted as though I did not care, and showed him no sympathy. He is now sitting in the corner weeping, and his sincere tears of repentance will wash away the residual stain from his neshamah, which will then be totally pure.*

"I thought that when I was the Kohen Gadol I had acted with kindness toward the penitent. Actually, I was much kinder to him today."

The *tzaddik* would certainly have preferred to embrace the remorseful man and soothe him, but he knew better. True kindness may require suppressing one's tender feelings when this is beneficial to others.

The Paragon
of Storytellers

T orah literature is rich in stories. The Talmud often re-
sorts to parables to drive home a point, because the
very same message delivered in the context of a story
appears to have a greater impact. Many of the *mag-
gidim* (preachers) illustrated their teachings with parables, and
the most famous of all, the *Maggid* of Dubno, used a parable to
explain why he always used parables.

Many of the chassidic masters would use stories as a vehicle
for their teachings. Best known for his stories is Rabbi Nachman
of Breslov, whose stories have been translated into English and
are readily accessible. However, whereas the parables of the
Maggid of Dubno are usually brief and quite simple, Rabbi

Nachman's stories tend to be lengthy and complicated, often leaving the reader wondering just what is the message he wished to convey. Indeed, Rabbi Nachman is alleged to have said that not until the coming of the Messiah will the full meaning of his stories be understood.

Rabbi Nachman was a great-grandson of the Baal Shem Tov. The accounts of his childhood reveal him to have engaged in solitude, meditation, and copious prayer. He would often set off to the woods, to be alone with G-d, free of all distractions. He was a prodigy, amassing a broad knowledge of Talmud and kabbalah at an early age. He fasted often and practiced mortification of the flesh. He was determined that physical desires not deter him from his spiritual aspirations. In his 20s he developed a devoted following, and he expounded profusely on Torah. His teachings were recorded by his disciple, Rabbi Nassan. His frail body succumbed to tuberculosis, and he died at age 39, without designating a successor. He promised his followers that he would never abandon them, and to this day he has remained the Rebbe of the Breslov chassidim, who are devoted to his teachings.

Rabbi Nachman was a controversial figure. Many of the chassidic masters greatly admired him, while others were highly critical of him and his rather unusual teachings. In particular, the Shpoler Zeide was his sworn opponent, and there were severe caustic exchanges between the two.

We must exercise great caution regarding the disputes between the chassidic masters. We are accustomed to people arguing over turf or because of rather selfish personal interests. This was definitely not the case in disputes between chassidic masters. We may not be aware, even to this day, why these spiritual giants were occasionally involved in sharp disputes, but just two examples can show us that these were not petty arguments.

Rabbi Levi Yitzchak of Berditchev is not only considered the most beloved of chassidic masters by later generations, but was highly revered by all his contemporaries. Rabbi Schneur Zalman said of him, "G-d is a *tzaddik* in Heaven, and Rabbi Levi Yitzchak is a *tzaddik* on earth." The Seer of Lublin said, "I thank G-d every single day that He has given us Rabbi Levi Yitzchak." Rabbi Shmelke of Nikolsburg said, "The longest period of time I can retain an uninterrupted communion with G-d is three hours. Rabbi Levi Yitzchak can be in constant communion."

This otherwise unchallenged *tzaddik* was the target of the sharp words of Rabbi Baruch of Mezhibozh, the grandson of the Baal Shem Tov. Rabbi Baruch never missed an opportunity to mock at Rabbi Levi Yitzchak and belittle him. It was widely known that Rabbi Baruch was sharply critical of Rabbi Levi Yitzchak.

O ne time *two merchants of Mezhibozh went to Berditchev for business, and went to see for themselves what Rabbi Levi Yitzchak was like. When they entered, they found Rabbi Levi Yitzchak to be standing in prayer, and in the midst of his prayer he ran over to one of the merchants, seized him by the lapels, shook him and said, "What can the angel Michael possibly say about you?" and then returned to his prayers.*

When the two returned to Mezhibozh, they hurried to Rabbi Baruch to tell him of Rabbi Levi Yitzchak's bizarre behavior, hoping to give him more material to scoff at him. When the merchant related how Rabbi Levi Yitzchak had accosted him, Rabbi Baruch suddenly shouted at him, "You scoundrel! You thief! I demand that you promptly return the money that you stole from your comrade." The man was shocked into admitting that he had stolen some money from his friend.

Rabbi Baruch then said, "The angel Michael is the defender of Jews, and when a Jew sins, the angel Michael pleads his case before the Heavenly Tribunal, and presents

*mitigating circumstances to obtain a more lenient judg-
ment, pointing out human frailties and the difficulty in
resisting temptation. For example, if a person steals because he is impoverished, the angel Michael enters a plea
that the person's destitute state caused his judgment to be
distorted, and that he stole only out of desperation. But
when someone who is well-to-do, like yourself, steals money from a fellow merchant, what kind of plea for lenience
can the angel Michael offer for you? That is what Rabbi
Levi Yitzchak meant."*

*Then Rabbi Baruch said, "Rabbi Levi Yitzchak is a tzad-
dik whose omniscience allows him to see everything. The
reason I constantly criticize him is because all Jews pray
daily for the coming of the Messiah and the restoration of
the service in the Temple in Jerusalem. But some of the angels say to G-d, 'What need is there for a restoration of the
Sanctuary? There you have Rabbi Levi Yitzchak, whose
prayers and service are every bit as great as that of the
High Priest in the Sanctuary.' I therefore criticize him to enter my protest and to show G-d that I am not satisfied with
his being a substitute for the High Priest, and that we must
have the redemption with the return of the Temple in
Jerusalem."*

Rabbi Baruch's attack on Rabbi Levi Yitzchak were thus hardly of the nature of a personal feud.

Much closer to home is a story about my great-grandfather,
Rabbi Shlomo, the first Rebbe of Bobov, who, like Rabbi Levi
Yitzchak, was the target of the sharp barbs of his uncle, the
Rabbi of Gorlitz. Rabbi Shlomo's mother once said to her
brother-in-law, the Rabbi of Gorlitz, "All your brother left me is
this one child. Why do you torment him so?" The Rabbi of
Gorlitz replied, "Don't you understand? My tormenting him pro-
longs his life." Rabbi Shlomo's mother nevertheless pleaded

with him to stop his torment, whereupon the Rabbi Gorlitz simply shrugged his shoulders. His sharp barbs ceased, and a few months later Rabbi Shlomo died. Although it may be beyond our understanding, the Rabbi of Gorlitz knew what he was doing. Such was the nature of "disputes" among the chassidic masters.

Let us return now to the stories of Rabbi Nachman. My favorite is:

A king was once informed by his chief minister that there had been a blight on the crops that year, which had been so affected that anyone who would eat of the grain would become insane. "But," said the minister, "there is no need for us to worry. I have set aside enough grain from last year's harvest for the both of us that will last us until the harvest of the following year."

The king shook his head. "No," he said. "I will not allow myself any privileges other than those shared by my subjects.

"We shall all eat of the same grain," the king continued, "and we shall both go insane together with the rest of the population. But here is what we shall do. You and I will mark our foreheads with an indelible imprint, so that when we go insane, I will look at you and you will look at me, and **we will know we are insane.**"

Sometimes I look at the world and it seems to me that everyone has taken leave of their senses. There is so much senseless bloodshed, whether in wars, in robberies, in domestic abuse, and in drive-by shootings. There is so much degradation and immorality. There is such a dearth of spirituality that mankind seems to have sunk lower than the level of brute beasts. There is so much corruption at all levels of government and commerce. While most people may not actively engage in such practices, they do essentially stand by and tolerate it. I often wonder, can it be that the whole world is insane and I am the only one who has retained sanity? Then I remember Rabbi Nachman's story, and I conclude that I too must be insane along with the rest of mankind, but the saving grace is that I am aware of it.

One story of Rabbi Nachman's has been erroneously attributed to Herschel of Ostropl.

A traveler was once stopped by a highway robber who pointed his gun at him and demanded his moneybag. The traveler said, "Don't shoot! I'll gladly give you my money. But I will ask a favor of you. If I come home empty handed, my wife will never believe me that I was robbed, and will accuse me of having squandered my money on gambling or on liquor, and she will beat me mercilessly. Please do me the favor of firing several bullets through my hat, and I can then prove to her that I was held up."

The robber saw no reason why not to comply. He took the moneybag and then shot several times through the man's hat.

"Thank you so much," the traveler said. "But you don't know my wife. She will say I punctured the hat and that these were not bullet holes at all. Here, take my coat and shoot several bullets through it at close range, leaving the powder marks. That will convince her for sure."

Again the robber complied and shot through the coat several times. When the traveler saw that the last pull of the trigger hit an empty chamber and that the bullets had all been used up, he promptly pounced on the robber, knocking him to the ground and retrieving his moneybag.

Given Herschel's ingenuity, this story would certainly have been appropriate for him, but it was told by Rabbi Nachman to convey a message. The robber represents the *yetzer hara,* who wishes to deprive a person of all his spiritual assets. Sometimes one may allow the *yetzer hara* to fire all his bullets, and when he has spent his ammunition, one pounces upon him and subdues him.

I have seen this in my practice. People who are entrapped by the *yetzer hara* into addiction may allow him to shoot at them numerous times, each shot representing another attempt of the *yetzer hara* to lead the person to his destruction. There comes a time when the person realizes that the alcohol and/or drugs are no longer providing him with the contentment he was seeking, and he is then in a position to abandon the lifestyle of addiction and turn toward a constructive lifestyle.

This is as true of other destructive pursuits as it is of addiction. The *yetzer hara* holds out all kinds of promises of happiness if one will only follow his advice and indulge oneself. All these promises eventually prove to be empty, and when one comes to that awareness, one can turn oneself toward the pursuit of spirituality.

The problem is that while the *yetzer hara* is firing his ammunition, a person may suffer considerable damage, some of which cannot be undone. A wise traveler would avoid the paths where robbers are likely to lurk, and travel only on paths that have proven to be safe.

There are paths in life which have been proven to be safe. Rabbi Moshe Chaim Luzzatto in the *Path of the Just* compares life to a maze, where there are many paths that lead to a dead end, and only one which leads to the goal. There is a lookout stationed high above the maze who shouts instructions to people who enter, directing them which path to take that will lead them to the goal and avoid the dead-end paths. The wise person will follow the instructions of the guide, whereas foolish people will insist on finding their own way, and may become hopelessly lost and never reach the goal.

The teachers of Torah, both past and present, are the guides who teach us what the correct path in life is, one on which we can avoid encounter with the "robber." If we ignore these instructions, we may fall prey to the *yetzer hara's* wily maneuvers. But even then, we should be alert enough to realize when the *yetzer hara's* ammunition has been exhausted, and then subdue him and proceed on the path to spiritual achievement.

≈)≈

As we know, the Baal Shem Tov showed great affection for the simple folk, who followed the Torah teachings with sincerity and unwavering faith. During the Baal Shem Tov's time, the wave of enlightenment caused many of the Jewish intelligentsia to deviate from traditional Judaism.

Here is another of Rabbi Nachman's stories.

A king went on a hunting jaunt with a number of his ministers. Suddenly they were struck by a severe storm, with lightning, hail, and ferocious winds. Everyone dispersed to find shelter, and the king found himself alone and abandoned. He wandered through the forest until he saw a small hut, and he knocked on the door.

The peasant who lived in the hut invited the king in, and gave him dry clothes, some of his simple food, and a straw mat on which to rest. Although he had no idea who his guest was, he provided for him as best he could, and at his request, showed the king the way out of the forest.

When the king returned to his palace, he dismissed all his ministers who had deserted him in the storm to find havens of refuge for themselves. He sent for the peasant, whom he elevated to a position of honor.

So it shall be when the Messiah comes. The intelligentsia who deserted G-d to pursue their own desires will be set aside, and the honors will go to the simple folk, who may not have had the rich intellectual resources with which to serve G-d, but by their sincere daily prayer and observance of the mitzvos to the best of their capabilities, made G-d welcome in their homes.

These rather brief stories seem to convey a simple message. Most of Rabbi Nachman's stories are quite long and complicated, with complex "plots." In the introduction to the volume of stories, Rabbi Nassan writes, "Let no one think that these are just stories. Every single word is sacred, containing secrets of the Torah and teachings in the Divine service." In conclusion let me state that when the Shpoler Zeide, the archopponent of Rabbi Nachman, heard of his untimely death, he retired to his study, removed his shoes and sat on the floor as if in *shivah*, and wept profusely. When his *shamas* asked him why he was mourning someone whom he had attacked so bitterly, the Shpoler Zeide said, "If people only knew what the world has lost by Rabbi Nachman's death, they would all weep profusely."

And When Life Is Over

Despite our awareness of our mortality and that there is no eternity to earthly life, death is nevertheless a most depressing experience for the survivors, and the contemplation of death can cause a great deal of anxiety. Yet, the awareness that some kind of existence continues when life on earth comes to an end may mitigate the sharp sting of death. There is much in chassidic teachings that makes this inevitable episode in life a bit easier to accept.

For example, while *chassidim* grieve over the passing of a Rebbe and feel ever so deeply the loss of their beloved master and teacher, the *yahrzeit* (anniversary of the death) of the Rebbe is observed in an upbeat spirit. *Chassidim* gather at a festive meal at which some of the teachings of the Rebbe are re-counted and some of the Rebbe's favorite chassidic melodies are sung. It is an occasion not of merriment, but a *seudas simchah shel mitzvah*, a *mitzvah* celebration. Why so? Because of the conviction that a *neshamah* (soul) is sent to earth to fulfill a specific mission, and inasmuch as the Rebbe certainly succeeded in fulfilling his assignment on earth, his *neshamah* rejoiced in returning to its abode in heaven to be rewarded by being in the immanent presence of the glory of G-d. *Chassidim* thus share in the *simchah* of the Rebbe's *neshamah*.

The perspective on death is exemplified by an incident that occurred with Rabbi Yosef Yitzchak of Lubavitch, who defied the order of the Russian government that he cease and desist preaching and teaching Judaism.

A Russian officer confronted Rabbi Yosef Yitzchak and pulled his gun on him, but the Rabbi did not flinch. *"Are you not afraid that I can kill you?"* the officer asked. *The Rabbi replied, "One who has a multiplicity of gods and only one world is frightened of dying. Those who have only one God and two worlds have no fear of death."*

When my father was diagnosed with cancer of the pancreas, he showed no signs of anxiety. He then told me that just a few weeks earlier his father had appeared to him in a dream and said, "There is nothing to fear. It is just walking out of one room and walking into another." My father said, "I knew then that my life was coming to an end, and I was only waiting to discover how this was to come about."

M y great-grandfather, the Rabbi of Hornosteipel, was a grandson of the tzaddik of Cherkassy, who had raised him when he was orphaned. One day the tzaddik sent for him and said, "Normally, when litigants come to a din Torah (rabbinic tribunal), the dayan (magistrate) is seated and the litigants must stand. The litigants today are myself and your grandmother. We are well along in years, and it is difficult for us to stand, so we will ask your indulgence in allowing us to remain seated. We have a dispute and we will rely on your judgment, because we know that your opinion will be honored in heaven.

"As we are approaching the end of our lives," the tzaddik continued, "we have a disagreement as to who should die first. Let me state my case. I do not want to be alone. It is much easier for a woman to be alone than for a man. Therefore, I wish to die first."

At this point the tzaddik's wife said, "What have I ever done wrong that I should deserve hearing Kiddush Friday night from anyone else than my husband? If you can tell me why I deserve such a fate, you can rule in his favor."

My great-grandfather was terribly upset by the awesome burden that had been thrust upon him. "Why are you even thinking about such things?" he said. "Both of you will live to see the coming of the Messiah."

The tzaddik of Cherkassy said, "We are not necessarily resigning ourselves to dying. I, too, believe that the Messiah will come today, and this will then be a moot issue. However, in the event that the Messiah should be delayed, if and when we should die, we need a judgment as to how it should occur."

My great-grandfather asked for some time to contemplate, and several hours later tearfully said to his beloved grandparents, "The Zeide will survive the Bobbe by six months."

After the Bobbe of Cherkassy died on the 13th day of Adar, one of the grandchildren was engaged, and the wedding date was set for within six months, so that the Zeide *could attend. Six months to the day, on the 13th of Elul, the tzaddik of Cherkassy died.*

The two chassidic masters, Rabbi Yisrael of Rizhin and Rabbi Meir of Premishlan were devoted friends, although the distance between them precluded frequent personal contact. When Rabbi Meir died, the *chassidim* of Rizhin kept this information from the Rabbi, knowing how deeply he would be grieved.

The Rabbi of Rizhin had two lit candles on his table, and one candle blew out. When the *shamas* lit the extinguished candle, the other candle blew out, whereupon the Rabbi said, "There is darkness in the world. Has anything happened that I have not been told?" It was then that the *chassidim* told of Rabbi Meir's death.

☙❧

At the *seder* one Pesach, when reciting the *Haggadah,* Rabbi Avraham of Slonim read the verse, "This year we are slaves, but next year we shall be free." He paused a bit and said, "As long as the *neshamah* is entrapped within a physical body, it is subject to the dictates of the body. When the *neshamah* leaves the body, it is free. This year we are slaves, but next year we will be free." Several months later, Rabbi Avraham of Slonim died.

☙❧

One *Hoshana Rabbah,* Rabbi David Moshe of Chortkov put on white garments, blessed his children, and began reciting the prayer of *Nishmas.* When he concluded the prayer, saying the final sentence "As David said, let my soul praise G-d," he breathed his last.

Whereas I usually avoid relating stories that seem weird, I feel obligated to relate this one. My father told me this story, and since he read it in the chronicles of the community of Cracow, which were destroyed along with everything else in the Holocaust, I feel it incumbent upon me to preserve this particular account.

My father had a great curiosity for historical events, and he spent much time reviewing the fascinating chronicles of the community of Cracow. The following story was recorded in the chronicles.

One day a young man came to the man who was in charge of the ancient cemetery in Cracow, and asked to purchase the grave immediately adjacent to that of the famed kabbalist, Rabbi Nosson Nota Shapira. The official told him that his request was absurd, because only a tzaddik of outstanding renown would be permitted to be buried near this revered personage, and no one had been found worthy of that privilege. The young man then began offering a huge amount of money for that grave, and as he increased his offer, the official was overcome by greed. He began reasoning, "I am already an old man, with perhaps just a few years of life left. This young man will live for decades. If I take the money, I will be able to enjoy it, and by the time this young man dies, I will have been long gone and forgotten." He then took the money and agreed to sell the gravesite to the young man.

The following morning the official was called to arrange the burial for an itinerant who had been found dead in a local inn. When he came to take the body, he was horrified. It was the very young man to whom he had sold the grave near the revered tzaddik. He was not about to disclose his greed to the community, so he prevailed upon the members of the burial society to give the young man a respectable place in the cemetery, but not, of course, that which he had purchased. The following night the young man appeared to him in a dream, complaining that he had violated their *contract, and demanding that he be moved to the grave he had purchased. On awakening in the morning, the official reasoned that the dream was nothing but the consequence of his having thought about the incident during the day, and he dismissed it. However, the following night the young man again appeared in a dream with a repetition of his claim, and on the third night, the young man said to him, "Look, we completed a legal transaction, and I demand compliance with our agreement. If you continue your refusal to honor our agreement, I will call you before a tribunal. Inasmuch as I cannot come down to an earthly tribunal, you will have to come up here."*

On awakening, the official realized that he had no choice but to confess his greed and disclose his misdeed to the community. He assembled the community leaders and related all that had happened, including the three dreams, with the final threat of being called to a heavenly tribunal.

The leaders of the community deliberated, and concluded that the young man indeed had legal rights to the grave. "However," they said, "we do not dare bury an unknown person near the saintly tzaddik, because if he is not worthy of being there, we will have offended the tzaddik. If this young man is indeed deserving of being near the tzaddik, then we hereby authorize him to move himself to the grave he desired."

On the following morning, visitors to the cemetery found the first grave empty, and a fresh grave near that of Rabbi Nosson Nota Shapira. They then built a little fence encircling both graves, and on the fresh grave erected a tombstone bearing the inscription, "Here lies an unknown tzaddik, who effected his own burial."

My father told me that he visited the ancient cemetery and saw the inscription on the tombstone.

I have tried to avoid stories which may appear farfetched. I have nevertheless recorded this one, since it, too, was recorded in the chronicles of Cracow that went up in the flames of the Holocaust, and having heard this story from my father, I feel it is my responsibility to preserve it.

One time a man presented himself to Rabbi Elimelech of Lizhensk, claiming to have been the chazzan (cantor) for the Baal Shem Tov, and he was accompanied by a member of his choir. He asked permission from Rabbi Elimelech to chant the Friday evening services. Rabbi Elimelech was reluctant, saying that musical artistry may distract him from proper kavannah (concentration), but his son, Rabbi Elazar, prevailed upon him to allow the chazzan to lead the services.

When the chazzan began to sing, Rabbi Elimelech felt himself being transported to the celestial spheres, in the presence of the heavenly angels, who were singing praises to G-d. At one point he asked the chazzan to leave the pulpit, because he felt that were the chazzan to continue to sing, his neshamah would leave his body, and he still needed more time on earth to fulfill his mission.

After Shabbos, Rabbi Elimelech asked the chazzan how he had achieved such sanctity in prayer. The chazzan stated that he had once complained to the Baal Shem Tov that he had no means for a livelihood, whereupon the Baal Shem Tov told him to become a chazzan.

"But I cannot sing," he said to the Baal Shem Tov.

"I will connect you to the celestial source of music," the Baal Shem Tov said, "and you will be able to sing. But let me tell you that one day you will be interrupted and asked to leave the pulpit. That will be a signal to you that it is the last time you will lead services."

"I know now," the chazzan continued, "that I am nearing the end of my life."

Rabbi Elimelech then asked the chazzan if he could re-late anything from his contact with the Baal Shem Tov. The chazzan said:

"Yes. One time we noted the Baal Shem Tov was smil-ing. When we asked the reason for his mirth, he said that a nobleman had built himself a palace in the countryside, but abandoned it after only a short period of use. Years lat-er, a pious person was traveling on foot along the countryside, when a sudden storm came upon him, with heavy hail and lightning. He took refuge in the abandoned palace, and when the storm abated, he continued on his way. He then heard a loud rumble, and turned around to see the palace falling in ruins.

"The Baal Shem Tov said, 'The purpose of the nobleman building that palace was that this traveler should have a place of refuge from the storm. Once it had served its pur-pose, it was no longer needed, and it collapsed. Seeing the precision of Divine providence in foresight, how could I not smile about it?'"

On the following day the chazzan fell sick, and that very night he died. On Wednesday of that week, the member of the choir came and asked that the burial society be called, and that a grave be prepared for him. "Last night the chaz-zan appeared to me in a dream, and told me that he was being asked to chant the Shabbos melodies for the tzad-dikim in Gan Eden (Paradise) and that he needed my accompaniment." The burial society was assembled, the member of the choir lit two candles at the head of the bed, and lay down. He began singing the opening verses of the Friday night services, and peacefully expired.

If death can be perceived as being a transition from one form of life to another, it loses some of its painful sting.

A Self-Made
Man

I s it appropriate to have favorites among *tzaddikim*? It is
hardly a matter of choice. Whether appropriate or not, one
does have a favorite. At least I do. The saving grace, perhaps, is that there is not just one favorite, but many.

Although it is not for us to pass judgment among these spiritual giants, we still have our own perspectives and images of
them. Thus, Rabbi Levi Yitzchak of Berditchev is a favorite in regard to seeing only the good in everyone, and in his
intervention before G-d on behalf of his people. Rabbi Schneur
Zalman is a favorite in chassidic philosophy. Rabbi Shmelke of
Nikolsburg is a favorite in his outstanding Talmudic scholarship.

Rabbi Zusia is a favorite in his absolute self-effacement. Rabbi Uri of Strelisk is a favorite in his fiery devotion which earned him the title "The Seraph." Rabbi Mendel of Kotzk is a favorite in his uncompromising demand for truth. Rabbi Moshe Leib of Sassov and Rabbi Dovid of Lelov are favorites in their love for people. The Rabbi of Rizhin is a favorite in the regal stateliness of his personality. Rabbi Dovid of Talna is a favorite for his keen wit, and so on.

But there is one *tzaddik* whose mention causes a tug on one's heartstrings, and one is overwhelmed with emotion. Indeed, just his name tells us the story, because this *tzaddik*, Rabbi Hirsh of Rimanov, has been perpetuated in chassidic lore as Reb Hirsh Meshores, or Reb Hirsh, the servant. The lowly appellation of "the servant" accompanies him throughout eternity. Imagine, a leader of thousands, venerated by the greatest chassidic masters, being referred to as "the servant"! Let us see how this came about.

R eb Hirsh was born to parents who were devout but simple people. The father, a Kohen, placed young Hirsh in a cheder to begin his Torah education. When Hirsh was 10, a virulent epidemic swept through the town, and he was orphaned of both parents in one day. A distant cousin adopted the child, but in a matter of several months the cousin was impoverished and simply could not afford to feed an extra mouth. Young Hirsh was then apprenticed to a tailor, who was to teach him the trade of needle and thread, and Hirsh was to earn his room and board by running errands, bringing in wood for the fire, and doing other chores.

The tailor, Reb Yudel, was a gentle and devout person, who tried to instill in Hirsh the character traits appropriate for a Jew. Hirsh was an obedient youngster, and would pray with great fervor, although he did not know the exact *meaning of all the Hebrew words in the prayers. He was forever inspired by his late father's last words, "Never forget, Hirshele, that you are a Kohen, and that 'the lips of a Kohen should safeguard knowledge' " (Malachi 52:7). Whenever Hirsh was free from doing chores, he did not join his peers in play, but would recite Tehillim (Psalms). However, he did not have the opportunity to further his knowledge of Scripture and Talmud.*

Hirsh was envious of the children who were privileged to learn Torah, and would fantasize that if only he had the opportunity to learn Torah, he might even become a tzaddik! But then he would castigate himself. What right did he have to indulge in such grandiose delusions? He was nothing but a tailor's apprentice, and even this lowly status was granted him only because people felt compassion for an orphan. But who was he really? A nothing, and a rather homely nothing at that. More than once he was the butt of the taunts of other children who mocked this strange child.

One day the news spread through town that the renowned tzaddik, Rabbi Moshe of P'shevorsk, was going to travel through the village, and Hirsh was seized by a craving to feast his eyes on the tzaddik. But Rabbi Moshe was a very private person, carefully guarded by his assistants from contact with people. There was just no way that he, the lowly tailor's apprentice, could get to see the tzaddik.

But the desire to see the tzaddik gave Hirsh no peace, and he then had a bright idea. Before dawn, he entered the deserted bathhouse through an open window, concealing himself under one of the benches, so that when the tzaddik would go to the mikveh (ritualarium) before morning services, he would be able to see him. Hirsh lay under the bench, silent as a statue, and watched how the tzaddik's assistant helped him off with his clothes, and after helping the tzaddik into the water, left the room. Hirsh then emerged from his hiding place, and watched how the tzaddik immersed himself in the water. He then quickly returned to his place of concealment, and after the tzaddik left the room, Hirsh hurriedly undressed and jumped into the water, hoping to have at least an indirect contact with the tzaddik, bathing in the water in which the tzaddik had purified himself.

Indeed, Hirsh felt that some transformation was taking place, as if the holiness of the tzaddik was entering his pores. His morning prayers that day were markedly different, because whereas he had previously prayed with silent tears, he could not contain his voice, and he cried aloud, often gesticulating wildly. The folk in the shul looked upon him as deranged. Who does this young boy think he is, acting as if he were being carried away by the fervor of his prayers? Hirsh tried to subdue his voice and his waving hands, but to no avail. And what was the substance of his prayer? "Master of the Universe! Open my mind and teach me Your Torah," and then Hirsh would cry because he felt his prayers were futile. One does not acquire knowledge of Torah by prayers, but by diligent study. However, he was busy all day as the tailor's apprentice, and there was little time or opportunity to study Torah.

Perhaps because he could not take the jibes of the townsfolk, perhaps because he thought he would find a better opportunity to study Torah elsewhere, Hirsh one day told Reb Yudel that he was leaving him. "Where will you go?" asked Reb Yudel. "Perhaps to Fristik, the home of the great tzaddik Rabbi Mendel. Perhaps there I will find a way to learn Torah," Hirsh said.

"Oy, Oy, Hirsh, I fear that you are more motivated by laziness than by a desire to learn. I am trying to make a tailor out of you, so that you will be able to support yourself."

But there was no stopping Hirsh. Reb Yudel gave him a few coins, and with just some bread and the clothes on his back, Hirsh began the long trek to Fristik.

The energy of youth carried Hirsh along his path, and every now and then he would rest his legs when a passing wagon offered him a lift. Sometimes the travelers shared their food with him. Hirsh's spirits were strengthened. True, he had no father, but the Father of all orphans was looking after him, providing him with compassionate people who offered him a ride and food. After several days, he arrived in Fristik, and soon found his way to the beis midrash (house of study) of the tzaddik, Rabbi Mendel. Some of the people there greeted him, and he told them he was an orphan, ignorant of Torah but anxious to learn, and that he was hopeful he could find some way of supporting himself and learning Torah, and perhaps do some chores for the tzaddik.

The people felt pity for this young boy, who obviously was not aware that few people have access to the tzaddik, who was a very frail person, tormented by much pain. The child appeared sincere, and they made it their business to give him food, and allow him to sleep on a bench in the beis midrash. Hirsh tried to study, and was overjoyed when one of the people would take a few minutes to teach him something of Scripture and the Mishnah. At other times he would try to learn himself, and would frequently have to bother those present to explain the meaning of a word or phrase.

Hirsh made it his business to scout the tzaddik's dwelling, and he saw the shamas (sexton), an elderly man, chop wood for the fire. Hirsh approached the shamas, offering his services, he would chop the wood for him, which the shamas gladly accepted. But Hirsh was allowed to carry the wood only to the door, and was not permitted entry into the house. Gradually, Hirsh won the confidence and even the affection of the shamas, who then allowed him to carry the wood into house. Hirsh offered his services in kindling the fire, but the shamas explained that this was impossible. "The tzaddik is very sickly and sensitive," he explained. "The fire must be made just so, because both inadequate heat or excessive heat are very irritating to the tzaddik. And moist wood must be avoided, because any smoke can trigger a dangerous cough." Hirsh understood, and carefully observed how the shamas arranged and kindled the wood. Again, his persistence paid off, and after several months the shamas yielded to the boy's entreaties, and allowed him to light the stove.

Hirsh was overjoyed with this opportunity, and carefully selected the wood, arranging it perfectly for a steady flame, accompanying each piece of wood with a verse from Psalms that he knew by heart, and thanking G-d for the privilege to be of service to the tzaddik. Soon Hirsh was attending the stove regularly, and this gave him the coveted opportunity to occasionally get a glimpse of the tzaddik when the door to the study was ajar.

Every day the shamas would prepare the tzaddik's bed. The tzaddik refused to sleep on a regular bed, having vowed to deprive himself of this comfort as long as G-d's people were in exile and the Divine Presence was absent from Jerusalem. The tzaddik's fervent efforts to hasten the coming of the Messiah were well known. The tzaddik slept on a mat of straw, supported by ropes stretched across a wooden frame. Hirsh watched how the shamas would carefully arrange the straw, and when asked to be allowed the privilege of preparing the tzaddik's bed, Hirsh was again told this was impossible. The straw had to be meticulously arranged so that the frail body of the tzaddik would rest comfortably for the brief period that the tzaddik slept.

But one day the shamas took ill, and had no option but to ask Hirsh to make the tzaddik's bed, cautioning him to do it exactly as he had seen him do it. Hirsh thanked G-d for this privilege, and as he carefully arranged the straw, recited the Psalms with great devotion, praying to G-d that his efforts succeed in giving the tzaddik his much-needed rest.

The following day, Rabbi Mendel asked his shamas who had prepared his bed the day before. The shamas began excusing himself, explaining that he had taken sick. "I never slept so peacefully before," Rabbi Mendel said. "My dreams were heavenly, and when I awoke to the midnight prayers, I felt the holiness of the Psalms inspiring me."

Let me digress here to explain that tzaddikim were able to sense spirituality in physical objects. The Seer of Lublin once lodged at an inn, and when he could not fall asleep, asked the innkeeper who had made the bed. The innkeeper told him that the bed had just recently been built, which was during the days of mourning prior to Tishah b'Av (commemorating the fall of Jerusalem). The Seer then said, "I could not sleep because I could feel the grief that had been infused into the bed."

Rabbi Mendel had thus sensed the love and devotion that Hirsh had infused into his bed, and told the shamas that henceforth Hirsh was to make his bed every day. Gradually, Hirsh took on additional duties, sweeping the floor, even helping the tzaddik with his clothes, and he eventually assumed the responsibilities of the shamas, who was approaching the age of retirement. The zenith of joy came when Hirsh was allowed to help the tzaddik don the second pair of tefillin after morning services. The tzaddik's intense prayers left him so totally exhausted that he did not have the energy to put on the second pair of tefillin by himself. Hirsh now became the tzaddik's constant attendant, and never left his side, earning for himself the *appellation of "Hirsh Meshores," which remained his title to this very day.*

When Rabbi Mendel moved from Fristik to Rimanov, his faithful attendant accompanied him.

The joy of serving the great tzaddik was so great that it obscured all the jibes directed at Hirsh. He was still ridiculed for his loud and active manner of praying, and as his every move began to resemble those of the tzaddik, he was denounced for the audacity of someone who was a boor, mimicking the great tzaddik, as though he too were a tzaddik. Even Rabbi Mendel's favorite disciple, Rabbi Naftali of Ropschitz, did not lose the opportunity to denounce the upstart. But Hirsh bore all the insults in silence. He had achieved the aspiration of his lifetime, and nothing else mattered. He continued to exhibit his lack of Torah knowledge by frequently asking people to translate rather simple verses and phrases for him.

Rabbi Mendel saw to it that Hirsh took a wife, but alas! misfortune haunted the young couple, because all their children died in infancy. Yet, Hirsh was not dejected. Even these grave personal losses did not detract from his joy of being the tzaddik's personal attendant. Hirsh's wife, however, could not share in his ecstasy, and wept before the tzaddik. Why was she being punished so, to lose all her children? Rabbi Mendel called in his attendant, "Hirsh," the tzaddik said, "what is the point of your bringing down neshamos (souls) which are so spiritual that they cannot adjust to the grossness of this physical world?"

The animosity of Rabbi Mendel's followers toward Hirsh continued to grow, and one time Rabbi Naftali asked the tzaddik to dismiss Hirsh. Rabbi Mendel shook his head. "The Psalmist says, 'He who walks the way of perfect innocence, he shall serve me' (Psalms 101:6) and that is Hirsh." Eventually they prevailed upon the tzaddik's son, Rabbi Nosson Yehudah, to ask for Hirsh's dismissal, and after 25 years of loyal service, Hirsh was dismissed. It was not too long after this that the tzaddik, Rabbi Mendel, left this world, and it is related that shortly before his death, Rabbi Naftali asked for the tzaddik's blessing, which the tzaddik gave by placing his left hand on Rabbi Naftali's head. "And the right hand is for whom?" Rabbi Naftali asked. "For Hirsh," the tzaddik replied.

After Rabbi Mendel's death, his son, Rabbi Nosson Yehudah, fearing that he would be pressured to assume his father's mantle of leadership, fled Rimanov to parts unknown. Reb Hirsh, to avoid any suspicion that he had aspirations of inheriting the leadership, left to join the court of Rabbi Naftali of Ropschitz, in spite of his awareness that the latter had been his adversary. Rabbi Naftali's court was graced by disciples who were Torah scholars of the highest rank, such as Rabbi Chaim of Sanz. In this company, Reb Hirsh kept his identity as one who barely had the elementary knowledge of an advanced cheder student. Rabbi Naftali was cordial to Reb Hirsh, but that was about all. It is related that when Rabbi Naftali's son asked his father why he did not show greater recognition to Reb Hirsh, Rabbi Naftali replied, "Reb Hirsh reaches the highest levels in heaven because of his profound humility. I do not dare jeopardize that."

Reb Hirsh remarried after his wife's death, and his second wife bore him a daughter. During the twelve years he spent in Ropschitz, it is unknown how he supported his wife and daughter, but this much is certain: They lived far below the poverty level. Yet Reb Hirsh was happy with his lot, even when his daughter was of the age when she was eligible for a shidduch, and without a dowry, prospects for marriage were dim. But Reb Hirsh felt that this was G-d's worry rather than his. A person's responsibility is to advance himself spiritually, because that is the one area that G-d has left to man's free choice. How much money will a person earn? Why, that is preordained by G-d. Why waste time on what G-d will take care of, when one has so much yet to learn in Torah?

One day a chassid of Rabbi Naftali came to the rabbi in a state of panic. He was a wealthy merchant, and his business had prospered, but in recent months things had taken a sharp turn downward. Although he still had some money, he was fearful that unless the trend reversed, he would be totally bankrupt before long. He had a large family and many obligations, and he was devastated by the prospect of becoming impecunious. He pleaded for a blessing from the Rabbi; nay, a promise that his fortune would pick up.

Rabbi Naftali told the man that a blessing was certainly in order, but that no one could make a promise. A rabbi is not G-d, and cannot control things. The merchant begged and wept, and would not be consoled with a blessing. He insisted on an assurance.

"Hear me," Rabbi Naftali said. "Reb Hirsh says that with sincere prayer and abundant tzeddakah one can reverse the harshest of Divine decrees. Perhaps that is what you should do."

"Hirsh?" the chassid asked. "You mean Hirsh Meshores out there?", and he promptly ran out to the beis midrash, threw himself at the feet of Reb Hirsh, and pleaded for help.

Reb Hirsh had always been secure that G-d would somehow provide for his daughter's dowry, and he believed that this was the vehicle G-d had chosen. "My daughter is in need of a dowry," he said. "I need 50 silver pieces, and by virtue of this mitzvah, G-d will bless you."

The merchant was stunned. "50 silver pieces? You jest, Reb Hirsh. That is a huge amount. Five pieces, even 10, is possible, but 50 is far too much." But Reb Hirsh stood his ground, and finally the man brought him 50 silver pieces.

No sooner had he given Reb Hirsh the money than he felt a heavy burden had been lifted from his heart, and he left in a spirit of elation.

Needless to say, from that day on the merchant's business prospered, and the word soon spread that Reb Hirsh's blessing had borne fruit. People began relating to Reb Hirsh with much greater reverence. Soon afterward, Rabbi Naftali passed on, and Reb Hirsh returned to Rimanov.

Nothing excites people like a report that there is a tzaddik whose blessings are fulfilled, and news of the incident of the merchant who prospered after Reb Hirsh's blessing spread rapidly. People who had suspected that Reb Hirsh's fervent prayers were but an act began rethinking, and concluded that they had made a grave mistake, and that all these years they had not appreciated that there was a tzaddik in their midst. They began flocking to Reb Hirsh for blessings, for cures for the sick, for children for the childless, and lo! Reb Hirsh's blessings produced results. And wonder upon wonder! Reb Hirsh began expounding on Torah, and pearls of wisdom poured forth from his lips. It was not the fervent prayer that had been an act! To the contrary, it was his asking for explanations of verses in Scripture and portions of the Mishnah that had been an act! Reb Hirsh had secretly become a scholar, but had led people to believe that he was ignorant.

At the yahrtzeit of Rabbi Naftali, when his disciples gathered, Rabbi Nosson Yehudah, the son of the saintly Rabbi Mendel, told the group that his father had said that Reb Hirsh was a true tzaddik. Soon the disciples of Rabbi Naftali, among them noted chassidic masters and accomplished Talmudic scholars, began making pilgrimages to Rimanov to the new Rabbi of Rimanov, Reb Hirsh Meshores.

Some distance away, the star of the Rabbi of Rizhin had risen, and the chassidic world was ablaze with admiration for this tzaddik. Reb Hirsh longed to meet the Rabbi of Rizhin, and as he traveled to Sadegura, where the Rizhiner now resided, groups of chassidim joined on the way, and he arrived at the head of a throng. The Rizhiner accorded Reb Hirsh the greatest honors, and told his chassidim that Reb Hirsh can reach those heights of heaven that are inaccessible even to angels.

Reb Hirsh had yet another daughter by his third wife, and the Rabbi of Rizhin proposed that she marry his grandson. The humble tailor's apprentice, whose lineage was of simple folk, was to enter into a relationship with the royalty of chassidism! At the engagement, the Rizhiner said, "It is our custom to relate our genealogy prior to an engagement. My father was the tzaddik Rabbi Shalom Shachna. My grandfather was Rabbi Avraham the Angel. My great-grandfather was the great Maggid, the successor to the Baal Shem Tov."

Reb Hirsh responded quietly, "My father was a simple and poor man. I was orphaned when I was 10, and I barely remember him. I was apprenticed to a tailor, a simple and devout man. He taught me the importance of doing an honest day's work, and he told me, 'Try to repair the defects in the old, and be cautious not to spoil anything new.' That is all I have to say."

The Rizhiner remarked, "Rabbi of Rimanov, you have outdone me."

Reb Hirsh became a famous chassidic master, with followers in the thousands. They brought him huge sums of money, which he promptly distributed among the poor, and when he died at the age of 70, his widow was penniless.

Reb Hirsh did not leave an estate, but he enriched us with the inspiration of the heights a person can reach if only one sets his mind to it.

In *Let Us Make Man* (CIS 1987), I referred to an interpretation by the Baal Shem Tov on the verse in *Genesis* which describes the Creation of the world, where G-d says, "Let us make man." Who is the "us" to whom G-d is referring, and in what way does G-d need anyone's participation in Creation?

The Baal Shem Tov explained the concept of man as a being that is created as potential, and who must achieve his own perfection to become man. A being created by G-d in a state of perfection would be an angel, not man. Hence G-d is addressing man himself, saying, "You and I together can make man. I will give you the potential, and you develop it to its fullest."

But man is by nature quite lazy, and is dragged down by inertia, often remaining at a lowly level, and failing to rise to the heights of which he is capable. Man often rationalizes his indolence, saying, "Spiritual heights are beyond my reach. I don't have the genes, I don't have the brains, and I don't have the means."

Reb Hirsh Meshores exposes these rationalizations for what they are: excuses, mere excuses, whereby one may succeed in deceiving oneself.

If anyone ever had justification for resigning oneself to the status quo, it was Reb Hirsh. With sheer effort and unwavering determination, he sought his goal and rose to dazzling heights, but never lost his humility. He was, and will forever be, Reb Hirsh Meshores.

Prayer

F ew subjects receive as much attention in chassidic writings as prayer. Rabbi Schneur Zalman said that he had heard that in Vilna the emphasis was on study of Torah, whereas in Mezeritch the emphasis was on prayer. "I knew something of Torah," he said, "but very little about praying, and that is why I chose Mezeritch." Other chassidic masters summed it up this way: "Torah is G-d's gift to man. Prayer is man's gift to G-d."

Chassidic writings point out that the word for prayer, *tefillah,* means "to bind," and that prayer is like a bonding between man and G-d. This aspect of prayer accounts for the attitude and emotions that it should evoke, an intense feeing of reverence and awe of the majesty of G-d. One should be so overcome with these feelings that one should be rendered speechless, and this is the reason why we preface the *Amidah* with the phrase, "G-d, open my lips." In other words, we pray for the ability to pray, for G-d to give us the courage to pray before Him.

In many prayer books there is a "prayer before prayer," which expands on the concept that we need Divine assistance in order to pray. The Mishnah states that the pious people of yore would meditate for an hour prior to praying, in order to achieve a proper state of mind (*Berachos* 30b).

The closeness between man and G-d that can be achieved in prayer might be such that the *neshamah* so clings to G-d that it cannot remain in a physical body. Hence, Rabbi Uri of Strelisk used to bid his family farewell before leaving for morning services, fully aware that his soul might leave him during prayer. He would instruct them that in the event he did not return, they should know that the manuscripts in his possession were not his own, but the teachings of his master, Rabbi Shlomo of Karlin. Rabbi Mendel of Linsk used to pray with such fervor that during the prayer of *Nishmas* he would faint, and would have to be revived and brought to consciousness with some nourishment. They used to have "*Nishmas* biscuits" ready in the *shul* for this purpose. The *tzaddik* of Cherkassy related that one of his father's *chassidim* prayed with such intensity that his father once went over and removed the *tefillin* from the man's head to interrupt his prayer. "I had to do it," he said, "because otherwise he would have expired."

The masters were well aware that not everyone could achieve this intensity of devotion, and that many common folk might not even know the meaning of some of the words in the *siddur*. Nevertheless, as long as the *kavannah* (intent) was sincere, the prayer was precious to G-d. There are many beautiful illustrations of this, my favorite being that of Rabbi Levi Yitzchak of Berditchev who delayed the start of services on Rosh Hashanah and explained to the worshipers:

"There is a young shepherd who was orphaned as a child, and did not have the opportunity of a cheder education, never learning to read Hebrew. He somehow came to know the letters of the Aleph-Beis. This morning, when he saw people streaming to shul, he felt bad because he did not know how to pray. He therefore said to G-d, 'Dear G-d, I would like to pray to You, but I don't know how. All I know is the letters of the Aleph-Beis. I will recite these to You, and You put them together to make the proper words.'

"That is why we must wait now," Rabbi Levi Yitzchak said, "because G-d is presently occupied arranging the letters recited by the shepherd."

It is because prayer brings a person into a closer relationship with G-d that it enhances one's spirituality. The *Midrash* states that the reason the matriarchs were barren for so long is because G-d wished them to pray. The matriarchs were to be the mothers of Isaac and Jacob, the fathers and foundation of the Jewish people. The level of spirituality that would prepare them for this immense responsibility could be reached only through fervent prayer, and they were therefore denied children so that they would pray intensely for their most cherished wish.

Chassidic masters said that when a person prays for his own needs, it should not be in a selfish manner. Who is to say that a person has adequate merits for his prayers to be answered? Rather, inasmuch as the Talmud states that when a person is in distress the *Shechinah* (Divine Presence) suffers along with him, one should pray to be relieved of his suffering so that the *Shechinah* should not suffer.

Prayers should also not be misconstrued as giving orders to G-d.

Rabbi Fishel of Strikov once told Rabbi Bunim of Pschis'che that he could no longer be a *rebbe* and receive *chassidim*. "If my prayers are of no avail, how can I allow *chassidim* to come to me?" What had happened was that a *chassid* who was desperate for money to provide a dowry for his daughter came to Rabbi Fishel for a blessing, and he gave him a *berachah* and told him to buy a lottery ticket. Rabbi Fishel prayed that the man would win the lottery, and when he did not, Rabbi Fishel felt his prayers were worthless.

Rabbi Bunim told him, "In our morning prayers we say, 'Who among Your creations can tell You what to do and how to act?' We cannot give G-d instructions. You had a right to give the man a *berachah* for wealth and to pray to G-d for this *berachah* to be fulfilled. Your mistake was in designating the method, *how* this was to happen. It is not your place to give G-d advice how to make a man wealthy."

The Talmud refers to prayer as *avodah shebelev,* the work of the heart, and sincere prayer must indeed be work. Some *tzaddikim* like Rabbi Levi Yitzchak were unable to restrain themselves in prayer, and shook violently or gesticulated. When someone criticized him for this, he asked, "If you saw a person drowning, and he was motioning wildly in his desperate attempt to stay above water or to attract help, would you criticize his behavior? When I try to concentrate on prayer and the *yetzer hara* tries to distract me, I am fighting for my life to retain my *kavannah* (concentration)."

Other *tzaddikim* prayed quietly and in a motionless posture, but their clothes would be drenched with perspiration from the intensity of their prayer. It is related that the mother of the five *tzaddikim* of Zidichov would check their clothes when they came home from *shul* in their childhood, and if their clothes were not wet with perspiration, she would reprimand them for not having prayed with proper *kavannah.*

Chassidic masters urged people to add personal prayers after completing the ritual prayers in the *siddur.* Rabbi Nachman of Breslov was an ardent advocate of composing individual prayers, and said that he owed much of his spiritual achievements to his personal prayers. There should not be anything too small or too insignificant to include in prayer. After all, a child does not limit his requests from his father to major items, and does not hesitate to ask his father for even trivial needs.

Faith and trust in G-d are the cornerstones of prayer. Some people who were not well versed in Torah nevertheless had a degree of faith and trust that merited Divine response to their prayers.

A chassid of the Tzemach Tzedek returned from a visit to Eretz Yisrael and told the rabbi that he was disappointed, having expected to find many people of greater spirituality there. "What makes you think you are a maven (expert) on people of spirituality?" the Tzemach Tzedek asked, and preceded to tell him this story.

In Eretz Yisrael there was a farmer who lived in the country and had no access to a rabbi. He was very devout, but totally ignorant of learning, so much so that he was unable to read the calendar. He would therefore go into the city once a month, and the rabbi would write out for him a detailed sheet of instructions as to which prayers he was to say each day of the upcoming month.

One year there was a terrible drought, and following the Talmudic guidelines, the rabbi proclaimed a day of fasting and teshuvah. It so happened that the farmer came into town that day and went to see the rabbi, whose wife told him that the rabbi was in shul and would be there all day because it was a fast day. The farmer went to the shul and complained to the rabbi that he had not given him any instructions to fast on that day or the special prayers that were to be said.

The rabbi explained that he had not been able to do so because this was not a regularly scheduled fast day, and he had no advance knowledge when he wrote out the

*monthly calendar that they would have to proclaim a fast
day to pray for rain. The man appeared puzzled, "Why do
you have to fast if there is no rain? If I need rain for my
farm, I just go out and look toward the sky, and say,
'Father, I need rain,' and then it rains."*

*The rabbi was impressed, and asked the man, "Do you
think you can do this for us as well?" "Why not?" the man
responded. He then went outdoors, lifted his eyes to the
sky, and in a tearful voice said, "Father, your children need
rain!" In just a few moments, gray clouds appeared on the
horizon, and soon abundant rain fell to the parched earth.*

*"Now," the Tzemach Tzedek said, "do you think you can
tell who is a spiritual person?"*

It is customary to give *tzeddakah* before prayer, not only because prefacing prayer with such a special *mitzvah* is
conducive to meriting Divine assistance in praying, but also because it is an act of sharing oneself with others. In some
siddurim there is an introductory passage at the beginning of
services, "I hereby take upon myself fulfillment of the *mitzvah*
of 'Love your neighbor as yourself.' " Of course, this is meant to
be said with sincerity, and not just verbalized. Caring for and
sharing with others is the key to one's prayers being received
favorably. There is nothing so dear to G-d as seeing His children
devoted to one another, and there is nothing that stresses Him
as much as divisiveness among His children.

That the sincere caring for another person is the major deter-
minant of the quality of prayer is illustrated by a story I related
in *Generation To Generation* (CIS 1987).

My great-grandfather, the Rebbe of Hornosteipel, was asked
by a *chassid*, "Why is it that my prayers go unanswered? Were
we not assured that G-d would grant the wishes of those who do
His will? Why is it that the prayers of a *tzaddik* are more effective than the prayers of an average person?"

The Rebbe replied, "A person's sincere wish is never denied, but that wish must be the person's foremost desire, and very few people pray for what is truly their foremost desire.

"Take, for example, the person who prays for success and wealth. He may indeed be impoverished and may very profoundly desire to become wealthy. Yet, if he were drowning and could not catch his breath, he would, of course, not think of acquiring wealth. At that point, his most fervent and only desire would be to breathe and remain alive, hence wealth is not really his first priority.

"The Talmud states that if a person forgoes his own needs to pray for the needs of another, that prayer is warmly received.

"The devotion of a *tzaddik* to his followers is so great," the Rebbe continued, "that their well-being becomes his first priority. The love of the *tzaddik* for his fellow Jew surpasses the love and devotion of a father for his favorite child. When a *tzaddik* prays for someone's health and success, his desire for that person's happiness is so intense, that even if the *tzaddik* were drowning at that point, his prayer would not be for his own survival, nor his wish to be able to breathe and remain alive, but rather that the other person's needs be fulfilled. This self-negation and self-sacrifice which the *tzaddik* achieves out of love for his fellow man is the reason why his prayers are answered."

The Rebbe knew of what he spoke. It is told that as a child, orphaned at a tender age, he was reared by his grandfather, the tzaddik of Cherkassy. Once one of the Rebbe's adherents came to Cherkassy to beg the Rebbe to pray for his salvation. He had not earned enough to meet the payments on the inn and dwelling which he was renting from the feudal lord, and the latter had threatened him with expulsion and imprisonment if his arrears were not promptly resolved. He could not envision any source of help, and asked the Rebbe to pray for Divine mercy, so that he and his family would not languish in prison.

To his horror, he found that the Rebbe was out of the city, and when he approached the Rebbetzin with his bitter plight, she suggested, "Go to the house of study and talk to my grandson. He may be able to help you."

"But your grandson is only a child of 10," the man said. "I need the Rebbe. Our very lives are in jeopardy."

Again the Rebbetzin said, "The Rebbe is not available now. Go talk with my grandson."

The man went to the house of study, where the 10-year-old child was engrossed in Talmud studies, and against his better judgment, unburdened himself to the young boy. The young boy listened sympathetically to the man's tearful tale of woe, sighed deeply, and said, "If only Grandfather were here, I am certain that he could help you. But there is nothing I can do for you."

In desperation, the man cried out, "Look, your grandmother sent me to you. Now, if you truly cannot help me, then I hold no grudge against you. But if you have the capacity to help me and refrain from doing so, then I shall never forgive you for what will befall my family. Not only will I not forgive you in this world, but I will not forgive you in the Eternal World as well."

The young boy was shaken. He slowly closed the volume of the Talmud and said, "Well, let us go first to the mikveh."

The man accompanied the young boy to the mikveh and stood by as the latter immersed himself beneath the surface of the water. After a few moments, the man became concerned that the child was not coming out of the water, and as the moments passed, far beyond what seemed to be the human endurance for surviving without air, the man became panic stricken. He tried to go down to the mikveh to extricate the child, but his limbs seemed to be paralyzed.

He soon forgot about his troubles, about his being in arrears, and about his imminent eviction or imprisonment. He was totally occupied with the child whose head remained immersed beneath the water. "Dear G-d," he prayed silently and fervently, "just let me see that young child emerge from the mikveh alive."

After what seemed to be not one but many eternities, the young boy emerged from the water. "Go home," he said. "You have nothing to worry about."

Several weeks later, the chassid returned to the Rebbe of Cherkassy and told him that upon his return home, the feudal lord had sent for him and apologized to him for having been so harsh with him. That previous night, the feudal lord related, he developed a choking sensation and was unable to breathe. In his panic he began to reflect that perhaps he was being punished by G-d for being so ruthless with his tenants. He then resolved that henceforth he would be more lenient with them, and soon thereafter his breathing returned to normal. "So," he said, "I will not only forgive you your arrears but I will also arrange more liberal terms for your future payments."

The Rebbe of Cherkassy listened to the story and shook his head sadly, "This is too tender an age for my grandson to place his life in jeopardy." But the pattern that was initiated at age 10 persisted for the next 53 years. The wants and needs of others took priority, always.

Too often our prayers are perfunctory. We certainly need the things we pray for, both for our individual needs and collective needs. Let us try to improve the quality of our prayers, so that they emerge from our hearts rather than just from our lips.

Simchah

Chassidus places great emphasis on *simchah* (joy). Let us remember that *chassidus* emerged in one of the darkest periods in our history, when the Jews in Eastern Europe were barely recovering from the massacres and pogroms of Chmielnicki, and were living under the anti-Semitic rule of the czar, subject to the whim of the *poritzim* (feudal lords) who showed very little mercy toward their Jewish vassals. The message of the Baal Shem Tov was that *simchah* is not contingent upon comfort and contentment, and that *simchah* is possible even when one is experiencing adversity and suffering.

How can one have *simchah* when one is in distress? By realizing that at all times one is fulfilling one's mission and purpose in existence. If one truly sees life as purposeful and sincerely believes that the sole purpose of existence is to do the Divine will, this can provide a feeling of achievement and satisfaction that need not be extinguished by physical suffering. Our oppressors can take away our material belongings and may even take our lives, but they are powerless to take our *neshamos.*

The *chassid* Reb Hillel of Paritch lost his home in a fire. Upon returning to examine the ruins, his students heard him recite a *berachah* (blessing). They were certain he was going to recite the *berachah* whereby one accepts harsh Divine judgments with an expression of faith, and they were surprised when he said, "Blessed is G-d Who has not made me a heathen." When they asked him about the relevance of this *berachah,* Reb Hillel said, "It is simple. When the house of a heathen burns down, the flames consume his idols as well, and he thereby loses his gods. I am grateful that I am a Jew, because even though I have lost my home, my G-d was not destroyed in the fire, and my G-d lives on."

Chassidus teaches that when one maintains an attitude of *simchah* even under adversity, this holds the greatest hope for salvation and emerging from that adversity. *Simchah* is considered to be a most potent force. In response to the Talmudic statement "The gates of heaven are never closed to tears" (*Berachos* 32b), one chassidic master said, "But prayers with *simchah* can break all locks and penetrate closed gates."

There is room for fervent, tearful prayers. Yet, prayers with joy are even more potent. Chassidic masters said that one should learn lessons from observing an infant. Infants are invariably happy, but when they want something, they cry for it. Joy and crying are not opposites.

This became evident to me on my first visit to the *Kosel.* Following the *halachah,* I tore my garment as a sign of grief, that the glory of our past was in ruins, and that we had lost our holy Temple. The following evening was Friday night, and I joined with many others, dancing with jubilation: We were at the site of the holy Temple, from which the Divine Presence had never departed, and soon, with the coming of the Redemption, our holy Sanctuary would again appear at this very site. Yes, dance and cry.

It is related that the prayers of the Maggid of Kozhnitz were never turned away, particularly when he included them in his midnight prayers, which were bathed in tears over the destruction of the Temple and the loss of the Divine glory when His children were driven into exile. The Maggid's tears flowed through the gates that were never closed.

One night, the Maggid's disciple, Rabbi Naftali of Ropschitz, was at an inn where a wedding celebration was in progress. Rabbi Naftali was told that the bride was unhappy because there was no badchan (jester) to lead the merrymaking. "Tell the bride to rejoice," Rabbi Naftali said, "because I am a badchan!" He then jumped on a table and began to lead the guests in merrymaking, composing lyrics impromptu, and expounding words of Torah wisdom in so clever and amusing a way that all the guests rejoiced.

When he subsequently came to Kozhnitz, the Maggid embraced him and said, "My dear Naftali, how I envy you. You can accomplish with joy what I cannot accomplish with the most heartrending tears.

"One night I was reciting my midnight prayers, and I was overcome with grief at the unfortunate state of our people and the exile of the Divine Presence from Jerusalem. Suddenly I realized that my prayers were not ascending to heaven. Upon investigating what the cause *was, I discovered that the heavenly angels were listening to your performance, as you brought joy to the newlyweds!"*

Rabbi Levi Yitzchak of Berditchev said that the greatest threat to the Jews of the Purim episode occurred when "On that day Haman went out joyful and exuberant" (*Esther* 5:9). This posed the greatest danger, because when one has an attitude of joy, one can accomplish virtually whatever he wishes. Haman's downfall began when he became despondent, having been compelled to honor Mordechai (*ibid.* 6:12).

The chassidic teaching of joy in feeling that one is fulfilling the Divine mission does not at all contradict the feelings of humility and awareness of how little one has achieved, an attitude that is required in Torah observance. The compatibility of the two can be seen in the story of the *chazzan* (cantor) who would chant the *al cheit* (confession) prayer with a lively and cheerful melody rather than with the habitual somber tone. When the Baal Shem Tov asked him why he did so, he said, "If I were assigned a housekeeping duty in the royal palace, would it not make me happy when I removed all the accumulated trash and made the palace a more beautiful and pleasant place for the king? The Divine Presence is in every person, and when I cleanse myself from my sins, I am making myself a more appropriate dwelling place for the Divine Presence, and that is reason to rejoice."

Being deprived of earthly goods may cause one to feel dejected, because there may be little one can do to significantly improve one's lot. But if a person feels he is spiritually impoverished, there is no reason for despondence, because one can at all times elevate oneself spiritually. In fact, a person who understands that his purpose in life is to grow spiritually by doing the Divine will, and senses that he must always do more, may actually relish this sensation, much as the person who is very hungry but who knows that he will soon partake of a delicious meal can actually enjoy the feeling of hunger, because of his anticipation of the pleasure of eating. Similarly, the sensation of hunger for spiritual growth, although it is in one sense uncomfortable, may also provide pleasure as one contemplates and anticipates doing *mitzvos*. For example, one has a pleasurable sense of anticipation when he awakens on the first day of Succos, knowing that in just a short while he will have the opportunity to fulfill the precious *mitzvah* of the four species. A person who realizes that the opportunity to do *mitzvos* is always before him can actually enjoy the feeling of anticipation even when one is still in a state of spiritual deprivation.

R*eb Zalman Sender's, a chassid of Rabbi Schneur Zalman, had been a wealthy man who had a turn of fortune and lost all his money. He presented the Rebbe with a petition, wherein he described his desperate situation, that he was deeply in debt and he was being hounded by his creditors, that members of his extended family were relying on him for support, and that he had daughters of marriageable age for whom he needed a dowry. He wept as the Rebbe studied his petition, and he pleaded for a blessing for success. The Rebbe closed his eyes in meditation, and after a few moments said to him, "Zalman, it is obvious that you have given much thought to your needs. Have you given equal thought to why you are needed?"*

Zalman was stunned as if struck by a lightning bolt. Being the chassid that he was, it suddenly occurred to him that as important as material wealth may be, it pales in significance to one's spiritual obligations. Man was not created to be wealthy, but to do the Divine will, to fulfill the needs of the neshamah. Zalman realized that he had not been giving due attention to the latter, and that he had allowed the distress of his material circumstances to distract him from what was truly important in life. While he was saddened by his particular financial plight, he was nevertheless buoyed by his awareness that he had a purpose in life for which he had been created. His existence in the universe was not an accident, and he was part of the Divine plan. The Rebbe had pointed out to him that he was important, that he was significant, that he was "needed," and he realized that his earthly "needs" had obscured his perspective on life.

Realizing that his first and foremost obligation was to perfect himself spiritually, Zalman returned to the beis midrash to recite Tehillim and to study Torah, particularly the works of mussar and chassidus that explained how a person is to fulfill one's mission on earth.

Zalman's dejection was mitigated by his rededication to spiritual growth, and he could thus have simchah in spite of his dire financial circumstances.

The Talmud states that a person's earthly fortunes are fixed and preordained, and that nothing one does will affect this predestination. On the other hand, a person is totally on his own to advance himself spiritually. How foolish it is to spend one's time and effort on that which is unchangeable and neglect that which is changeable! The Rebbe's brief comment helped put Zalman on the right path, and he was able to achieve an attitude of *simchah*.

Just a bit of analysis will help in assigning priorities to our efforts. Let us think about the physical pleasures we enjoy in life. Every single one of them is ephemeral, and as delicious as yesterday's meal may have been while we were eating it, it provided no residual pleasure for today. On the other hand, we can at the present time still enjoy the feeling of a *mitzvah* performed years ago. For example, the feeling that one has given *tzeddakah* and helped a destitute person can provide a pleasant feeling which one may retain long after the deed. As one accumulates *mitzvos,* one acquires spiritual joy, and even if we feel we have not yet accomplished enough, we can nevertheless enjoy the anticipation of doing more.

A proper perspective on life can enable one to have an attitude of *simchah* even in difficult times.

T*he prayer for appearance of the new moon must be said before the moon reaches its fullness. One month the skies were continually cloudy, and the Baal Shem Tov was upset that he would not have the opportunity to say the monthly prayer, and on the last appropriate night, he prayed for the skies to clear so that the moon could be seen and the prayer recited. But alas! the hours went by and the clouds remained thick as ever.*

Several of the Baal Shem Tov's disciples were studying Torah, and at one point became so ecstatic with the realization of how privileged they were to have the Divine Torah, by the study of which one could identify with Almighty G-d Himself, that they began to sing, then joined hands and danced. They danced near where the Baal Shem Tov was meditating, and invited the master to dance with them. As they were dancing, someone announced that there was a break in the clouds and the moon was visible. They all rushed out to say the designated prayer. The Baal Shem Tov later commented that what he had been unable to achieve even with his fervent prayers was achieved by the simchah of the song and dance.

Joyous dancing is customary among *chassidim,* who say that there is symbolism in dancing. "In order to dance, one must life one's feet off the ground, and this symbolizes that one elevates himself and separates from earthiness."

The graceful dancing of the chassidic master, the Shpoler Zeide, is legendary, and his peers used to say that his dancing constituted a Divine service of the highest order. The Zeide related the following.

"**D**uring my years of wandering from village to village, I heard about a Jewish vassal who was imprisoned in a dungeon for failure to pay the rent to the poritz (feudal lord). Once a week they would lower food and water through a hole in the ceiling, and the prisoner was to remain confined there until the poritz's birthday.

"On the poritz's birthday, there would be a great party for all the neighboring poritzim, at which time the prisoner would be brought out, and would be given a costume of the hide of a bear. Someone would put a chain around the neck of the prisoner, who had to walk on all fours like a bear, and then had to dance on all fours according to the band leader's tempo. If the 'bear' failed to dance to the guests' satisfaction, he would be thrown to the dogs. If the guests were pleased, the prisoner would be freed. Needless to say, a person who had been in prison for months and who had survived on starvation rations would hardly be able to dance adequately to satisfy the guests, and the prisoner's doom was a foregone conclusion.

"As I was contemplating how to rescue the imprisoned Jew, the prophet Elijah appeared to me and told me to take the place of the Jew and dance for him. When I told Elijah that I was a very poor dancer, he taught me how to dance gracefully.

"I found the dungeon, and was able to lower myself via a rope through the hole in the roof. I brought some food and drink for the prisoner, and changed clothes with him. I told him that when they came to take him, they would *undoubtedly leave the gate open, since he was the only one there, and that he should then make his escape.*

"When they brought me before the party, the poritz announced that he would himself lead the 'bear' in the dance, and that if the 'bear' danced better than he, he would be free to whip the poritz to his heart's content.

"The band started playing, and the poritz held the chain and began dancing. I then danced around him with much grace, as Elijah had taught me. As the guests applauded, the band quickened the tempo of the music, and I danced faster and more gracefully than ever. The poritz, who had been drinking heavily, fell to the floor, and I then jumped upon him and began beating him. Some of the other poritzim intervened and begged me to stop the beating, and I was set free."

Chassidim love to tell the story of the Shpoler Zeide's dancing. While we are not so fortunate as to be taught by Elijah, we can nevertheless utilize the *simchah* of dancing to set free the *neshamah* that is imprisoned within our physical bodies, just as the Zeide's dancing set free the Jew from the dungeon.

The Childhood of a Tzaddik

The Talmud says that the character of the blossom foretells the nature of the fruit. We are fortunate that several accounts of the younger years of various *tzaddikim* have been preserved for us.

One of the outstanding luminaries of the past century was Rabbi Abraham of Sochatchov, who was a child prodigy, learning Talmud at age four, and baffling accomplished scholars with his keen understanding of complex *halachic* issues at age seven.

When he was a child of six, his father sent him home from *shul* on Yom Kippur morning to eat something, and said, "Don't forget to make *Kiddush*, son. For adults who fast, there is of course no *Kiddush* on Yom Kippur, but since you are permitted to eat, you are also required to say the *Kiddush*."

Rabbi Abraham responded, "No, Father, there is no need for *Kiddush*. Actually, a minor is not obligated to do any of the *mitzvos*, but we do them as a matter of training, to prepare us for when we will be *bar mitzvah*, so that we will be familiar with the way of doing *mitzvos*. But when I will be 13, I will be fasting on Yom Kippur, so there is no reason for me to train myself now for a *Kiddush* that I will never recite as an adult!"

⤝⤞

W hen Abraham was eight, his father, who was a noted Talmudic scholar, would hold intricate discussions with him. One time young Abraham offered an interpretation of a difficult Talmudic passage which his father dismissed as incorrect. Many years later the father reviewed this particular topic, and realized that the child had been correct after all. He asked the son whether he recalled their discussion of many years earlier.

"Every word of it," Rabbi Abraham answered.

"Well, I must admit to you that I have just reviewed that Talmudic passage, and you were correct in your interpretation," the father said.

"I knew that all the time," Rabbi Abraham said, "but to have refuted you would have been in violation of the Torah obligation to respect one's father. Just because I was correct did not give me the right to be disrespectful."

⤝⤞

W hen Abraham was a child of six he once passed by a fruit peddler and upset the cart, causing the fruit to spill onto the street. The peddler complained to the father, requesting to be compensated for his son's mischief.

"Why did you do that?" the father asked.

"I had to," the child replied. "The peddler had placed damaged fruit in baskets, and covered them with a thin layer of good fruit, thereby cheating the people who thought the whole basket was like the top layer. I had to do it to protect people from being cheated."

The account of Abraham's prodigious knowledge of Talmud spread far and wide, and when he was 11, he was recommended as a *shidduch* for the daughter of the *tzaddik* of Sanz. As was the custom in those days, marriages were arranged when the couple were yet children. The *tzaddik* of Sanz questioned young Abraham, and was impressed by the boy's genius. He later requested a second session to further interrogate him.

"Well and good," young Abraham said. "The Rabbi of Sanz may interrogate me a second time, provided that I first have the opportunity to test his knowledge of Talmud." The audacity of this comment upset Abraham's father.

Young Abraham explained, "Why is a prospective son-in-law tested in Talmud? It is because the Talmud says that one should be sure to take a Talmudic scholar for his daughter. But the Talmud also says that one should seek to marry the daughter of a Talmudic scholar. Then why does the prospective son-in-law not test the father-in-law to be certain that he is a scholar?

"It must be," young Abraham said, "that one does not test the prospective father-in-law because one relies on the fact that when the father-in-law was young, he was tested as a prospective son-in-law. However, the Rabbi of Sanz has interrogated me once, and if he is not satisfied with one test, then I am not satisfied with the fact that he was tested once. I therefore have a right to retest him as well."

The *tzaddik* of Sanz was impressed by Rabbi Abraham's sharp wit, but was concerned about his boldness. He sought the counsel of his master, the *tzaddik* of Belz, who advised him against the *shidduch*, and said, "You will do even better." The *tzaddik* of Sanz then took as his son-in-law my grandfather, Rabbi Mordechai of Hornosteipel.

A t age 11, Rabbi Abraham fell gravely ill, and his father asked Rabbi Mendel of Kotzk (who later became Rabbi Abraham's father-in-law) to pray for the child saying, "He is a great Torah scholar." He was surprised when Rabbi Mendel said, "I don't consider his learning as being of much value." The father was upset by the Rabbi's belittling his son's scholarship, and mentioned this to the young boy.

"Of course," the young boy said. "The Talmud states that when Rabbi Tarfon was ill, his mother asked his colleagues to pray for him, and told them how extremely diligent he was in his respect for her. 'He does not even let me step on the cold floor,' she said. 'He puts his hands under my feet to serve as a mat.' The Rabbis responded, 'So what? He hasn't even begun to fulfill the mitzvah of parental respect.'

"Why did the Rabbis say that?" young Abraham asked. "It was because when a person has fulfilled mitzvos adequately, he may have completed his mission on earth, in which case his life may come to an end. Inasmuch as Rabbi Tarfon was sick, the Rabbis wished to indicate that he had not yet fulfilled mitzvos sufficiently; hence, he needed to remain alive longer.

"That is why the Rabbi of Kotzk dismissed my Torah study as inadequate, in order to point out that I must yet live to learn Torah properly."

When Rabbi Abraham's father relayed this to Rabbi Mendel, the latter said, "I knew he was bright, but I did not know that he could detect my intentions." Young

Abraham later grew up to be one of the outstanding Torah scholars of the century, whose Talmudic works are highly regarded to this day.

Rabbi Yehudah Leib of Gur (*Sfas Emes*) was orphaned when very young, and was raised by his grandfather, Rabbi Isaac Meir, who required the young boy to arise at dawn to study Torah. One time the youngster studied Torah all night and went to sleep shortly before dawn, and when he awoke two hours later, his grandfather, who did not know that Yehudah Leib had studied all night, reprimanded him sharply for oversleeping. The young boy accepted the rebuke respectfully.

The youngster's friend, who knew the truth, said to him, "Why did you not explain to your grandfather that you had studied until dawn?"

Young Yehudah Leib replied, "In the Torah we find that the tribes of Reuben and Gad wished to receive their share of the land Transjordan, which they planned to settle after they had helped their brothers conquer Canaan. Moses, assuming that they were seeking to avoid participating in the conquest, rebuked them sharply.

"Why did they not simply explain their intention to Moses and avoid the reprimand? It was because it is not every day that one has the opportunity to be reprimanded by Moses, and to these tribes, this was a valuable experience.

"Had I interrupted my grandfather, I would have missed the opportunity to receive a reprimand from him. That is something far too precious to lose."

When the *tzaddik* Rabbi Yisrael of Rizhin was a child, he was playing outdoors one Friday afternoon, and his older brother told him that it was time to come in because Shabbos was near. The child looked up at the sky and said, "It is not yet Shabbos. I can tell by looking at the sky. When Shabbos enters, the entire heavens change in appearance."

Young Yisrael learned Chumash (the Five Books of Moses) at the age of five, and would anticipate every question asked by the Torah commentator, Rashi. When they learned the portion describing Jacob's dream wherein he saw a ladder reaching the sky and angels were ascending and descending on it (Genesis 28:12), the teacher paused, expecting the child to ask Rashi's question on the reverse order, namely, that the angels should first be descending from the sky and then ascending. When the child was silent, the rebbi asked, "Doesn't this verse bother you?"

"No," said the child.

"Aren't you curious why the order is reversed? Angels must first descend from the sky before ascending the ladder."

"But this was only a dream," said young Yisrael, "and dreams don't have to conform to logic."

≈⋍

A man once came to the Rabbi of Rizhin's court, and told the shamas (sexton) that he was desperate for the tzaddik's help. When he was told that the tzaddik was ill and could not receive anyone, he broke down crying.

The Rizhiner's oldest son, Rabbi Sholom Yosef, was then a child, and he asked the man what the trouble was. The man said that his craft was fashioning metal pots, and that the poritz (feudal lord) had given him several ingots of copper to make a large pot for him. Some of the workers must have stolen some of the copper, because when he brought the pot to the poritz it was weighed and was found to be considerably less than the weight of the ingots. The poritz was furious and threatened to throw him into the dungeon for the theft.

Young Sholom Yosef said, "Do you have six rubles? Give me six rubles and you will be all right." The man gave the child six rubles and left.

Sometime later the man reported to the Rizhiner that the poritz had weighed the pot a second time, and found that the weight equaled that of the ingots, and apologized to the man for having accused him of stealing. He told the Rizhiner that the son's blessing had come through. The Rizhiner called the child and asked him to explain his action.

"I had just come from a walk," young Sholom Yosef said, "and I passed by a wedding party and heard a great commotion. The chassan and kallah were two orphans without family, and the community had arranged a modest wedding. When the groom discovered that the bride had not provided a talis for him, as is customary, he said he would not go to the chupah (wedding canopy) unless he had a talis, and the wedding was in jeopardy. Just then I met this man. When he gave me the six rubles, I ran off and bought a talis and the wedding took place with great joy. I was certain that the zechus (merit) of this mitzvah would deliver the man from his tzaros (troubles)."

When the Seer of Lublin, Rabbi Yaakov Yitzchak was a child, he would escape from *cheder* to the woods, where he would spend hours in solitude. This greatly distressed his father who used to reprimand him, "Roaming in the woods is appropriate for youngsters who do not learn Torah. You belong in the *cheder*. What are you seeking there in the forest?" To which young Yaakov Yitzchak responded, "I am looking for G-d." His father said, "There is no need to go to the forest to look for G-d, because he is everywhere." The child replied, "Yes, I know that G-d is everywhere. He is also within me, and it is G-d within me that I am trying to find. I cannot do this when I am disturbed by people around me!"

M any years later when the Seer was already famous as a chassidic master, he was traveling with several of his disciples when the horses suddenly took off on a side path, and the driver could not bring them back to the road. The horses eventually stopped in a small village, and by that time it was late Thursday night. Inasmuch as it was a short winter day, the Seer said that he would not attempt to return home on Friday, and that they would have to spend Shabbos in the village. Not having any provisions or much money with them, they relied on being invited to people's homes for the Shabbos meals, and they would sleep on the benches in the beis midrash.

Indeed, Friday night after services, the worshipers invited the strangers to their homes for meals. After everyone had left, the Seer was still in the midst of his prayers, and when he finished, only one elderly man remained in shul. This man said to him, "I have only a meager meal, but you can share it with me."

At the meal the host asked his guest where he was from, and when the Seer responded, "Lublin," he asked, "Do you by any chance know the Rabbi of Lublin?" to which the Seer responded affirmatively.

"I hear he is a great tzaddik," the host said. "Can you tell me something about him?"

"Why are you interested in him?" the Seer asked.

"He was a student in my cheder," the man said. "He used to run away from cheder and spend hours in the woods, and I used to beat him for this. He was not a bad child, and I was curious why he was always running to the forest. One day I followed him, and I saw him sit between two huge rocks, raise his hands to the sky and cry out Shema Yisrael. I never beat him again after that. I knew then that he would one day be a great tzaddik. I would so love to see him now, and ask his forgiveness for having *beaten him. But I am old and weak, and I cannot make the trip. How I would like to see him yet before I leave this world!*

The Seer then revealed his identity to his childhood teacher. "There is no need for forgiveness," he said. "Those beatings helped make a mentsch of me."

After Shabbos was over, the Seer and his disciples decided to delay their return home until daybreak. At morning services they heard that during the night the Seer's teacher had died, and the Seer was able to attend the funeral of the teacher of his youth, whose fervent wish to see the great tzaddik who had once been his pupil had been granted.

When the *tzaddik* of Sanz was a child, his father took him to the Seer of Lublin, who loved to spend time with this bright youngster. One time, when the Seer was receiving many supplicants in private audience, he abruptly stated that he needed some time for meditation, and everyone would have to leave. Little Chaim'ke was curious and hid in a closet to observe what the Seer was doing in solitude. He noted that the Seer paced to and fro, reciting the first *mishnah* in *Berachos*.

After a few moments had passed, the Seer went to the closet and found the young hideaway. He embraced the child and said, "Chaim'ke, let me tell you what I did. People come to me for advice. The only sound advice I can give is based on what I can see of a person's situation. The *Midrash* tells us that at Creation, G-d created a very bright light, but because there would be sinful people who are unworthy of this light, G-d replaced it with a weaker light, and concealed the original light. This original light is concealed in the Torah, and with this powerful light one can see everything clearly.

"When I felt I was no longer seeing things clearly, I had to restore my vision, which I did by reciting the *mishnah*. The study of Torah enables one to use the light that is concealed therein."

Many years later, little Chaim became the *tzaddik* of Sanz, to whom thousands of people came for advice. Being the great Torah scholar that he was, he utilized the teachings of the Seer of Lublin that one can see everything by the light of the Torah in order to answer the many questions of his followers.

Channeling
the Energy

orah observance is predicated on the hope that people will use their *seichel* (intelligence), as Moses says in his last words, "If only they were wise and would comprehend this" (*Deuteronomy* 32:29). Solomon repeatedly emphasizes the virtue of wisdom, and repeatedly condemns the *ksil,* the person who acts foolishly not because of an inherent lack of intellect, but because, as Rabbi Samson Raphael Hirsch explains, he allows his judgment to be distorted by his emotions and desires, which results in the utter disregard of rational considerations. Rabbi Hirsch states:

> A *ksil,* on the other hand, will have had opportunities to gain knowledge. Having disdained them, however, and

still disdaining them, because he overestimates man's intelligence in general and his own in particular, in foolish conceit he allows himself to form opinions and hold onto them by sheer force, never heeding objections from a higher source, not even from the Highest One. So, wisdom bids such arrogant fools, who consider themselves so wise, to first try to gain some insight into their own capacity for understanding, before granting unlimited confidence to their own intelligence, before forming an authoritative opinion about things and matters, and before spurning any superior advice. "Get to know your 'heart'," the narrower range of its understanding, and the impact that sensual desires have upon it. Only then can you ultimately become open, accessible to the Divine wisdom (*The Wisdom of Mishle,* Feldheim, 1976, Page 53).

It was this type of *ksil* whom Rabbi Naftali of Ropschitz could not tolerate. Why be a fool when you have the option to be wise? Rabbi Naftali was once asked why he was so intolerant of fools. "After all," he was told, "the Talmud states that whether a person will be wise or foolish is preordained prior to one's birth *(Niddah* 16b). If a person is a fool, it is because of a Divine decree. How can you then condemn him?" Rabbi Naftali answered, "True, but it is also a Divine decree to eat matzah on Pesach, yet one can comply with this decree by eating a piece of matzah the size of an olive. If one thinks he performs the *mitzvah* more admirably by eating a larger piece of matzah, he is free to do so. Granted, it was Divinely decreed that a person should be a fool. Would it not have been enough for him to comply with the Divine decree with just a minimum amount of foolishness? Why must he try to fulfill the Divine decree so admirably as to be such a great fool? That is what angers me."

Humans share many emotions with animals: hunger, anger, lust, greed, etc. The one feature that gives us our uniqueness as human beings is *seichel*. Is it not the epitome of folly that allows us to be dominated by that portion of ourselves that is animal, that we share with lower forms of life, and to ignore the *seichel*, our distinct human feature?

The animal component of the human being is the source of many of our drives, and can provide the energy for our system to operate. We have the option of allowing them to flow along the animalistic channels, or redirecting them into behavior that is uniquely human. If we are truly proud of our humanity, we would do the latter.

Chassidic teachings often refer to the process of "rechanneling energies." The Baal Shem Tov taught that energy should not be stifled, but rather redirected. If we suppress a drive, we must exert force to maintain that suppression, and while this may enable us to avoid improper action, it drains us of energy and does not contribute to anything productive. On the other hand, redirecting a drive avoids the expenditure of energy and suppression, and allows the potential in the drive to be used in reaching higher spiritual levels.

For example, a person may be attracted to an object of beauty, and assuming that one is a believer, one should think, "From where does the beauty of the object derive? It was obviously put there by G-d, Who is thus the origin of all beauty. Why then should I be attracted to a remote and mere derivative, when I can be attracted to the Source of all beauty, to G-d Himself?" We should put our *seichel* to good use. Think of some pleasurable experience that you had recently, such as a delicious, gourmet, pleasurable meal. No doubt it was most tasty and pleasant at the time, but how much pleasure do you have from it now, perhaps only two days later? Then think of a good deed that you did several years ago, as for example having helped out a needy person or family. You will find that it still gives you a good feeling now. If on the one hand you have fleeting pleasures, and on the other hand long-term pleasures, isn't it simply a matter of good judgment to choose the latter? Indulging our physical drives at the cost of neglecting our spiritual potential is simply a matter of not applying *seichel.*

The Rabbi of Kotzk cites a Scriptural source for redirecting emotions. The Torah relates that when the patriarch Jacob was reunited with his beloved son, Joseph, after 22 years of separation, Joseph wept. Rashi comments that Jacob did not weep because he was occupied with reciting the *Shema* (*Genesis* 46:29). Why, asked the Rabbi of Kotzk, could Jacob not have waited for a few moments to recite the *Shema*? Why did he have to do it at the precise moment that he embraced Joseph?

The Rabbi of Kotzk answered that Jacob felt himself overcome by an intense emotion, when he was reunited with Joseph for whom he had grieved so long, assuming him to have been dead. Feeling the enormous passion in his heart, Jacob thought, "An intense passion and sensation of love such as this is unlikely to occur again. Let me say the *Shema,* and channel this passion into love for G-d, as the *Shema* states, 'You shall love G-d with all your heart.'" Always seeking ways to enhance his devotion to G-d, the patriarch channeled his intense feelings of love toward love of G-d.

W*hen Rabbi Yosef Yitzchak of Lubavitch was a small child, his father, Rabbi Shalom Dov, saw him asleep in his crib, and felt an intense urge to kiss the beautiful baby. He then reasoned that when the Temple was in existence, Jews would bring sacrifices to G-d, and that he now had an opportunity to offer his expression of his intense love for the child as a voluntary offering to G-d. He therefore wrote a chassidic essay on the verse "How Great Are Your Deeds, O G-d." Had he expressed his emotion by kissing the child, this feeling would have been largely dissipated, having accomplished nothing other than a momentary gratification. By channeling this feeling into a theological essay, he utilized this enormous* *emotional energy for a higher purpose. When Rabbi Yosef Yitzchak reached an age of reason, his father presented him with the essay that had been inspired by his love for him as an infant. This essay is still referred to as "A Chassidic Kiss."*

Channeling energies is essentially a matter of focus. If a person is focused on making money, he will be alert to every opportunity, and take advantage of it for his purpose. If one is focused on devotion to G-d, then one is alert to every opportunity to serve G-d, and when any situation occurs that lends itself to be directed to the Divine service, one will take advantage of it. It is all a matter of mindset, which is why the *Shulchan Aruch* begins with "I constantly have G-d before me." This constant awareness permits one to channel energies to this ultimate goal.

As the Sun in Its Brightness

R abbi Moshe Chaim Luzzatto in his epochal work, *Mesillas Yesharim* (Path of the Just), states that there is nothing sweeter in the world than revenge. Just think. You have been harboring your resentment against someone who offended you grievously, and now he is at your mercy, and you have the opportunity to give him his just desserts, which may finally relieve you of the gnawing pain of carrying the grudge. Yet the Torah forbids you to do so. "You shall *not* take revenge" (*Leviticus* 19:18). Is this not an unrealistic command? Are we expected to be superhuman? How can one restrain oneself in a moment of such a sweet opportunity?

No, it is not a superhuman feat. To the contrary, it is a very human feat. If we think it to be superhuman it is only because we have so lean an understanding of the greatness that is within human reach. As with other traits, we can learn them from people who truly deserved the title "*adam*," the person that G-d designed. When Rabbi Schneur Zalman was asked to describe his master, the great *Maggid* of Mezeritch, he said, "He was an *adam hashalem*, a complete human being." Our *tzaddikim* served as models of what it is to be an *adam hashalem*, and it is from them that we can learn what it means to be human, to restrain our animal instincts.

R*abbi Moshe Sofer, better known as the Chasam Sofer, did not have an easy life. He fought vigorously to protect traditional Torah values against encroachments by secularists who were seduced and who were seducing others, particularly the youth, to reject Divine authority and embrace rationalism. Their attacks against Rabbi Moshe, who stood like a fortress for tradition, were often vicious.*

When Rabbi Moshe assumed the rabbinate of Mattersdorf, he found that one of the community elders, Rabbi Hillel Tokef, had a stronghold on the community. Hillel was a learned man, and his wealth as well as his connections with important government officials earned him the seat of honor in the synagogue, as well as the respect of the entire community.

Hillel was an observant Jew, who spent the entire Shabbos in Torah study and prayer. True, there was gossip that there was activity in his flour mill and in his inn on Shabbos, but then, that was not necessarily a violation of Shabbos. A person like Hillel would hardly transgress the Shabbos. He must certainly have made a contractual agreement with a non-Jew, approved by a rabbi, where he transferred ownership of these businesses on Shabbos, which might allow them to remain open for business.

It was known that Hillel was rather unhappy that his son, Reuven, had been infected with the enlightenment virus. Reuven, or Robert as he was now known, looked with disdain on the archaic Jews who were confined to the ghetto, and who were not familiar with the cultural delights. Robert had cast off Torah observance, and did not conceal his smoking on Shabbos.

When Rabbi Moshe assumed the position in Mattersdorf, the townspeople, knowing of his refusal to compromise on Torah values, respectfully urged him not to provoke Hillel Tokef. "Hillel is a pious Jew, and it is not his fault that his son has deviated. He must have somehow legitimized his business being open on Shabbos. Furthermore, he is a powerful person who can cause trouble for anyone who crosses him."

Rabbi Moshe was not impressed. The Torah is not his to compromise, and it specifically states "You shall not tremble before any man" (Deuteronomy 1:17). He sent a message to Hillel to produce whatever documents he had that authorized him to allow his business to operate on Shabbos. When this message was ignored, he sent a summons to Hillel and to Robert.

When father and son ignored the summons, Rabbi Moshe set aside his honor and went to see them. Hillel greeted the Rabbi with dignity, offering feeble excuses for not heeding the summons. Robert, however, spoke with chutzpah. "Rabbi, you were born and raised in Frankfurt, yet you prefer the oppression of the ghetto?"

Rabbi Moshe was not interested in a philosophical debate. The issue is the sanctity of Shabbos, which is the question under discussion. Robert remarked that the Tokef family, who are the pillars of the Jewish community and control its economy, deserve special consideration.

"Special consideration?" thundered Rabbi Moshe. "Shabbos does not discriminate! Everyone, from the highest to the lowest, is bound by Torah law to observe Shabbos."

Robert laughed derisively, and Hillel's failure to restrain his son's audacity was the last straw for Rabbi Moshe. On that day he issued a proclamation deposing Hillel from the community leadership, and forbidding anyone to associate with Robert.

The community, stunned by the Rabbi's fortitude, nevertheless followed his leadership. They no longer patronized Hillel's businesses, and made an extra effort to compensate the community coffers for the loss of the Tokef contributions.

Sheepishly, Hillel produced a document which some rabbi had drawn up, technically transferring his business to a non-Jew for Shabbos. Rabbi Moshe pointed out that this was a worthless document and ordered Hillel to cease operations on Shabbos.

"I am not in control of my business," Hillel said. "My son is now in charge."

Just at that time, Rabbi Moshe was invited to assume the rabbinate of Neustadt, a community which promised him adequate funds to establish a large yeshivah, and which would accept his authority in all matters of halachah. The opportunity to expound Torah and provide leadership where it was desired could not be resisted.

Rabbi Moshe bid farewell to Mattersdorf, and on Shabbos delivered a heartrending address, encouraging the community to remain loyal to traditional Torah principles.

That night the community was aroused by shouts of "Fire!" The thatched huts were tinder for the flames which engulfed the Jewish quarter. The flames started from the Tokef mill and inn, and quickly spread to the frame homes, threatening the synagogue. Devout Jews ran into the building to rescue the Torah scrolls. By dawn the fire had subsided. The Jewish quarter was a heap of ash. Miraculously, the synagogue and the Rabbi's house had escaped destruction. The Jewish quarter was otherwise totally destroyed.

The populace gathered around the Rabbi, who said, "As we bemoan our misfortune, let us be grateful to G-d that not one life was lost. The community will rise from its ashes to new heights." As if in unison, the people shouted, "And you, Rabbi, will be in Neustadt!"

"Not until Mattersdorf is rebuilt," Rabbi Moshe responded.

This time it was not Rabbi Moshe's Torah scholarship, but his administrative skills that shone. Appealing to nearby communities, Rabbi Moshe organized building crews, and amassed building materials, furniture, food, money, and whatever was necessary to rebuild the town. Slowly but surely, brick homes began to replace the wooden huts, and the community came back to life. Throughout the restoration, Rabbi Moshe lifted the spirits of the community with inspiring words of Torah. Hope replaced despair, and the community was rebuilt.

But lo! The Tokef family came under suspicion of arson! As a result of loss of patronage, Tokef had apparently been in arrears on his rental, and the poritz accused Tokef of deliberately setting the fire to receive the insurance money. Witnesses reported that they saw smoke in the mill on Shabbos. How could this be, since Jewish businesses were closed on Shabbos? They also testified that Robert was seen on the premises on Shabbos. What would a Jew be doing in his business on Shabbos? Although there was as yet no firm evidence of arson, these facts were enough for an indictment.

Inasmuch as Rabbi Moshe was universally respected by the secular authorities, he was called to court to testify.

When Robert saw the Rabbi enter the courtroom, he turned pale. The man whom he had so brazenly offended now had his life in his hands. Hillel looked at the Rabbi with eyes that pleaded for mercy.

Rabbi Moshe took the stand and declared in a firm voice, with an attitude of unwavering certainty. "The Tokef family are not observant. They have been operating their business on Shabbos for some time. That is why there was activity in the mill, and why Robert was on the premises.

"Neither father nor son are capable of deliberately setting the fire. Hillel is a traditional Jew, and Robert's espousal of the principles of the enlightenment, with the championing of justice and protecting peoples' rights, would not stoop to arson. Furthermore, Robert was so devoted to the business, which he hoped to build up, that he could not resist staying away even on Shabbos. It is unthinkable that either the father or son could do so dastardly a deed."

The words of the Rabbi were convincing, and the indictment was dismissed. Rabbi Moshe promptly left the courtroom without glancing at Hillel and Robert, to spare them the embarrassment of looking him in the eye.

The Talmud states that those who suppress their desire for revenge are people who love G-d, and who shine like the sun in midday. The *Midrash* says that G-d said of King Saul, "See what a noble creature I have created." He certainly said this of Rabbi Moshe Sofer as well.

Keeping It Simple

T he chassidic masters had great respect and affection for people who, although unlearned, were most sincere in their faith and devotion to G-d. Various quaint stories have come down about the piety of these folk, and the chassidic masters said that the purity and sincerity of their prayers were enviable.

O ne Yom Kippur eve Rabbi Levi Yitzchak of Berditchev delayed the start of Kol Nidrei. His demeanor was one of worry and distress, and to his followers this indicated that he knew that it was not a *propitious moment for attaining forgiveness for the many sins Jews had committed. Rabbi Levi Yitzchak scanned the assembled worshipers and then said, "I don't see Berel, the tailor."*

"Berel is not here," someone said.

"Then go fetch him!" the Rabbi said. "We cannot begin Kol Nidrei without Berel."

The congregation was bewildered, because Berel was hardly a personage whose presence warranted delay of services for the entire congregation. When Berel finally appeared, Rabbi Levi Yitzchak asked, "Why weren't you in shul, Berel?"

"Because I have nothing to do anymore with G-d. He has been unfair to me, and I have no way of taking my complaints against Him to court, so all I can do is protest. That is why I am not davening."

"Tell me your complaints against G-d," Rabbi Levi Yitzchak said. "Perhaps I can settle things for you."

"Very well," Berel said. "Two weeks ago the poritz sent for me, and said that he wanted me to sew him a peltz (fur coat) for the winter. I took my sewing box to the poritz's mansion, and he gave me the skins for the coat. When the coat was finished, there were a few skins left. Now the poritz had given me all the skins to use for the coat, and if I was skillful enough to complete the coat and still have some left over, they were properly mine. Furthermore, I have a daughter to marry off, and I need every cent I can get, and as far as the poritz was concerned, the skins could have all gone into the coat. I therefore put the leftover skins in my bag and left.

"After I had walked back to town, having gone several kilometers, a horseman came after me. 'Berel!' he said, 'The poritz wants you back right away.' I panicked, figuring that the poritz had counted the skins in his coat and had discovered that I had not used them all, but had not

returned the excess. This could lead to my imprisonment in his dungeon for life. I dropped my bag and mounted the horse, back to the mansion.

"When I came in the poritz said, 'Berel, the coat is beautiful, but you did not sew on a hook for hanging up the coat. That is not how you finish a job, Berel.'

"I raised my eyes to heaven in gratitude, and I sewed on a hook. I retraced my steps, but alas! My bag was gone. It was clear to me that this was the work of G-d, who considered my taking the extra skins as stealing, but this was not so. The poritz had not asked for an accounting. He gave me the skins to make the coat, which I did. The extra skins were legitimately mine, and G-d was wrong in taking them from me. I then decided that if that was how He acts toward me, I am no longer going to do His will.

"I came home and sat down to eat without washing my hands and without saying a berachah. That night I did not daven, nor the following days. On Rosh Hashanah I did not go to hear the blowing of the shofar. If G-d can be so unjust toward me, I will have nothing to do with Him. That is why I did not come to shul for Kol Nidrei."

Rabbi Levi Yitzchak said, "But Berel, it is Yom Kippur, a time for forgiveness. Can't you find it in your heart to forgive G-d? After all, on Yom Kippur G-d forgives everyone's sins."

Berel thought for a moment, then said, "Very well. I will forgive Him, but only if He in turn forgives everyone's sins without exception, regardless of how severe they may have been."

Rabbi Levi Yitzchak was overjoyed. He lifted his eyes toward heaven. "Master of the Universe," he said, "do You hear? Berel says he will forgive You, but only if You will forgive everyone's sins. I, Levi Yitzchak the son of Sarah Soshi, Rabbi of Berditchev, decree that this is an *equitable settlement. You are forgiven, and all transgressions that Jews have committed during the entire year must be forgiven.*

"Now let us say Kol Nidrei," Rabbi Levi Yitzchak said.

The efficacy of simple, unquestioning faith and trust is also evident in the following story.

R*abbi Yeshayah Horowitz, often referred to as the "Shelah" — which is the name of his epochal work — had a sister who was married to a simple but pious man, who made his living by hauling with his horse and wagon. One Shabbos, the Shelah delivered a sermon in which he said that a person's earnings are preordained each Rosh Hashanah for that year, and that regardless how much effort a person exerts, he will never exceed that which was allotted for him.*

On the following day, the Shelah's brother-in-law returned from shul late in the morning, and explained to his wife that he had davened at a leisurely pace, and then spent some time reciting Tehillim. After breakfast he took a Chumash (volume of the Torah) with a Yiddish translation and began studying it.

"What is wrong with you today?" his wife asked. "Why aren't you going to work?"

"No need for that," he said. "The Rabbi said that whatever earnings were decreed for a person will be his regardless of how much he exerts himself. It is senseless for me to exert myself needlessly. Whatever is meant for me will come to me, and I can use my time reciting Tehillim and studying the Torah."

"Don't be foolish," his wife said. "You misunderstood the Rabbi. That is not what he meant."

But the man would not be budged. He insisted that he had understood the Rabbi very well, and there was no need for senseless exertion.

The wife ran off to her brother. "You must be careful what you say in your sermons. My husband took you literally and now refuses to work, saying that whatever was destined for him will be his. He now wants to stay at home and recite Tehillim all day. How will we have enough to manage?"

The Shelah responded, "What I said was true, but most people do not have the requisite faith in G-d for this to be effective. If your husband is sincere, he will be well provided for." The poor woman left broken hearted.

Later that day there was a knock on the door. A man had noticed an idle horse and wagon and inquired if they were for rent. The husband let the horse and wagon to the man for a small fee.

The man who rented the horse and wagon was a highwayman who had robbed travelers of their valuables and had buried his loot, which he was now going to retrieve. He drove to the hiding place, dug deeply to unearth the loot, and loaded it on the wagon. When he went back into the pit to see if he had left anything behind, the walls of the pit collapsed, burying him. After a while, the horse was hungry, and with no one to feed it, made its way home along familiar roads, bringing the unclaimed riches to its owner.

The Shelah later said to his sister, "If anyone with less faith than your husband had tried to do this, it would be of no avail. It was his absolute, simple, and unquestioning trust in G-d that resulted in his being provided with a fortune that will let him study Torah for the rest of his life."

The sincere prayer of the pious simple folk was considered to be especially effective.

T he Baal Shem Tov related that a very harsh heavenly decree had been issued, which many tzaddikim
were unable to overturn, even with their most fervent
prayers.

"What we were unable to do," the Baal Shem Tov said,
"was accomplished by a pious woman, who, upon hearing the tearful prayers of the congregation, addressed G-d:
'Master of the Universe! How can You not accept the sup-
plications of Your children? I am only a human being, and
my mercies are limited. Yet when any of my children cry,
it breaks my heart, and I would do anything to stop their
tears. But You are infinite and Your mercies are infinite.
Listen how all Your children are crying. Surely You do not
have a heart of stone. You must help them and relieve
their suffering!'

"It was this simple but fervent prayer that caused G-d to
annul the harsh decree."

34

Never Too Late

Ideally, *teshuvah* should occur before one has repeated a misdeed or allowed a sin to linger so long that it has profoundly affected one's thoughts and emotions. Extirpating deeply ingrained ideas and behaviors can be very difficult, and they should not be allowed to take root. However, a person should never feel that he is so far gone that he is beyond *teshuvah*. Sincere *teshuvah* can redeem even a long history of sinfulness. The Talmud states that if a person makes a marriage contract contingent upon his being a *tzaddik,* it must be considered valid even if he is an outspoken *rasha* (sinner), because he may have had a sincere thought of *teshuvah* (*Kiddushin*

49b). Even a momentary thought of *teshuvah,* if sincere, can transform a *rasha* into a *tzaddik!* The Talmud relates the case of Elazar ben Doradia, who was a wanton, degenerate sinner, yet was admitted to *Gan Eden* (Paradise) because he was genuinely remorseful, and actually cried himself to death (*Avodah Zarah* 17a).

The Rabbi of Tolna was very fond of music, and the most renowned cantors visited his court. The famous cantor, Nisi Belzer, occasionally led the services in Tolna. In Nisi Belzer's choir was a young boy, Meir, who had been orphaned from his father, a devoted chassid of the Rebbe of Tolna, at an early age. Meir was very musical and had an unusually sweet voice, and Nisi relied on him for major solo renditions. However, Meir had a wild streak, and being without a father to discipline him, he often behaved mischievously. One Rosh Hashanah, when Nisi signaled Meir to begin a solo, Meir purposely sang a totally different portion of the liturgy. Nisi became angry, but to everyone's surprise, the Rebbe signaled Meir to repeat his solo, and the Rebbe wept during his singing.

After the service was over, the Rebbe said to the youngster, "May you always sing these sacred songs, and may they be your salvation."

Nisi could not contain the boisterous youngster, who gradually drifted away from Torah observance, and entered a conservatory of music. He became an outstanding opera star, and eventually married a non-Jewish woman. After many years of success under the bright lights, Meir's fortunes declined. His wife left him, he became depressed, and his once dulcet voice lost its character. He was about to be released from the operatic group when he asked for one more chance to redeem himself at a concert. He strode onto the stage, and suddenly began singing the liturgy of *his youth, the very solo the Rebbe had asked him to repeat. The orchestra stopped playing and the curtain was promptly lowered, and Meir was shown the exit door.*

With no job and no home, Meir joined a group of beggars who traveled from town to town, and one Shabbos he found himself in Tolna. He joined the throng of people who attended the Rabbi's Shabbos meal, and of course, no one recognized the one-time child wonder. When the Rebbe asked someone to sing one of the Shabbos songs, a voice suddenly rang out, "I will sing!" The Rebbe then said, "Let the man sing. Perhaps the singing will be the rectification for his errant ways."

Meir began singing the liturgy which the Rebbe had asked him to repeat many years earlier, and both Meir and the Rebbe wept with the rendition. Only afterwards did a few of the older chassidim recall the incident with the young choir boy, and realized that the Rebbe's words, "May this song be your salvation," was prophetic.

Meir remained in Tolna and became a sincere *baal teshuvah*. Shortly after that, he died, and the Rebbe of Tolna personally assumed the responsibility of saying *Kaddish* for him.

It is not unusual that someone who has conducted himself improperly and does *teshuvah* late in life may be so deep in remorse and so depressed on having squandered an entire lifetime that, like Elazar ben Doradia, he weeps himself to death. However, *teshuvah* should be a key to life, rather than contributing to death. Perhaps this is what the prophet meant, "I do not desire the death of the wicked one, but rather the wicked one's return from his way, that he may live" (*Ezekiel* 33:11). This is why it is so important for *teshuvah* to begin as early as possible, so that one may have the opportunity to live a new life.

Wisdom Surpasses Prophecy

There are many stories of wondrous happenings wrought by *tzaddikim*. The Talmud relates numerous incidents of Rabbi Chanina ben Dosa, as well as of other Talmudic personages, where the laws of nature were suspended to bring about a desired result. Miraculous phenomena have continued to occur throughout the ages, according to the Talmudic statement that G-d fulfills the wishes of a *tzaddik* (*Moed Kattan* 16b). However, many *tzaddikim* tried to camouflage the potency of their words and their prophetic foresight, explaining them away as natural occurrences or just logical conclusions. Many miraculous phenomena are attributed to the great *tzaddik*, Rabbi Yehoshua Leib Diskin, who was Rabbi of

Brisk and later of Jerusalem. Most of these could not possibly be camouflaged as natural happenings, yet Rabbi Yehoshua Leib dismissed any effort to attribute great powers to him, explaining away every such occurrence.

R abbi Yehoshua Leib was a man of few words, and every word he did speak was carefully measured. It was also known that his silence was significant. His non-response to a question was assumed to be a negative response, and woe onto him who transgressed the advice of the tzaddik.

In his early years, when he was Rabbi of Lomza in Poland, there was to be a national celebration for the opening of the highway that would join St. Petersburg with Warsaw. The inaugural ceremony involved a trip by the czar along the entire length of the highway, stopping at various cities on the way, one of which was Lomza. The Jewish population of Lomza, knowing the hostile attitude of the czar toward Jews, was particularly diligent in decorating the Jewish quarter properly, with abundant displays of the Russian flag and portraits of the ruler. The leader of the Jewish community, Israel Dubinsky, consulted Rabbi Yehoshua Leib about the participation of the Jewish community in the welcoming ceremonies. Rabbi Yehoshua Leib listened attentively, and, while agreeing with the program, said, "But you should not participate personally."

Dubinsky left the Rabbi in bewilderment. How could he, as head of the Jewish community, not greet the ruler personally? Would this not be considered an affront? He shared his concerns with other community leaders, and decided that he would indeed represent the community in greeting the czar.

Dubinsky led the royal entourage on a tour, and showed them the new hospital which had just been built, *and which was lavishly adorned with the czar's portraits. The czar inspected the building, and several times re-marked on apparent defects in the structure or on the layout. Each time Dubinsky explained to the czar why the structure was this way and the reason for the particular layout. Abruptly he was seized by several police and escorted to the jail.*

The rules of decorum in Russia were that when the czar made a critical comment, one was supposed to admit that the czar was correct and promise to rectify the situation. To justify oneself was tantamount to saying that the czar was wrong, which was considered an offense against the crown. With much effort, the community prevailed upon the authorities to commute Dubinsky's prison sentence to a fine, and after the money was raised, Dubinsky was released.

The word quickly spread among the Jews of Lomza that Rabbi Yehoshua Leib had foreseen the events prophetically, and that he therefore had warned Dubinsky not to greet the czar personally. When word of this came to Rabbi Yehoshua Leib, he dismissed any claim to prophetic powers, and explained: "I knew Dubinsky to be a sincere, straight-minded person who is not likely to know much about protocol, and he would therefore act according to his logic, which could get him into trouble. There was no supernatural foresight involved."

The moral of this story? One should not second guess the instructions of a Torah authority. The Torah states "You shall not deviate from the word that they (the Torah scholars) will tell you, right or left" (*Deuteronomy* 17:11). In matters that are not a question of *halachah*, it is not obligatory to ask the advice of a Torah authority, but if one does so, it is most foolish not to heed it.

The keen wisdom of *tzaddikim* is again evident in the following story.

A chassid of the Rabbi of Tolna was a lumber merchant, and had reached an understanding with the poritz to buy a section of his forest for lumbering. No contract was written, and when the price of lumber fell, the merchant wished to renegotiate the deal, claiming that he was not legally bound by the verbal agreement. The poritz knew that according to civil law the merchant was right, and he therefore suggested that they take the dispute to the Rebbe for a decision according to Jewish law.

The Rebbe listened to both sides, then ruled that although there was no legal contract, the Talmud pronounces a severe curse upon one who reneges upon a verbal agreement, and that certainly the merchant would not wish to subject himself to this. He therefore found in favor of the poritz.

The poritz was most pleased with the decision in his favor, but remarked, "In our courts there is a much longer process, and if a litigant is displeased with the court's decision, he can appeal it to a higher court, and there are several levels of appeals available to him. Suppose the merchant wished to appeal your decision. What recourse does he have?"

The Rebbe smiled and said, "One time a wolf attacked a flock of sheep, and the animals dispersed. The wolf pursued one of them, but before he had a chance to seize it, a lion emerged and pounced upon the sheep. The wolf protested that the prey was his, because he had caused the sheep to leave the flock, but the lion said that he had as much right to the sheep as the wolf, since neither had paid for it. They agreed to take their dispute before the fox, who was the wisest of all the animals.

"The fox ruled that the sheep should be divided equally between the two, and proceeded to cut the sheep in half. Noting that one portion was larger than the other, he nibbled away a bit, but then, seeing that now this portion was smaller, he nibbled away a bit of the other. This 'equalization' process continued until the fox had consumed almost the entire carcass, leaving nothing but the bones for the wolf and lion.

"In your courts," the Rebbe continued, "there are indeed many appeals, with the result that the lawyers on each side nibble on the disputed assets. By the time a final decision is reached, all that is left for the litigants are the bare bones. We may not have an appeals process, but both litigants are likely to benefit from our judgment."

The Rebbe said this in 1840. Was it by his wisdom or prophetic foresight that he so accurately described the judicial system of our own times?

Priorities

Although we cannot assign values to *mitzvos,* and indeed, the Talmud states "Be as scrupulous in performing a 'minor' *mitzvah* as in a major one, for you do not know the reward for the respective *mitzvos*" (*Ethics of the Fathers* 2:1), we nevertheless find the Talmud emphasizing the importance of certain *mitzvos,* as when it says "The study of Torah is equivalent to all other *mitzvos* combined" (*Peah* 1:1), and "Even when G-d overlooks other transgressions, He does not overlook neglect of Torah study" (*Eichah Rabbah* 2:1). It follows then, that if we see something given even higher priority than Torah study, we can understand how extremely important it must be.

In Jerusalem there was a Torah scholar, Rabbi Zelig Braverman, whose devotion to Torah study was absolute. Rabbi Zelig would be home for Shabbos, and immediately after Havdalah (prayer at the departure of Shabbos) he would take two loaves of bread and go to the yeshivah where he remained until Friday afternoon. He would catnap at the table where he studied, and never slept in a bed. When lack of money caused the yeshivah to extinguish the lights early, Rabbi Zelig would study by the light of the moon, and on moonless nights, would review the many portions of the Talmud he knew by heart. When his son was married, Rabbi Zelig reluctantly interrupted his Torah study to attend the ceremony, and immediately afterward returned to his studies, leaving the celebration of the wedding to the family and guests. Nothing took priority to the study of Torah, except. . .

One Torah scholar complained to Rabbi Zelig that his wife frequently berated him for not helping her with the housework, because he was spending all his time in the beis midrash studying. "When does your wife leave home to do the shopping?" Rabbi Zelig asked, and upon receiving the answer, Rabbi Zelig said, "Do not worry, all will be well."

The next morning, when the man's wife left the home, Rabbi Zelig entered, washed the dishes, swept and washed the floor, and set everything in proper order. He continued doing this for two years, and the secret was not revealed until he fell sick, and the wife, assuming that it had been her husband who was helping with the housework, wondered why he had suddenly stopped doing so.

Rabbi Zelig, who did not stray from Torah study even to participate in his son's wedding celebration, found time to do housework in order to preserve peace and harmony between a couple.

During World War I, when most of the Jewish population of Brisk fled the city, the standards of Torah observance plummeted precipitously. *Shochtim* (ritual slaughterers) of questionable competence and reliability took over the provision of kosher meat for the remaining population.

After the war, when life began to return to normal, a meeting was held in the home of the Rabbi of Brisk to plan for the provision of properly slaughtered meat. One of the unauthorized *shochtim* came to the meeting, which could not, of course, be held in his presence. It was pointed out to him that his attendance at these proceedings was inappropriate, but the *shochet* refused to leave, saying, "This is the Rabbi's home, and I will leave only if the Rabbi orders me to leave."

To everyone's great surprise, the rabbi remained silent, and the meeting was about to dissolve when the uninvited *shochet* abruptly left on his own. The Rabbi then said, "The Talmud relates that the destruction of the Second Temple was the result of the Divine wrath because one person was publicly humiliated (*Gittin* 57a). Had I ordered this man to leave, that would have been public humiliation. How could we think of restoring Torah observance to the community at the cost of humiliating someone?"

Our great Torah personages had their priorities in order.

R abbi Yisrael of Salant was a guest at someone's home, and when he performed the ritual washing of the hands before the meal, he used the minimum of water required by halachah. When his students respectfully pointed out that halachah praises one who uses more liberal quantities of water for the hand-washing, Rabbi Yisrael replied, "Yes, but one cannot be more virtuous at another person's expense. If I use more copious amounts, the person who fetches the water from the well may have to make an extra trip. If I wish to go beyond the minimum *requirements for hand-washing, it must be at my own expense and not someone else's." Our priorities may depend on our evaluation of our spiritual needs. We may sometimes take too much for granted, and neglect important aspects of our spirituality.*

The Steipler Gaon was a person who accounted for every moment of the day. His entire life was absorbed in the study of Torah.

One day a friend of mine entered the Steipler Gaon's study, and the Gaon, who was hard of hearing, was unaware of the man's presence. My friend noted that the Steipler Gaon was without a Talmud volume before him, a rare phenomenon indeed, but was swaying to and fro, softly mumbling some words. Approaching closer, he heard that the sage was reciting the Thirteen Principles of Faith, and translating them from the Hebrew into Yiddish: "I believe with perfect faith. . ."

The Thirteen Principles of Faith are listed in the *siddur,* but not everyone recites them daily, perhaps because we have more important things to do, like rushing off to work. The Steipler Gaon, for whom a single moment devoid of Torah study was intolerable, nevertheless felt it was necessary to take precious moments away from Torah study to reinforce his belief in G-d and the fundamentals of Judaism.

Yes, great people do have their priorities in order.

Empathy

I t is only natural that when we see someone in distress, we feel sorry for him. That is *sympathy*. If we truly feel his suffering along with him, that is *empathy*.

The Torah relates that Moses went among his Israelite brethren and saw their travail (*Exodus* 2:11), upon which the *Midrash* notes that Moses put his shoulders under the huge boulders that they were carrying. Rabbi Chaim Shmulevitz comments that Moses did this in order to personally feel their suffering, for otherwise he would be lacking in empathy (*Sichos Mussar* 5732:23).

Sympathy for others may lead us to do something which will relieve our conscience. Empathy goes beyond this, because when we feel the suffering of others, we dedicate ourselves more fully to their plight.

R abbi Moshe of Kobrin had as a chassid one Reb Yitzchak, a poor and devout man, who never gave his poverty much thought. He was able to fully rejoice in the performance of mitzvos, and while his prayer was intense, he never prayed for better fortune. Who was he to tell G-d to whom He should distribute worldly assets? Whenever he had an audience with his Rebbe, his requests were for spiritual growth, for guidance how to improve the quality of his prayer and performance of mitzvos, but he never mentioned his poverty.

In the culture of the shtetl, having a dowry was essential to a girl's matrimonial aspirations, and alas! since Reb Yitzchak had no dowry to give his daughter, the matchmakers did not concern themselves with her. Reb Yitzchak's wife pleaded with him that the next time he visited the Rebbe he should ask for a blessing that he should earn enough to provide for his daughter's dowry. Reb Yitzchak assured his wife that he would do so, but when he came to Kobrin he totally forgot about all earthly matters, and asked the Rebbe only for spiritual guidance. On his way home he prayed that G-d enlighten his wife to realize that material assets are not of importance. He had a difficult time explaining to his wife that once he crossed the Rebbe's threshold, such matters did not enter his mind.

Reb Yitzchak's wife lost patience with him and one day said, "If I cannot rely on you to ask the Rebbe for a blessing, then I will go to him myself." Reb Yitzchak then gave his wife a solemn promise that he would ask the Rebbe.

Having made a sacred vow, Reb Yitzchak had no choice but to put his plight before the Rebbe. Rabbi Moshe listened attentively and then said, "I will bless you with wealth, Yitzchak, but first you must do as I say."

Rabbi Moshe took out two gold coins and gave them to Reb Yitzchak saying, "You must follow my instructions without the minutest deviation. You are to go home and use this money to buy the finest food and delicacies and the best wine available. You are to set the table for yourself, and only you may eat from this food. Eat to your satisfaction, but neither your wife nor your children may taste a morsel of it. Then come back here, but remember my orders. Only you are to eat therefrom."

Reb Yitzchak was a loyal chassid, and did as he was told. His wife and children, whose meager rations left them hungry, watched as he sat down to a sumptuous meal. Their eyes and sunken cheeks testified to their hunger, and he saw their mouths water as he lifted the fork with the roast duck to his mouth. Seeing the expressions on the faces of his wife and children, he could hardly swallow the food. Had it been rocks it would have been easier to eat! He tried to take a drink of wine, but it was like hemlock to him. Yet, the Rebbe said he must eat, and the torment Reb Yitzchak experienced eating the delicacies in the presence of his hungry family and not sharing anything with them was the worst torture he had ever felt in his entire life. "Please, G-d," Reb Yitzchak prayed silently, "take my soul from me, but do not allow me to feel this terrible pain."

When Reb Yitzchak returned to Kobrin, the Rabbi said to him, "I will bless you to become wealthy, Yitzchak, and you and your family will have an abundance of everything. How much will you be able to enjoy what you have, knowing that there are poor people who have nothing to eat all day? You now know what it feels like to have an abundance when there are others who are deprived. The blessing for wealth is yours for the asking, Yitzchak. Do you still wish it?"

"Never!" exclaimed Reb Yitzchak and he returned home empty handed.

Reb Yitzchok's wife then visited the Rebbe personally, and did ask for the blessing. His fortunes indeed improved, and he became wealthy. Both he and his wife gave generously to the poor, but Reb Yitzchak never ate another meal at home. He donated liberally to the soup kitchen, and ate there along with the poor. The experience of eating heartily while others were hungry was one that he never forgot.

38

When the Guilty Are Innocent

C hassidic lore is particularly replete with stories: miraculous cures and rescues wrought by chassidic masters; accounts of their total devotion to G-d; the fervor of their prayers; the manifestation of love for another person that surpassed all standards of humanitarian altruism; their incomparable insights into and interpretation of Torah; the lifestyle of their followers, their *chassidim*. It would not be an exaggeration to say that my concepts of Judaism, of G-d, and of Torah were molded in very great measure by chassidic stories, by tales of how great and righteous people internalized the teachings of the Torah in their everyday lives.

This is not unusual. The Midrash states that the Torah considers the narration of the servants of the patriarchs to be worthy of more space than the learned discourses of the patriarch's descendants (*Bereishis Rabbah* 60:11). This is because accounts of how these *tzaddikim* actually behaved conveys very emphatically what G-d wants us to do.

Some chassidic stories are enchanting, perhaps even entertaining. Many are inspirational, indicating the height of spirituality which a mortal can attain.

It is certainly true that versions of stories conveyed from person to person over several generations will come to vary in many details. Some may not be entirely accurate. It matters little. *Chassidim* say that anyone who accepts all these stories as factual is being credulous, whereas anyone who denies that they could have happened is a heretic. Since they *could* have happened — and they reveal essential truths — what difference does it make whether they did or not?

Furthermore, the kinds of stories told about people are a valid measure of their character. The Chofetz Chaim once was requested to testify in court, and begged to be released from being sworn in, since he had been cautious never to take an oath. The attorney tried to impress upon the judge the impeccable honesty of this great sage, and told the judge that when the Chofetz Chaim once saw someone stealing his candlesticks, he promptly renounced his ownership so that the thief would not be transgressing the Torah prohibition against theft. "A man like that is not going to give false testimony," the attorney said.

The judge was skeptical. "And you expect me to believe that story is true?" he said.

The lawyer responded, "Your Honor, nobody tells stories like that about me or you."

So, whether factual or not, these stories tell us a great deal.

I used to look forward to Saturday night, because at the *melaveh malkah* (the meal following the close of Shabbos), my father, following tradition, would tell a chassidic story. This practice also had an important psychological impact. Shabbos was a day of rest, not only rest from work, but also rest from stress and worry. On Friday evening the Jew is required to divest himself of all weekday thoughts, and focus only on things spiritual, particularly his relationship to G-d. Having unburdened oneself of the myriad problems of the workweek, one's spirit may soar.

But as darkness moves in Saturday night, and one bids farewell to Shabbos, the many stresses of the week may return. Tradition offers a balm. People get together for a meal, usually an austere meal of herring, borscht, and boiled potatoes, and sing about the prophet Elijah who will soon appear with the tidings of the Redemption. The *melaveh malkah* is the meal dedicated to King David, whose throne will soon be reestablished in the Holy Land. And stories are told about chassidic masters, stories which bring a message of courage, hope, and joy, and banish the potential depression.

Some of the stories I have heard or read are more than just stories, in that they convey important teachings. Many chassidic masters were critical of relating miraculous events, because they do not teach us anything. Furthermore, a true believer knows that even nature is G-d's doing, and there is nothing miraculous about G-d doing anything. A miracle is nothing but an unusual occurrence. Rabbi Schneur Zalman said, "In Mezeritch there were abundant miracles lying in heaps on the ground, but no one bothered to stoop to pick them up." The dedication to the study of Torah and devotion to G-d did not permit any diversion to bother "picking up" miracles.

Nor should one really marvel that *tzaddikim* were able to bring about wondrous occurrences with their fervent prayer. The Talmud (*Berachos* 34b) states that when the son of the great sage, Rabbi Yochanan ben Zakkai, fell ill, he prayed for his recovery but his prayers were not answered. He then asked Rabbi Chanina ben Dosa to pray for him, and the son promptly recovered. Rabbi Yochanan's wife asked, "Do you mean to say that he is greater than you?" to which Rabbi Yochanan replied, "No. It is just that I am like a minister in the king's court, and I see the king only by appointment. Chanina is like a servant in the palace, and although of lesser rank than a minister, he can come and go at will." Many *tzaddikim*, like Rabbi Chanina, were "servants" in the Divine palace, and gained "access" at will.

The performance of miracles is based on the Talmudic statement that a *tzaddik* has the power to decree something and G-d will fulfill it. Those who were more selective about what kinds of stories to tell about the chassidic masters used to say, "It is more important to relate how a *tzaddik* fulfilled the will of G-d than how G-d fulfilled the will of a *tzaddik*."

Do not get me wrong. I love to read about how the blessings of *tzaddikim* materialized, and the wondrous deeds they wrought. Nothing can be sweeter than reading oneself to sleep Shabbos afternoon, under the soporific effects of the *kugel* and *cholent,* and going into dreamland amidst the stories of the wondrous deeds of *tzaddikim*. But this is not the object of this book. These are not just stories, but teachings, teachings conveyed in a manner that will impress themselves better on our minds, so that we can guide our lives according to the principles of Torah, principles which, as the Talmud states, are brought to life by narrations of the lives of our *tzaddikim*.

This particular story requires a preface, a historical preface. *Chassidus* began with the teachings of the Baal Shem Tov, who appeared on the scene during one of the most bitter times in Jewish history, which unfortunately is so full of tragic episodes. Prior to the unspeakable horrors of the Holocaust, the worst massacre of Jews was probably that of 1648, when the Cossacks under the leadership of Bogdan Chmielnicki went on a wild rampage of pogroms, wiping out many Jewish villages. Even prior to this forerunner of Hitler, Jewish life in Russia was precarious. The feudal lords had unrestricted powers of life and death in their fiefdoms, and most of them were virulent anti-Semites. Jews were not allowed to live in the large cities without special permission, and were totally disenfranchised. Poverty was widespread, and hope for a better life was all but non-existent.

The Jew lived with his faith in the Divine promise of the ultimate Redemption, which, as the Talmud tells us, would be preceded by the "pangs of Messiah," severe oppression and persecution. Many people saw the pogroms of 1648 as the fulfillment of this prediction, and the Jews survived the anguish only by hanging on to the hope that soon there would be salvation.

Thus, when in 1655 there appeared a charismatic person, one who seemed to be a respectable scholar well versed in the *kabbalah,* who declared that he was the Messiah, the craving for salvation was so great that many people, including noted Torah scholars, believed what they so desperately wished to believe: The Redemption was at hand. This false messiah, Shabtai Tzvi, soon gathered an enormous following, but everything came to a tragic end and he ultimately converted to Islam. The hopes of the oppressed and persecuted Jews were once again dashed, and their physical distress was aggravated by depression and despair.

It was upon this scene that Israel Baal Shem Tov appeared, carrying a message of hope and joy, to lift the spirits of his downtrodden brethren. They were all children of G-d, he said, chosen as His people, and privileged to be His servants. This was something so great that it obscured all the distress they were experiencing. While we are not privy to the Divine secrets as to why His chosen people are subjected to suffering, there is no denying the facts. Abraham, Isaac, and Jacob were the fathers of a chosen people. Approximately three million Jews experienced the many miracles of the Exodus from Egypt, and stood at the foot of Mount Sinai where they saw the Divine glory and heard the thunderous voice of G-d. These were historic facts, eyewitness accounts transmitted from generation to generation. At Sinai we accepted the Divine mission, and each day we read the *Shema* and reinforce our commitment to G-d. Each day we recite the verse of the Torah "… beware for your soul lest you forget the things that your eyes beheld (receiving the Torah at Sinai) … and make them known to your children and your children's children" (*Deuteronomy* 4:9). Each day we thus re-experience being selected by G-d as His people. The feudal lord and his henchmen may have power over our physical bodies, but so what? We were not selected by G-d because of our great numbers or physical strength, but because of our spirit, our *neshamos* which are inherited from the patriarchs. The *neshamah* is the essence of our existence, and while the feudal lord can imprison the body of the Jew in the dungeon, the spirit of the Jew remains forever free. This was the message of hope and joy the Baal Shem Tov brought to the brokenhearted and hopeless Jews of Russia.

The Baal Shem Tov was undoubtedly a charismatic leader, and this message of hope was like cool water to a parched throat. He quickly gathered loyal and devoted disciples, and *chassidus* began to capture the hearts of the populace. But the Baal Shem Tov and his disciples were adherents of *kaballah,* and it appeared that they sometimes even favored *kaballah* over an accepted *halachah.* Here it was again, a charismatic leader, a kabbalist, gathering a throng with a message of hope.

Coming so soon after the debacle of Shabtai Tzvi, the Torah authorities feared for a repetition of that disastrous episode. Judaism could not afford the risk of another false messiah. This new movement, which threatened to become another messianic cult, had to be curtailed. Vigorous and aggressive action was called for. The only tool available for social control was *cherem* (excommunication). Several pronouncements of excommunication against the *chassidim* were issued, with the support of some of the leading Torah authorities of the time, declaring, among other things, that no one was to marry into a family of *chassidim* and that the meat slaughtered by a chassidic *shochet* was not kosher.

We must understand the purity of heart of the original *misnagdim*, the opponents of chassidism. There was no question in their minds that *chassidus* presented a grave threat to Judaism, and it was thus their sacred duty to defend the faith. Their sincerity in their zeal and how this was perceived by the Baal Shem Tov is illustrated by a story I heard from my father, and which I cited in *Generation To Generation* (CIS 1989).

The city of Brody in Poland was a citadel of the *misnagdim*, and the great Talmudist, Rabbi Chaim Tzanzur* of Brody, was among them. One time when the Baal Shem Tov visited Brody, the zealous misnagdim took after him with a vengeance. Rebbe Chaim Tzanzur, although sympathizing with them, was not wont to do physical battle, and remained in the house of study.

Later that day a woman called upon Rebbe Chaim to pass judgment over a question relating to family purity. After studying the question, Rebbe Chaim ruled in the affirmative.

That night before retiring, Rebbe Chaim reviewed the events of that day, as was his custom every night, to see whether all his actions of that day were as they should have been, or perhaps there were things upon which he should improve. As he pondered the question of law regarding family purity which the woman had raised, it suddenly occurred to him that he had ruled incorrectly. He recognized that his ruling had undoubtedly been responsible for causing a person to inadvertently transgress.

Rebbe Chaim was beside himself with self-flagellation. How could he have overlooked the correct ruling? He decided that this oversight could only have resulted from some misdeed, some transgression which he himself had

---

* Not to be confused with the chassidic rebbe, Rabbi Chaim "Sanzer" Halberstam.

committed, which in its aftermath had resulted in this mistaken judgment.

But what? Rebbe Chaim began to scrutinize his past behavior, to find what he had done wrong, what sin he had committed that had resulted in so serious a consequence as a distortion of judgment that had led an innocent person astray. But search as he might, he could find no misdeeds except for one: He had failed to join his colleagues in pursuing the Baal Shem Tov.

As dawn broke, Rebbe Chaim arose, and went out to the street to fill his pockets with stones with which he would pelt the Baal Shem Tov. After searching among the many inns in the city, he found where the Baal Shem Tov had spent the night, and hurried to atone for his dereliction. But when he met the Baal Shem Tov, the latter was reciting the prayers upon arising, and the saintly image of the Baal Shem Tov precluded any stone throwing.

After completing the prayers, the Baal Shem Tov greeted Rebbe Chaim. "Shalom aleichem, Rebbe of Brody," the Baal Shem Tov said. "You have no reason to worry. Your ruling was perfectly sound!" And the Baal Shem Tov proceeded to review the question of law involved and satisfied Rebbe Chaim that his original ruling had indeed been correct, and that it was rather his reconsideration that had been erroneous.

Rebbe Chaim, overjoyed that he had not after all been the cause of anyone's transgression, left the inn and emptied his pockets of the stones that he had gathered. But as he did so, the Baal Shem Tov followed him, picking up the stones, kissing them, and putting them in his bosom. "Stones that were gathered with kedushah (holy motivation) dare not roll in the dust. These stones, too, have become sacred, and they should be stored with other objects of mitzvah."

When my father related the Baal Shem Tov's words, he would choke up and his eyes would moisten. Whenever I relate this story, I feel a lump in my throat the size of a cantaloupe. The sincerity of people of widely divergent views, who remained adversaries, superseded their personal considerations.

But even the drastic maneuver of *cherem* did not stifle the movement, whose enthusiastic message of *simchah* fanned the sparks of hope and faith among the masses. The successful spread of the movement confirmed the worst fears of the leadership, who became more zealous than ever in condemning *chassidus.*

However, toward the end of the third generation of *chassidim,* i.e., the disciples of the disciples of the *Maggid* of Mezeritch, the successor to the Baal Shem Tov, there began to be some mellowing of the fierce opposition in some areas. The suspicions about the authenticity of Torah observance and study among *chassidim* began to give way, and it became evident that this was not another messianic cult. The *chassidim* were obviously diligent in observing the *Shulchan Aruch,* and they had outstanding Torah scholars, such as the two acknowledged Talmudists, the brothers Rabbi Shmelke of Nikolsburg and Rabbi Pinchas of Frankfurt. In the city of Berditchev, which was a Jewish metropolis, Rabbi Levi Yitzchak had won the hearts of a majority of the population with his Torah scholarship, saintliness, and incomparable love of people. This great *tzaddik,* who had suffered unimaginable persecution in previous communities where he had served as rabbi, found relative peace in Berditchev, although a nucleus of obstinate *misnagdim* did make their presence felt. For the most part, however, the Jews of Berditchev, even those who were not adherents of Rabbi Levi Yitzchak, related to *chassidim* with respect.

But another source of difficulty developed. In Rizhin, there was a young chassidic master, Rabbi Yisrael, who was a grandson of the *Maggid* of Mezeritch. Inasmuch as he bore the Baal Shem Tov's name, Yisrael, his followers considered him the second Baal Shem Tov, and indeed said that the Baal Shem Tov's *neshamah* had come down to earth for a second time in the person of the Rabbi of Rizhin. In contrast to all other chassidic masters, who lived a very austere lifestyle, the Rizhiner, as he was called, lived in pomp and wealth. His court was similar to a royal palace, and since he traced his ancestry to King David, it did not take much for his followers to conclude that he conducted himself regally because he was indeed to be the Messiah, who was to be from the Davidic lineage. This resurrected the zeal and fervor of those who had begun to think more benignly about *chassidim*. Perhaps *chassidus* was acceptable, but Rizhiner *chassidus* remained suspect.

The fame of this new star in the chassidic firmament had spread to Berditchev, and had inflamed the curiosity of the young scholars. Who was this young master, to whom thousands pledged allegiance and whom they showered with lavish gifts? It was said that when he was but 16 and was in the presence of the venerable chassidic master, the *tzaddik* of Apt, his *gartel* (sash) came loose, whereupon the white-bearded sage bent down, picked up the *gartel* and wrapped it around this youngster, saying, "I am fulfilling the mitzvah of *gelillah* (binding) of the Torah scroll." The passion of these young men to observe this phenomenon first hand could not be contained, but knowing of the fierce opposition that was aroused by mere mention of the word "Rizhin," they knew that they could never obtain their families' permission to go there. The young men therefore made a secret pact among themselves, and one Thursday night, taking advantage of it being *mishmar* night, when it was customary to study Torah all night long and their absence at home would not be noted, they took off for Rizhin. When they failed to return home Friday morning, their whereabouts were sought, and by the time it was discovered they had gone to Rizhin, it was too late in the day for the fathers and fathers-in-law to retrieve them. Immediately after Shabbos, the disgruntled parents traveled to Rizhin to retrieve their wayward sons and sons-in-law. Once in Rizhin, they sought an audience with this young leader of a new sect, to upbraid him for enticing young scholars to his court, diverting them from their study of Torah.

The Rabbi of Rizhin welcomed the contingent, and listened patiently and attentively to their complaints. Then he said softly, "What can I say? You have just grounds for your grievances. You are right, and since you are right, these young men must be wrong."

The irate group was somewhat placated to hear the Rabbi admit that these young men were guilty in leaving their homes in stealth, in defiance of the wishes of their parents. "But before you leave," the Rabbi said, "Let me tell you something about being right."

"In the days of my grandfather," the Rabbi said, "the opposition to chassidus was fierce. No one would have anything to do with these people, who were considered defectors from Judaism. In Vitebsk, for example, a group of men who were followers of my grandfather, the Maggid of Mezeritch, were ostracized and expelled from the local shul. They found themselves a small hut which they refurbished, and they gathered there for services and to study Torah. This was known as the shtibel. Of course, no respectable member of the community would be seen anywhere near the shtibel of these outcasts. Indeed, the rabbi of the community had issued a cherem, and no one dared communicate with any members of the shtibel.

"Little wonder. There were many stories about how far these people had strayed from Judaism. They were known to violate the Shulchan Aruch by praying late in the morning, beyond the prescribed limits. Furthermore, their behavior in their shtibel was atrocious. The community shul was treated with great respect. People sat in their places during services, read quietly out of the siddur, and behaved with the utmost reverence as befits a place of holiness. But in the shtibel? Why, they walked to and fro when they prayed, sometimes shouting the prayers or singing at the top of their voices as though this were a tavern quartet! It was also reported that after services they drank a l'chaim in the very room where they prayed, and they occasionally joined hands and danced in a circle. Whoever heard of such irreverent behavior in a place of prayer?

"But Vitebsk remained a peaceful town. Traditional Jews went about their business, and no one paid any attention to this radical sect.

"One of the young scholars in Vitebsk, a newlywed son-in-law of one the town's prominent citizens, was a respected student of Torah. His father-in-law was the envy of the community for having arranged such a fine match for his daughter. The young man was totally devoted to Torah study, spending all his days and often nights in the house of study, and held great promise of becoming one of the Torah luminaries of the generation.

"One time this young man came across a difficult passage in the Talmud which he could not explain. He discussed it with the other Torah scholars, who agreed that it was indeed enigmatic. He searched in the various commentaries for an explanation, but to no avail. Although he proceeded with his studies, his mind always drifted back to this enigmatic passage, and it tormented him, giving him no peace of mind by day and haunting him at night. When he mentioned to a friend how surprised he was that none of the commentaries in the beis midrash seemed to be bothered with this problem, his friend said, 'Why don't you go down to the shtibel? They have many books there, and they may have some that we do not have in our library.'

"The shtibel? That forbidden place, where no one dared set foot? Absurd.

"But once the thought was implanted in his mind, it gave him no respite. One night, hoping that under cover of darkness no one would notice him, he went into the shtibel. No one paid much attention to him as he searched the bookshelves, withdrawing several volumes and leafing through them, and then—there it was! This particular author had raised the very question which had been nagging him for weeks. Excitedly he rushed on to see the answer to his question, and yes, it was valid. Of course! Why hadn't he thought of it himself? In a state of rapture and relief he kissed the book, thanked G-d for having led him to the solution of the problem, held the book close to his heart, kissed it again, and replaced it on the shelf.

"Just then someone said to him, 'Young man, what are you so excited about?' He turned to the questioner, and explained how he had been tormented for weeks by a difficult passage in the Talmud, and only now did he find its resolution. The man inquired just what the difficult passage was, and the young man told him.

" 'Strange,' the man said, 'my friend and I had just studied that portion of the Talmud recently, and we did not find it difficult at all.' He then proceeded to explain the passage with the interpretation that the young man had found in the book in the shtibel collection. But what surprised the young man was that to this person this particular interpretation was obvious, whereas he had missed the obvious, and had been subject to torment for weeks. He bid the man a polite farewell and left the shtibel.

"Our young man could not help thinking: Why is it that chassidim have a reputation of not being erudite in Torah? Something which had eluded him, an accomplished scholar, for weeks, appeared elementary to this chassid. But he put the issue out of his mind and returned to his studies.

"It was not too long after this incident that our young man was stymied by a contradiction in the Rambam. There were two halachos (laws) which seemed to be contradictory, yet the Rambam held both halachos to be valid. How could this be? If a glass is full, it is not empty. It cannot be both full and empty at the same time, yet this is essentially what the Rambam seemed to be contending. Again, the available sources in the house of study he attended did not shed any light on the problem. Rather than subject himself to continued torment as he did the first time, he made his way to the shtibel. But this time he did not care if he was seen. What a mistake people had made in excommunicating the chassidim! They appeared to be dedicated, Torah-observant Jews after all.

"It was shortly before noon that the young man entered the shtibel. While most of the people were engaged in learning, there was one man walking to and fro with a folded talis on his shoulder, in preparation for the morning prayer. Now? Shortly before noon? Why, the time limit for the morning service had expired hours ago! How could this be?

"As he was standing there, the young chassid he had met on his previous visit greeted him warmly. 'What brings you here?' he asked. The young man explained that he was having difficulty reconciling two contradictory statements in the Rambam. 'I have not been learning that particular subject,' the man said, "but I think that there are two others here that are learning that topic. Let's ask them.'

"Our young man posed his question to this pair of scholars, one of whom responded, 'Ah, yes. The apparent contradiction in the Rambam,' and then proceeded to explain that there was a fine distinction between the two cases, and there was therefore a different rule applied to each instance. There was, in fact, no contradiction at all.

"Our young man was impressed. 'Tell me,' he said, 'I have been a diligent student of Torah for years. This is the second time that I have been unable to understand something, first in Talmud, then in the Rambam, and to you it appeared to be so elementary. What is your secret that you seem to grasp things so easily?'

"By this time several others had joined in and the young man was invited to sit down. One of the group then began.

" 'As you know, my friend, the Torah is truth, as we say in the blessing, it is a Toras Emes. And this is because G-d is truth, and G-d and the Torah are one and the same, as our Sages say, that when G-d gave the Torah to the Israelites, he thereby gave Himself to us. When we study Torah and seek to take the Torah into our minds, we are actually absorbing G-d into ourselves. The study of Torah allows us to become united with G-d, to become one with G-d.

" 'Torah and falsehood are polar opposites, and cannot coexist. The bond between man and G-d can only exist where there is no falsehood. The minutest amount of falsehood sets up a barrier between man and G-d, hence between man and Torah. To be able to grasp Torah, one must be truthful in every way.

" 'But the Midrash tells us that when G-d sought the counsel of the angels prior to creating man, Truth said, "Do not create man because he is full of falsehood." G-d disregarded the counsel of Truth and did create man. Yet it is true that man is full of falsehood.

" 'Which person knows himself thoroughly? All of us live with some degree of self-deception. We are vulnerable to the cunning of the yetzer hara (the evil inclination) which drives us to indulge in earthly pleasures, in animalistic behavior, in pride and vanity. But who is aware of these defects within himself? We generally think ourselves to be free of them, but oh! how we deceive ourselves. Even meditation and soul-searching is not enough, because when we meditate and investigate ourselves, the yetzer hara participates in this and blinds us to what he does not wish us to see.

" 'How then can one escape this self-deception? We go to a tzaddik, who is our teacher, our guide, our mentor, and who cares for us as a father does for a child. With his deep powers of perception and understanding of our character, the tzaddik penetrates into our soul with his vision and sees where we are mired in self-deception. He helps us peel away the layers that the yetzer hara has deposited. He teaches us how to pray to G-d to help us come to the truth. When we leave the tzaddik we feel rejuvenated and refreshed. It is as though he has taken our neshamah, cleansed it, and restored it within us in a state of purity. When we return home we review the teachings of chassidim, helping one another in pursuit of the truth. As we strive for truth with sincerity, we receive Divine assistance in our venture, as the Talmud tells us, that without Divine help, no one could withstand the wiles of the yetzer hara. The more we approach truth, the stronger our bond becomes with Torah, which is truth, and that is why we may have a clearer perception of Torah.' "

" 'But then tell me,' the young man said, 'That person over there who is just starting to pray. Does he not know that one must pray earlier in the day?'

" 'Ah, yes, my friend,' the other responded. 'But you know the Talmud says that the pious people of yore would meditate for an hour before prayer in order to prepare themselves adequately for communion with G-d. But those were the ancients whose brilliant minds and purity of devotion were so great that they could achieve the proper attitude for prayer with just one hour of meditation. How can we compare ourselves to them? That man was here shortly after dawn today, having already immersed himself in the mikvah prior to coming here, and he has spent these past hours in teshuvah and in studying the holy writings to do teshuvah properly. Can he be expected to approach G-d in prayer when he feels that his sins constitute a barrier between him and G-d?'

"Our young man's visits to the shtibel increased in frequency, and he was sharply rebuked by his father-in-law for violating the ban of excommunication. When his father-in-law's reprimands fell on deaf ears, he brought the son-in-law to the rabbi, who sharply denounced him for associating with the forbidden cult.

" 'But you have excommunicated people of whom you know nothing,' the young man protested. 'They are sincere, devoted, and pious Jews. You acted on hearsay. The excommunication has no validity because it is based on a false premise.'

"The rabbi would not listen. He insisted that the ban must be obeyed. The father-in-law then threatened that if he persisted in violating the ban, he would have no choice but to insist that he divorce his daughter and leave. He extracted a solemn oath from the young man that he would not visit the shtibel again and would cease associating with the people of the shtibel, an oath which the young man gave with a heavy heart.

"How often he craved to visit the shtibel! Occasionally he would pass by and meet one of the chassidim outdoors. He reasoned that he was not violating his oath because he was not going into the shtibel, and the chance encounters outside could hardly be considered 'associating.'

"As the month of Elul approached he noticed an increased activity and fervor among the chassidim. They were planning to go to the tzaddik in Mezeritch for the holy days. How he longed to be with them, to open his neshamah to the tzaddik, to have him cleanse it and restore *it to him in its pristine state. How he dreamed of the tzaddik peeling away the layers of self-deception like the layers of an onion, and bringing him to an awareness of his true self, in possession of the truth, so that his grasp of the Torah could be more thorough.*

"As Rosh Hashanah drew closer, the urge to join the chassidim in their trip to the tzaddik increased in intensity, and his battle to subdue it in compliance with his vow began to weaken as he realized more and more that both the ban of excommunication and the oath that he was compelled to give were based on totally false premises and were therefore null and void. Three days before Rosh Hashanah, when he saw the chassidim loading their wagons, he ran to take his talis and tefillin, not telling anyone that he was leaving, and jumped on board.

"Our young man was warmly received by the Maggid, and whenever the Maggid expounded on Torah, he felt that every word was directed toward him. The Maggid was looking into the recesses of his soul, guiding him to cleanse out the contamination that the yetzer hara had put there. He prayed like he had never prayed before, and the words of the Torah he studied sparkled before his eyes like scintillating jewels.

"The two weeks in Mezeritch were two weeks in paradise, but on return to Vitebsk he was not permitted into his own home. Instead, he was hauled off to the rabbinical court where the rabbi decreed that he must bear the consequences of his errant behavior, violating a sacred oath. He was compelled to give his wife a divorce.

"Forcibly separated from the wife and child he so loved, the young man fell into a deep depression. He could not eat nor sleep. He secluded himself in an abandoned hut, where his energies slowly dissipated and he died.

"Many years later, the father-in-law and the rabbi of the community passed on, and the young man called them

before the Heavenly Tribunal, claiming that they were responsible for his premature death. The father-in-law defended himself, saying that he had merely abided by the ban of excommunication that the rabbi had proclaimed. The rabbi defended his judgment, stating that the young man had broken a sacred vow, and had stipulated that he would divorce his wife if he transgressed his vow.

The tribunal ruled that the father-in-law was in the right, and that the rabbi was also in the right. Clearly, the only one who could be found to have been in the wrong then, was the young man, who was therefore guilty.

"And my mission," concluded the Rabbi of Rizhin, "is to defend the guilty who are innocent."

≈)≈

What conclusions are we to draw from this story?

Most of us will probably sympathize with the young man, who sought the truth with sincerity and who was unjustly deprived of the wife and child he loved, and driven into a fatal depression. Personally, as a *chassid,* I may be very angry with his father-in-law and with the rabbi who ruled against him. However, there was a reason I prefaced this story with that of the holy *misnaged,* Rabbi Chaim Tzanzur.

There is an important distinction between Torah philosophy and secular philosophy. In the latter, two opposites cannot both be correct. In Torah we have the principle "These and these are the words of the living G-d" (*Eruvin* 13b). Hillel says something is permissible, Shammai says it is forbidden, yet both are right. Why? Because when a person begins with sound Torah principles as a foundation, and uses his reasoning powers sincerely and solely in the pursuit of truth, seeking only to do what is right, without personal interest or ulterior motive, then the conclusion he reaches is right. In the Divine system two opposites can be right.

However, we cannot conduct ourselves purely by our reasoning. Only one of the two opinions can be adopted, and the Talmud generally rules according to the opinions of Hillel, which have become the *halachah* that guides our behavior. Shammai is no less right than Hillel, but we must conduct ourselves according to the "right" of Hillel and not according to the "right" of Shammai, even though to G-d, both are equally correct and precious. Shammai's reward in heaven is no less than Hillel's, but we are not permitted to act in accord with Shammai's opinions when the *halachah* is not decided that way.

The era in which the young man defected to the *chassidim* was one in which many *misnagdim*, like Rabbi Chaim Tzanzur, were sincere in their opposition. The rabbi had no choice but to implement the proper *halachah*. His ruling — and hence the father-in-law's actions — were right, even if I, with 20/20 hindsight, disagree with the reasoning which found the basis for the rulings which led to their decision. At any point in time a magistrate must rule according to the data he has before him.

Is the system unjust? Not in the long run. There is a world where all grievances are eliminated, where all misconceptions are elucidated, and where truth shines forth and illuminates everything. This world of absolute truth, where all wrongs will be righted, will not be available to us until we take leave of the physical world which is so restrictive.

The Rabbi of Rizhin tried to advance time a bit. Today, many years later, we know that both the Baal Shem Tov and Rabbi Chaim Tzanzur were right. The Rabbi of Rizhin wished the parents of these young men to see then what we know now.

It may be a delicate judgment call, but there are situations where those that are, in retrospect, right are guilty, and those that are, in retrospect, not right are innocent.

39

The Teacher and the Disciple

Trends and changes usually occur gradually over a number of generations, hence I am somewhat surprised to have witnessed a distinct change in my own lifetime, a change which gives me great concern, and that is the quality of the relationship between teacher and student. I have reason to believe that the strong bond that used to exist between the two has been eroded. For example, I remember students identifying themselves according to who their teacher was, as when my older brothers would say, "I am Reb Shloime's *talmid*" (student), referring to the venerated Torah scholar, Rabbi Shlomo Heiman, or when others said, "I am a *talmid* of

Reb Aharon," referring to the sage Rabbi Aharon Kotler. Rarely do I hear this today, and instead, students refer to the institution where they study rather than to a rebbi.

This is of concern to me because a personal relationship has a much greater impact upon a person than an institutional relationship. Indeed, the Talmud says that the relationship of a teacher to a student should be like that of a parent to a child (*Sanhedrin* 19b). Furthermore, the Talmud states that parents and teachers are never envious of their children or students who surpass them in excellence (*ibid.* 105b), and this is because they see the latter as extensions of themselves. Lacking such perspective, we may find that a teacher may actually feel threatened by the superior progress of a student, and this could have an inhibiting effect on the latter's growth and progress.

The relationship of a teacher to a student reached its zenith in *chassidus,* and indeed, it was not only the teacher-student relationship that was so intense, but the rebbe-*chassid* relationship as well. One *chassid* bemoaned that King Solomon had not experienced a rebbe-*chassid* relationship. "Had Solomon known this he would not have chosen the analogy of romantic love in song of *Song of Songs* to describe the relationship between G-d and Israel, but rather that of a *chassid* to his rebbe."

Reb Pinchas of Shklov was a *chassid* of Rabbi Schneur Zalman, and would visit the Rabbi several times a year. One year he was not well, and remained home for Succos. At one point he said to his friends and family, "The Rabbi is thinking of me at this very moment."

Indeed, at that very moment Rabbi Schneur Zalman was saying to his *chassidim,* amongst whom were some who lived in Shklov, "Reb Pinchas is not well. We wish him a *refuah shleimah* (a complete recovery)." When the *chassidim* returned to Shklov and discovered that Reb Pinchas had made his comment at the exact moment that Reb Schneur Zalman had remembered him, they became very angry with him. "How dare you exhibit clairvoyance!" they demanded.

Reb Pinchas said, "It is not clairvoyance at all. You see, the first time I went to the Rebbe, I gave him part of my *neshamah,* and over the next several visits I delivered my entire *neshamah* to him. I am no longer my own self, because I have given myself totally to the Rebbe. I am no longer a separate entity from the Rebbe. Therefore, what he thinks, I can feel."

The relationship between teacher and disciple can be seen all the way back to Moses and Joshua, and to Elijah and Elisha. We can better understand the Talmudic statement that a teacher is not envious of a student who surpasses him in the light of statements made by our great Torah personalities. Thus, the Arizal said, "I was not put on earth for any purpose other than to teach Rabbi Chaim Vital." The Baal Shem Tov said, "Master of the Universe! I may not deserve reward for anything I have done in the world, except for having given you Yossele (Rabbi Yaakov Yosef of Polnoah, his eldest student)." When the teacher perceives his student as his own fulfillment, there can be no envy.

The Talmud describes the relationship between Rabbi Yochanan and his disciple, Rabbi Shimon ben Lakish, who so progressed in his study of Torah that he became a peer to his teacher. When Rabbi Shimon died, Rabbi Yochanan grieved so intensely over his disciple's death that he soon died. Life without his beloved disciple was not worth living.

The bond between the chassidic masters and their disciples was similar to a lock and key, with each part being essentially non-functional without the other, and the relationship between the two being a perfect match. Rabbi Uri of Strelisk sought a teacher from among the great masters of his time. His first visit was to Rabbi Elimelich of Lizhensk, the undisputed *tzaddik* of his generation. He learned much from the great *tzaddik,* then made his way to Rabbi Yeiva, whose study of Torah and devotion to G-d was angelic, yet he did not become his disciple. He went to Rabbi Pinchas of Koritz, the eldest of the chassidic masters, who greeted him warmly but told him, "I am not your

Rebbe. Continue your search." This is also how he fared with Rabbi Zusia of Hanipoli. He then went to Rabbi Shlomo of Karlin, and was immediately overcome with an unprecedented sense of awe and reverence. "Let the reverence for your teacher be as dear as the reverence of Heaven," says the *Mishnah* (*Ethics of the Fathers* 4:15). Rabbi Uri knew immediately that he had found his Rebbe. The key fit the lock, and each knew that he was destined for the other.

Perhaps the intense bonding with one's teacher stemmed from the awareness that without a guide and mentor, one was at risk of making wrong judgments and deviating from the Divine will, which is why the *Mishnah* says, "Accept a teacher upon yourself" (*Ethics of the Fathers* 1:6). To a disciple, being without a teacher was like being without oxygen. It is related that the Rabbi of Ostrovtza was orphaned from his Rebbe, the Rabbi of Grodzhisk, and at the latter's funeral, he pleaded with the Rabbi of Porisov to accept him as a disciple. The converse was also true, with the rebbe knowing that just as a nursing infant stimulates the mother's production of milk, so a disciple's learning increases the master's knowledge. It is for this reason that the chassidic masters were possessive of their disciples, and felt a deep loss when a disciple left them.

The reverence of a disciple for the chassidic master has no parallel elsewhere. When Rabbi Shalom of Kaminka was asked to repeat some of the teachings of his master, the Rabbi of Belz, he said, "My master revealed to me only 1/1000 of what he knew, and I understood only 1/1000 of what he taught me. I can put only 1/1000 of this into words, and you will grasp only 1/1000 of what I tell you. What point is there, then, in my trying to teach you anything from my master?"

One of the most painful defections was that of the Rabbi of Izhbitza who left his master, Rabbi Mendel of Kotzk. He was once visited by a friend, the Rabbi of Vorka, who asked him why he had left the master. "It was the Divine will that I do so," the Rabbi of Izhbitza said.

The Rabbi of Vorka shook his head. "Scripture tells us that when young Samuel heard the voice of G-d calling him, he ran to his master, the High Priest Eli, who told him that it was the voice of G-d calling to him (*Samuel I* 3:3-10). Could not Samuel have reasoned on his own that it was the voice of G-d? The answer is that even if one hears the voice of G-d directly, one should still take counsel from one's master. We are always vulnerable to misinterpret the Divine word. No one should act on his own without the master's approval."

We may understand the significance of the Rabbi of Vorka's remark by noting that immediately preceding the Book of *Samuel,* the Book of *Judges* closes with the tragic observation, "In those days there was no king in Israel; a man would do whatever seemed proper in his eyes" (*Judges* 21:25). Being without a guide and mentor may result in anarchy, which is as dangerous morally as it is politically.

Gain Through Loss

One of the most difficult adjustments a person must make is to adversity. Ever since we were expelled from *Gan Eden,* mankind has been subject to hardships. It is often difficult to be accepting of unpleasant happenings, particularly when we feel we don't deserve them.

The question "Why do bad things happen to good people?" has tormented mankind since time immemorial, and we have already alluded to this. There is much in chassidic and *mussar* writings that can help a person accept the difficult realities of life.

The *Midrash* tells us that the patriarch Jacob wished to dwell in tranquility. After surviving the persecution by Esau, the repeated deceptions by Laban, and the episode of Dinah, Jacob wished to live in peace. But G-d said, "Peace and tranquility are reserved for *Gan Eden*. In the physical world, you struggle and suffer," and Jacob was then subjected to the agony of thinking his beloved son Joseph had perished.

Why is it necessary for us to struggle and suffer? This is a secret which G-d has not divulged. "Man was born to suffer" (*Job* 5:7). This is a fact of life. But we can be helped to accept this reality, and the teachings of our great Torah scholars can provide this help.

R abbi Nota of Chelm had a chassid who was very well-to-do, who said to him, "I am very wealthy and I lack for nothing. But recently there is little voice within me that tells me that not all is well. It is as if I have a premonition that my fortunes are about to take a turn. It is one thing if a person is born into a life of poverty and accepts poverty as a way of life. Not so with me. If I lose my fortune, the change will be disastrous, and I doubt that I will be able to adjust to it."

"What kind of changes have you made in your home recently?" Rabbi Nota asked.

Assuming that the Rabbi was inquiring about laxity of Torah observance, the chassid said, "G-d forbid, Rabbi. Everything is as it was. Shabbos is totally Shabbos, my kosher standards are as rigid as ever, and I faithfully study the Torah daily."

"That's not what I am after," the Rabbi said. "What physical changes have you recently made in your household?"

The chassid thought for a moment, then said, "Yes, I did make a change, but it is hardly significant. I had a set of expensive crystal glassware, but I would get upset when a crystal goblet fell or was chipped. I therefore set it aside, and bought silver goblets which are more resistant to damage."

"There you have your answer," Rabbi Nota said. "Every person is destined to experience a certain amount of adversity. You were fulfilling your quota of unpleasantness when a piece of crystal was damaged. When you eliminated that source of unpleasantness, you invited adversity from other sources. Put away the silver goblets and use the crystal again. You will then have sufficient aggravation from the crystal being chipped so that you will not need any other."

And so we have an explanation for the custom in Jewish homes that when a glass or dish breaks, we exclaim, "Mazel tov!" My father used to add on the verse from Psalms (124:7) "The snare broke and we escaped." If we were destined to experience some loss, we satisfied this decree by the loss of the glass or dish, and now we could go on to be happy.

A *chassid* once complained to his Rebbe about various distresses he was experiencing. The Rebbe told him the following story:

A *wealthy man accused one of his employees of stealing from him. The employee protested that he was innocent, but his plea fell on deaf ears. The wealthy man took him before a judge, and although the evidence was very flimsy, the judge showed favoritism toward the wealthy man and found the employee guilty, ordering him to make restitution. The employee said he did not have the money, and the judge then ordered that he be given 20 lashes.*

Some time later the real thief was exposed, and the employee then sued his employer for damages. The judge awarded the employee compensation of $100 for each of *the lashes he received. The employee then said to the judge, "Why did you only fine me with 20 lashes? If you had given me 50 lashes, I would be so much richer now."*

The Rebbe said to the chassid, "Now you complain about your distress. Just wait until Judgment Day, and you will see how much benefit you will derive from having sustained this suffering. You will then wish you had suffered even more."

Some *tzaddikim* comforted people who were going through distressful periods by pointing out that in order for a seed to sprout and produce a new plant, it must first disintegrate. Only then are the growth enzymes that are contained within it released, so that they can synthesize the elements in the soil into a thriving plant. So it is with a human being, who may sometimes have to go through great difficulty in order to be able to rise to success. The prototype for this is the story of Joseph, who rose to the monarchy of a mighty empire, only after the devastating experiences of being sold into slavery and unjustly imprisoned.

In addition to personal gain coming only after a loss, there are many instances where an individual's personal adversity resulted in a communal gain. Some of the greatest Torah personalities were catapulted into positions of leadership only after suffering a loss. There are numerous stories of how these great scholars wished to spend their entire lives in the study of Torah, and refused to accept requests to become communal rabbis because the obligations of leadership would distract them from the study of Torah. For years they enjoyed uninterrupted devotion to learning because they had an income from their dowries or were supported by in-laws, and it was only after an economic crisis which deprived them of their support that they were forced to accept a rabbinical post for a livelihood. We were thus blessed with the greatest of leaders whose light might otherwise have remained concealed, or revealed only in their scholarly works. Their personal loss became Judaism's gain.

Τ he Rabbi of Kotzk had a wealthy chassid who was an accomplished Torah scholar, and who supported the Rebbe's household. One time the Rebbe refused to accept his gift of money, and explained:

"A person must have faith and trust that Hashem will provide for him, and one should not feel secure in relying on one's own wealth or on another person.

"I have come to rely on your support," the Rebbe said, "and this threatens to erode my reliance on Hashem. I am afraid that in order to restore my trust in Hashem, you may lose your entire fortune, so that I will once again rely directly on Hashem instead of on you. I don't want you to experience this loss, therefore I no longer wish to accept any money from you."

The chassid protested. "I do not care what will happen to me. I have the privilege of supporting the Rebbe. This is my mitzvah, and I will continue to do it, come what may."

Sure enough, the chassid's fortunes took a turn for the worse, and he eventually became impecunious.

On a subsequent visit to the Rebbe, the chassid said, "I have no regrets. I accepted this with full awareness of what might happen. However, I am now asking the Rebbe's blessing for parnassah (a livelihood)."

"The time has come for you to share your Torah scholarship with others," the Rebbe said. "There is a vacancy in a nearby community for a rabbi, and I advise you to apply for that position."

The chassid did so, and became a widely recognized Torah scholar.

Rabbi Baruch of Mezhibozh was reciting the prayer before Kiddush Friday night, and as he read "I thank You G-d *for all the kindnesses that You have done for me, and for those that You will do for me in the future," he paused and reflected, "Why must I thank G-d in advance for future kindnesses? Why not just wait until those kindnesses occur, and thank Him then?" After a few moments of meditation, Rabbi Baruch said, "Ah, I understand. When those kindnesses in the future occur, they may be packaged in a manner that I will not recognize them as kindnesses, but perhaps experience them as sufferings, and I will then not be in a position to appreciate them and be grateful for them. That is why I must thank G-d for them in advance."*

After a few moments, Rabbi Baruch began to weep. "How tragic," he said, "that G-d will be doing kindnesses for me, and I will not be able to recognize them as such."

Every one has had experiences which, at the time they occurred, seemed to be nothing less than calamities, yet after a period of time, we see how these incidents were actually beneficial. We should be able to learn from such experiences so that when we encounter adversities, we can cope with them more effectively, recognizing that they are undoubtedly precursors of better things.

Pleading for One's People

I n the Talmud we occasionally find the sages addressing one
another as "Moses." Why? Because Moses was the prototype of a Torah scholar.

Another similarity we find between Moses and later *tzaddikim* is that they emulated Moses in pleading the case of Israel
before G-d. In the Torah we find how Moses repeatedly inter-
ceded when the Israelites evoked the Divine wrath, and he
ingeniously pleaded for them, achieving Divine forgiveness.
Many *tzaddikim* followed in his footsteps, invoking His Divine
mercy on His people.

Rabbi Levi Yitzchak of Berditchev was outstanding in this respect. He interpreted the verse (*Numbers* 23:21) "He perceived

no inequity in Jacob, and saw no perversity in Israel; Hashem his G-d is with him," as meaning that one who sees no fault in his fellow Jew is one who merits the Divine Presence with him.

R abbi Moshe of Kobrin would say, "Yes, you heavenly angels are indeed holy. But you are in the celestial spheres, with no need to eat or drink, no family for whom you must care, no worries concerning a livelihood. Come down to earth once, and share in human stress and needs, and let us see whether you can still be angelic."

The Shpoler Zeide once convened a group of chassidic masters and summoned the Almighty to a din Torah (rabbinic court). "Since G-d gave us His Torah, He must observe its ordinances. The Torah says that Jews are servants unto G-d, and it also ordains that a master must provide ample food and all the necessities of life for his servants and their families. Why then, Master of the Universe, does such great poverty prevail among Your servants? Why are You not providing better for them? And if You will claim that they are lax in serving You, where in the Torah does it say that a master may refuse to provide for a servant because he is lazy? Furthermore, if it were not for the yetzer hara that discourages them from performing the Divine will, all Jews would serve G-d diligently. But You created the yetzer hara, hence their dereliction is not all their fault.

"We, the convened rabbinical court, therefore decree that You, Master of the Universe, must provide more amply for Your servants."

≈⌒≈

The Baal Shem Tov was intolerant of preachers who reprimanded congregants. One time, when he heard a preacher sharply rebuking the worshipers for their dereliction in Torah study and performance of *mitzvos,* the Baal Shem Tov went to the Holy Ark and said, "Please, Heavenly Father, do not listen to this man. He makes his living by preaching, hence he must give sermons of this type. He is desperately in need of money because his daughters need a dowry. Please, Heavenly Father, bless him with wealth so that he will have no need to find fault with Your children."

*R*abbi Levi Yitzchak of Berditchev saw a man greasing the wheels of his wagon while he was wearing his talis and tefillin. Instead of being enraged at this sacrilege, Rabbi Levi Yitzchak turned his eyes toward heaven and said, "See, Master of the Universe, how holy Your children are! Even when he is engaged in greasing his wheels, he nevertheless remembers to pray to You."

*A*nother time, Rabbi Levi Yitzchak addressed G-d, saying, "Master of the Universe, the Midrash says that the relationship between Israel and G-d is compared to that of a husband and wife. Each partner must bring something to the marriage. Israel brought a noble ancestry, the patriarchs Abraham, Isaac, and Jacob. But of course, You have no ancestry, because You are eternal. The only thing You could bring to the marriage is Your enormous wealth, since the Torah says, 'The gold and silver is Mine' (Haggai 2:8). Therefore we request that You comply with the terms of the marriage agreement, and provide Israel with all its material needs."

A woman once came to the Maggid of Kozhnitz, complaining that her husband wished to divorce her, because she was not attractive. "It is not my fault, holy rabbi," the woman cried. "When I was young I was very beautiful, but now that I have grown old and lost my beauty, he wishes to abandon me. That is not just."

The Maggid began weeping, and turning his eyes to heaven, he said, "Master of the Universe, this woman's complaint is indeed heart rending. But are we not in the same relationship with You? In our youth, when You delivered us from Egypt, we trusted You implicitly and followed You into the barren desert. Now that we have grown old and have lost the beauty of our youth, is it just that You abandon us?"

The devotion of the tzaddikim to G-d and their loyalty to the Torah was absolute, yet their love for their brethren was no less. Inasmuch as it is indeed true that love blinds one to the faults of the beloved, so did their love for their fellow man blind them to their defects.

42

The Chassidic Existentialist

W hile all the chassidic masters were unique, one is most prominent in his uniqueness. Rabbi Mendel of Kotzk and his followers are quite different from all other masters and their *chassidim*. We have already encountered the Rabbi of Kotzk, with his fierce pursuit of truth. But even this is an understatement. For the Rabbi of Kotzk, there was no compromising on truth. Anything that is not entirely genuine is worse than worthless. And since everything in the world is subject to dissimulation, the only absolute truth is G-d. Therefore, anything other than G-d held no interest for him.

The world being what it is, with absolute truth often being sacrificed for the sake of expedience, the Rabbi of Kotzk had no use for the world, which he totally dismissed, saying, "The entire world is not worth even a single groan." Pragmatic philosophies had no place for him. Something is either entirely true, or it is false. His comment on the principle of the "golden path," or "mean of virtue," was "the middle of the road is for the horses." If one seriously pursues truth, one cannot avoid extremes.

Many of his contemporaries were critical of the ideology of Kotzk. Absolutism is the realm of heavenly angels. Yes, we can make great demands of human beings, but one cannot demand absolute perfection of anyone dwelling within a physical body. The Rabbi of Kotzk rejected such arguments. "Stop pampering the body, and it will not be an impediment to angelic perfection." Relentless pursuit of truth will unite a person with G-d, and that is the sole purpose of one's being on earth. Little wonder that Rabbi Mendel of Kotzk was often referred to as "the Seraph."

It is not for us to try to understand the personality of a Seraph, and although Rabbi Mendel's goals may be beyond our reach, there is reason to study them. If we reach for the stars, we may at least grasp a small piece of the sky.

As far as the Rabbi himself is concerned, we must be satisfied with his teachings rather than with his lifestyle, and his teachings are also most unique. Torah scholars generally recognize a given thought as "That must be something the Kotzker said." For example, "Some may think it is a miracle to bring the dead back to life. My mission is to bring the living to life." Or, "Some tzaddikim say that they actually see the patriarchs in their succah. I do not see them, but I believe they are there, and believing is superior to seeing."

But while we cannot hope to fathom the Seraph, we may benefit from observing some of his followers, and how his teachings impacted on them.

R eb Hirsh was one of Rabbi Mendel's chassidim. One time he met a friend of his youth, and asked him, "What are you doing with yourself these days, Yitzchak?"

Yitzchak replied, "Thank G-d, I have the opportunity to study Torah all day."

"So what are you doing with yourself, Yitzchak?" Reb Hirsh repeated. "Ay, Ay, Yitzchak. How you deceive yourself! Yitzchak, my friend, you saw a portrait of the great Gaon Rabbi Akiva Eiger, and you are envious of the fame and respect this great Torah scholar achieved. You, too, Yitzchak, wish to become a great Torah scholar, so that people will revere you and will display your portrait as they do that of Rabbi Akiva Eiger. That is what you are really doing all day, Yitzchak. You are painting your portrait.

"Rabbi Akiva Eiger was not only a great Torah scholar, Yitzchak. He was the essence of humility, and just as Moses received the Torah because he was the most humble of all men, so Rabbi Akiva Eiger became the outstanding Torah giant because of his profound humility and total self-effacement. He never aspired to have his picture displayed. Be honest with yourself, Yitzchak. The Torah is the Torah of truth."

Chassidim of Kotzk were relentless in their battle against self-deception. The master had drummed this into them, as when he once entered the beis midrash and cast a sharp, penetrating glance at this disciples.

"What do you think you have done today?" Rabbi Mendel thundered. "You think you have davened well and have learned Torah diligently, and so you are wise and are tzaddikim. But have you gained even a grain of truth? All you are is vain. Your vanity and self-deception is sickening." And with that, Rabbi Mendel returned to his study, leaving his disciples in a state of shock.

⁐◌⁀

O ne chassid of Kotzk asked another, "How do you define what a chassid is?"

"A chassid is anyone who wishes to become a chassid,"
the other answered.

"But then, who would not wish to become a chassid?"

"Someone who thinks he already is a chassid."

This is the teaching of Kotzk: If you are pursuing holiness and
are in the search of spirituality, you are on the right track.
However, if you feel you have already become holy and have
achieved spirituality, then you have already lost it.

O ne chassid came to Rabbi Mendel, complaining that
he had a very serious problem, because he was
without parnassah (livelihood).

"Are you sure that is your most serious problem?" Rabbi
Mendel asked.

"Yes," the chassid answered.

"Then pray to G-d for parnassah," Rabbi Mendel said.

"But I do not know how to pray properly," the chassid
said.

"Then why do you say that parnassah is your most serious problem?" Rabbi Mendel said. "Not knowing how to
pray properly is a far more serious problem than that."

I have already told you the well-known story which follows,
but I repeat it in part here to bring out a specific point.

O ne wealthy chassid used to support Rabbi Mendel
and his disciples. One time Rabbi Mendel said, "You
must stop giving me money, because I may begin to rely
on you instead of on G-d." But the chassid stated that he

had no intention of discontinuing his support for the Rabbi.

"I must warn you," Rabbi Mendel said, "that if you do not cease, then you may well lose all your wealth, so that I would drop my reliance on you and return to rely on G-d."

If I must lose my wealth, so be it," the chassid said, "but as long as I have it, I will continue to support the Rabbi."

This is what Kotzker *chassidim* were made of.

It was not easy to be a *chassid* of Kotzk. The demands Rabbi Mendel made of his *chassidim* were beyond the reach of many people. Indeed, Rabbi Mendel would at times chase away people who sought to become his *chassidim*, knowing that very few were likely to live up to his demands.

R*abbi Leib Eiger, grandson of the great Talmudist Rabbi Akiva Eiger, became a follower of the Rabbi of Kotzk. His father, Rabbi Shlomo Eiger, was quite displeased with this, and sent two emissaries to Kotzk to urge Rabbi Leib to return home. The emissaries noted that a group of chassidim who were engaged in a discussion abruptly stood up in reverence for a man who entered the room.*

"Is he a great scholar?" the emissaries asked.

"No," the chassidim answered. "In fact, he is rather unlearned."

"Then is he wealthy?" they asked.

The chassidim laughed. "Wealthy? Why, he subsists on tzeddakah."

"Is he unusually wise?" they asked.

"No one could ever accuse him of that," the chassidim said.

"Then why did everyone rise when he entered the room? What is it about him which warrants such a show of respect?" the emissaries asked.

"Because he is very humble," the chassidim answered.

The emissaries laughed. "Humble? How could he not be humble? He is ignorant, poor, and dull. What does he have to be vain about?"

The chassidim replied, "You see, a person who studies Torah understands the virtue of humility, as does a wise person. A wealthy person who found that his wealth did not bring him happiness is also more likely to be humble. It is most often precisely the ignorant, the poor, and the dull that do not appreciate humility, and it is often people who are thoroughly devoid of any character strengths that are the most vain. When we see a person who has no redeeming qualities, yet he is humble, that is indeed a person who deserves to be respected."

That was the logic of Kotzk.

W hen Rabbi Leib Eiger did return home after spending several years in Kotzk, his father asked him what he had accomplished there. "I came to know that G-d runs the world." Rabbi Leib said.

"And for that you had to spend years in Kotzk? Just ask the chambermaid, and she will tell you that G-d runs the world," his father said.

*"Yes," Rabbi Leib answered. "She **says. 'I know.' "***

All that is necessary to know is that G-d runs the world, but one must truly know it.

One young man came to Kotzk, and complained to one of the older chassidim that he was having a difficult time battling his yetzer hara. What is there that he could do to resist the yetzer hara's seduction?

"Believe in G-d!" the chassid said.

"That is not enough," the young man replied. "I do believe in G-d, but I still am subject to yield to temptation."

"That is because you do not really believe in G-d," the chassid replied.

"One time a king wished to test the loyalty of his subjects. He therefore assigned someone to circulate among the people and incite them to break the laws of the land. Some people entered into a discussion or argument with him. The wiser among them said, 'How is it possible that so mighty a king would allow someone to freely incite people to break his laws? It can only be that this is a test which the king himself has set up to test our loyalty. There is therefore no reason to get into a discussion with this person. Even he does not really want people to transgress the laws. He is only fulfilling his assignment, and the wisest thing to do is simply to ignore him.'

"You see, young man," the chassid continued, "if you truly believe that G-d is everywhere, sees everything, and is in total control of everything, you would immediately realize that He would not tolerate an independent yetzer hara to urge you to break His laws. Obviously, the yetzer hara is there only to test your loyalty to G-d. There is no reason to argue with him. Even he doesn't want you to do what he tells you to do. Just ignore him and he will go away."

That is the ideology of Kotzk.

The Heart
and the Mind

J ust as the stories about the *chassidim* of Kotzk give us
some insight into the ideology of Kotzk, so do the stories
about *chassidim* of Chabad give us a flavor of this school
of chassidic thought.

One of the luminaries of Chabad *chassidim* was Reb
Hillel, whose erudition in both *halachah* and more esoteric aspects of Torah was legendary. Yet, this great scholar was
totally self-effacing before Reb Shalom Yosef.

W ho was this great Reb Shalom Yosef? He was a simple man, a carpenter by trade, whose knowledge

of Torah was very sparse, perhaps not even extending to a full knowledge of simple Hebrew. But when Reb Shalom Yosef prayed, it was a happening. Pools of tears marked the place where he stood in prayer.

One time Reb Hillel asked Reb Shalom Yosef, "Just what is it that moves you to cry so profusely?"

Reb Shalom Yosef answered, "I do not understand much about the master's teaching, but I did hear him say that every person has a Divine neshamah a soul, which is part of G-d Himself.

"This pure neshamah was sent down to earth to reside in a body like mine, a body which craves so many gross earthly pleasures, which must be anathema to the Divine neshamah. How agonizing it must be for the neshamah to have to dwell in so unpleasant a place. I cry out of pity for the Divine neshamah that was condemned to be imprisoned within my body."

The great scholar, Reb Hillel, used to repeat Reb Shalom Yosef's words, and would weep as he did so. He felt that even with his great Torah knowledge, he had been unable to reach the level of sincerity and devotion that this simple man had achieved.

The portrait of Rabbi Schneur Zalman, the author of *Tanya*, is displayed in the house of virtually every Chabad *chassid*. One *chassid* was a notable exception, and when he was asked why he did not have a picture of the Rebbe in his home, he said, "When I study the *Tanya*, I get a better image of the Rebbe than when I look at his physical likeness."

Chassidim placed much emphasis on music. Chabad music is rich in joyous melodies, and also in tunes composed in march or waltz tempo which are set to the words of portions of the liturgy. There are also *niggunim* (melodies) which are referred to as *dveikus,* or devotion. These are rather somber refrains which are conducive to meditation. Chabad *chassidim* often used these *dveikus niggunim* as preparatory to a discourse on *chassidus.*

O ne young chassid asked why so much time was devoted to these dveikus niggunim, and was told by one of the older chassidim, "We listened to the Rebbe chanting this niggun, and how it brought him into intimate contact with G-d. When we sing this niggun, we feel ourselves being in the Rebbe's presence, knocking on his door and crying, 'Rebbe, have mercy. The yetzer hara is relentless in pursuit of my neshamah. Save me from his grasp!'"

"Speech is the vehicle whereby the intellect reveals itself. Music is the vehicle whereby we express our emotions. The true emotion of the soul is to be reunited with its source, with G-d, but there are many obstacles which stand in its way. When one meditates with the help of a niggun, one cuts through all the obstacles, and reaches a state of intimacy with G-d. That is why there was the beautiful music of the Levites in the Temple in Jerusalem. The person who entered the Sanctuary was transported to the celestial spheres.

"And what about the lively melodies which you sing?" the young man asked.

"These are the tunes to which we dance. You see, when you dance, your feet are lifted off the ground. You break contact with the earth, and you are a few inches closer to heaven."

F or all their serenity, chassidim of Chabad had a sense of humor. One of the chassidim of Rabbi Schneur Zalman was euphoric after listening to one of the Rebbe's discourses, and after leaving the Rebbe's study, he tied *himself with his sash high on one of the poles in front of the Rebbe's home.*

Other chassidim asked him, "Reb Shmuel, what in the world are you doing up there?"

Reb Shmuel answered, "A watchmaker displays a clock in his window, so that people would know that he fixes watches. A shoemaker displays a shoe, so that people will know where to go to get their shoes repaired. I put myself on display here so that people will know that the Rebbe repairs broken spirits."

One *chassid* was a shoe merchant, and was very much absorbed in his business.

"This is strange," the Rebbe said to him. "I have seen people put their feet into shoes, but this is the first time I've seen anyone put his entire head into shoes!"

Chabad chassidim would emphasize the teachings of Rabbi Schneur Zalman, that the only real entity in the world is G-d, and that if one truly understood this, one would see nothing in the world other than G-dliness. Certainly one could not be vain, because how could one be vain if one barely exists?

If a Chabad chassid saw someone who appeared a bit self-satisfied with his Torah study and prayer, he might say, "That a person needs an ear canal in order to receive sound is understandable, but why does one need the whole ear appendage?" And he would answer, "That is so that someone can grab you by the ear and pull you out of the quicksand of vanity into which you are sinking."

The difference between the *chassidim* of Kotzk and the *chassidim* of Chabad can be understood through this dialogue. It was characteristic of Chabad *chassidim* to pray very slowly and deliberately and to frequently pause for silent meditation. The Kotzk *chassidim*, on the other hand, would pray very rapidly.

A Kotzk chassid said to his Chabad friend, "If you have a garden and wish to prevent animals from getting in and destroying your plants, you would build a solid fence, with the slots close to each other. If you left a large space between the slots, animals can find their way in.

"Similarly, if you leave spaces between the prayers, the yetzer hara can find his way into your thoughts. That is why it is better to pray rapidly, with no 'slots' for meditation."

The Chabad chassid said, "That is all well and good, but what happens if when you build the fence, there is already an animal in the garden. A solid fence will trap him in. It is therefore better to leave a space between the slots that allows you to chase the animals out.

"Most of us already have the yetzer hara within us. If we do not pause and meditate, we may have no way of banishing the yetzer hara from our prayers."

In Deference
to Authority

S etting aside one's own opinion in deference to the accepted authority may be a difficult challenge, but is a most important concept in Torah living. We are often convinced of the correctness of our own position, and maybe most reluctant to yield to authority. The prototype of this is in the Talmud, when the great sage, Rabbi Yehoshua, and Rabbi Gamliel, the great sage who was also the formal authority, disagreed on which day was Rosh Chodesh (first day of the month), and when Rabbi Gamliel ordered Rabbi Yehoshua to come before him with his weekday on the day which Rabbi Yehoshua considered to be Yom Kippur, the latter complied.

Rabbi Gamliel thus addressed him as "My master and superior in learning, and my student, in that he humbled himself before my opinion."

Whereas erudition and thorough knowledge of *halachah* is the *sine qua non* for making a Torah decision, there is something unique about being a *posek*, and people of greater learning have deferred to the *posek*.

T*he Vilna Gaon did not function as the posek in Vilna, leaving these decisions to the appointed local rabbi.*

One Friday afternoon, a woman who lived near the Gaon discovered something questionable about the food she had prepared for Shabbos, and sent her son to the local Rabbi for a decision as to whether it was kosher. Before the son returned, the husband decided to ask the opinion of the Gaon, who lived nearby. Since it was late Friday afternoon, a quick decision was necessary about the suitability of the food for Shabbos, and the Gaon agreed to consider the question, ultimately ruling that the food was forbidden. The son later returned from the local rabbi with a response that the food was permissible.

When the rabbi heard of the Gaon's ruling, he came to the Gaon and said, "You are by far superior to me in your knowledge of halachah, but I am the local rabbi, and my authority should not be undermined. I am therefore requesting that you, my master, come with me to their home tonight, and we will both partake of the food which I have ruled as kosher."

The Gaon did as he was asked, and went with the rabbi to the neighbor's home, where they were served the food in question. Just as the Gaon was about to eat, one of the Shabbos candles sputtered, squirting tallow into the Gaon's dish. The Gaon was thus spared having to eat something which he had ruled forbidden, yet he had indicated his willingness to allow himself to be overruled by the local rabbi, who was inferior to him in Torah scholarship.

That is the mark of greatness. Like Rabbi Yehoshua, the Gaon deferred to authority, setting aside his own convictions.

Closer to our own times, it is known that Rabbi Aharon Kotler, the unquestioned Torah scholar of his generation, yielded to Rabbi Moshe Feinstein in issues of practical *halachah*. The reason for this is that practical decisions of *halachah* require the particular mindset of a *posek*. A great scholar, whose theoretical knowledge of Torah may be immense, nevertheless may not have the mindset of a *posek*.

T*here is also another consideration, as evidenced by Rabbi Yechezkel Landau, the author of the incomparable Noda BeYehudah, whose students once posed a hypothetical question to him, only to successfully challenge his ruling.*

The Noda BeYehudah responded, "When a practical halachic question is brought to a posek, there is special Divine guidance to lead him to a correct ruling, so that there not be, G-d forbid, a transgression committed. Such Divine guidance is not forthcoming when the question is of a hypothetical nature, and the ruling will not immediately affect anyone's behavior. Had this very same question been presented to me as a practical rather than a theoretical issue, I would certainly have ruled otherwise."

We are fortunate that our generation has been blessed with a large enrollment in *yeshivos,* and there are many fine Torah scholars who have studied *halachah.* We must remember that even erudition in Talmud does not qualify one to render *halachic* opinions, and that the authority of a *posek* must be respected.

What is meant by the mindset of a *posek*? Let me provide one example.

A young couple consulted me because the wife, who had just recently recovered from depression, discovered she was expecting, and was concerned that this might precipitate a relapse of the depression. After thoroughly evaluating the case, I suggested that they contact a posek, and I would provide him with the pertinent medical information.

Two days later I received a call from Reb Moshe, and I told him that there was indeed reason for concern about a recurrence of the depression.

"I understand," Reb Moshe said, "but let me ask you this. Suppose this family were millionaires, and the young woman could have adequate rest, with all her household duties being cared for by hired help. Would that change your opinion?"

I replied that if the woman could be relieved of her many responsibilities, this would reduce the stress on her and significantly diminish the likelihood of depression.

"Then it is not her condition that constitutes a threat to her, but rather a lack of money. That places a responsibility on us to raise sufficient money so that the woman can go through the pregnancy and preserve her emotional health. I will undertake to raise money on my end, and if there is anything you can do to help, it would be appreciated. After all, it is those of use who know the circumstances of this case that bear the responsibility."

The happy ending is that she did receive help, gave birth to a healthy child, and did not have a recurrence of depression.

That is the mindset of a true *posek*.

Great Torah scholars deferred to a *posek* even when they knew the latter was in error. My great-grandfather, the Rebbe of Hornosteipel, was recognized as an outstanding Gaon and *posek*, yet he too deferred to the local rabbi, who was by far his inferior.

A t a *Rosh Chodesh* feast, attended by learned rabbis of various communities near Hornosteipel, it was noted that the drumstick of a portion of chicken showed that the bone had been broken and had healed. This constituted a question as to the kosher status of the chicken. Although my great-grandfather and the other rabbis around the table recognized that this was indeed kosher, my great-grandfather insisted that the problem be brought to the attention of the local rabbi, who was benevolently known as Yankel, the rabbi.

Much to everyone's surprise, the messenger who was sent returned and said that Rabbi Yankel had ruled that the chicken was not kosher. My great-grandfather promptly instructed everything to be removed from the table, and that all utensils that had been used must be kashered. The rabbis in attendance were furious, and ran off to Rabbi Yankel, pointing out to him that his ruling was in error. With bowed head, Rabbi Yankel came to my great-grandfather, to apologize for his oversight.

My great-grandfather said, "Reb Yankel, it is only human to make an error, and I have no problem with that. But you should have understood, that if the ruling was that it was non-kosher, I would have made that ruling myself. Inasmuch as I knew it was kosher, I did not want to issue a ruling that was in my own favor, since I have a personal interest in its being kosher. The fact that I sent the question to you should have alerted you that I had

*already decided that it was kosher, but I wanted an out-
side opinion to confirm it, since I might not be totally
objective.*

*"Nevertheless, since you had ruled otherwise, I have
instructed that all the utensils we used be kashered. That
is out of respect for your authority as the local rabbi."*

By Special Merit

There are many stories of *tzaddikim* whose birth was a reward for their parents' exceptional devotion to G-d. The prototype for this is, of course, the patriarch Abraham. The *Midrash* states that according to natural law, Abraham and Sarah could not have a child, but their profound devotion to G-d warranted a miraculous reversal of natural law.

While we cannot vouch for the factual validity of all these stories, the importance lies in their message. *Mesiras Nefesh*, absolute devotion to G-d, makes a person deserving of Divine blessings. This concept is embodied in the various stories, and the concept is certainly of unquestionable authenticity.

Raphael Dubzinsky was a pious Jew who lived in a village in Poland, and like so many of his countrymen who were barred from living in the larger cities and from various types of livelihood, Raphael operated an inn which he rented from the local poritz. Raphael was known for his honesty and was respected and loved by all, Jew and Gentile alike. Raphael and his wife were content, but their happiness was marred by their being childless.

One time a new priest came to village, who was a virulent anti-Semite, and Raphael's popularity vexed him no end. He issued an edict that none of his parishioners were permitted to patronize the Jew, but inasmuch as the inn had been a place for drinking and camaraderie for years, the edict went unheeded. Similarly, his pressure on the poritz to revoke Raphael's lease on the inn bore no fruit.

Raphael sold his entire supply of beer and spirits to a non-Jew every Pesach, so the priest issued an injunction that no one was permitted to buy the Jew's chametz, under threat of excommunication and eternal damnation.

When Pesach arrived and no one wished to buy his chametz, Raphael left the doors to his inn wide open and made a public announcement: "I hereby renounce ownership of all my beer and spirits. Whoever wishes may come in and take it." He and his wife then left to spend Pesach with relatives, and although he knew that he would now be penniless, Raphael rejoiced during the festival.

When he returned home, Raphael asked the first townsfolk whom he met whether everyone had enjoyed all the free drinks. "What do you mean enjoyed free drinks?" they said. "We could not even get close to your place with those vicious dogs you had guarding it."

Raphael did not know what they were talking about, but when he came to the inn, he saw two vicious looking *dogs there. The dogs approached him gently, sniffed him, and then took off. Raphael realized that G-d had intervened to protect him from economic ruin. But he had one problem: His chametz had been guarded and thus had remained in his possession over Pesach, and as such he was forbidden to derive any benefit from it. Raphael began opening the spouts of the barrels to dispose of the beer and spirits. His wife screamed at him, "What are you doing? You did what you were supposed to do and divested yourself of ownership of the chametz. You may use it and sell it. Ask the rabbi!"*

The rabbi ruled that the wife was indeed right. When Raphael opened the doors and left his inn open to all, declaring publicly that all who wished were free to help themselves, he had indeed abandoned ownership of the chametz. The fact that G-d had miraculously protected him did not change things, and he was therefore now permitted to reclaim his former goods.

But Raphael was not at peace with himself. "The chametz was in my inn, and if because of a technicality it is halachically permissible, I still do not wish to benefit from it," and proceeded to pour his entire stock down the drain.

When the wife poured out her bitter heart to the rabbi, saying, "Now we are both childless and penniless," the rabbi said, "Have no fear. The virtue of his intense devotion to Torah will merit your having a child whose spirituality will illuminate the world."

That year the woman gave birth to a son, who later became the chassidic master, Abraham of Czechanov.

Two stories are told about the birth of the *Maggid* of Kozhnitz, and each one carries a message.

A woman once came to the Maggid asking for his blessing for a child, since after a number of years of marriage she and her husband were still childless.

The Maggid replied, "My parents, too, were childless for many years. Then my mother sewed a coat for the Baal Shem Tov, and after that I was born."

The woman exclaimed, "I will gladly sew a coat for you, a beautiful coat."

The Maggid shook his head. "No, my dear woman," he said. "That will be of no avail. You see, my mother did not know this story."

The Maggid's mother had no ulterior motive. Her gift to the Baal Shem Tov was sincere and altruistic, which gave it such great merit. This woman's gift would be lacking this unselfish motivation, hence it would be lacking in merit.

Another story has it that one Friday night the Baal Shem Tov was unusually joyful during the meal, and noting his disciples' curiosity, he told them that after Shabbos he would reveal the source for his joy.

After Shabbos the Baal Shem Tov took his disciples on a trip to a village, where he sent for Reb Shabsi, the bookbinder. When the latter came the Baal Shem Tov asked him, "What did you do this Friday night that was so special?"

Reb Shabsi appeared embarrassed, but answered, "My earnings have been very meager, and this past week I had no money to buy even candles or challah for Shabbos. I told my wife that I refused to ask for tzeddakah or even a loan, and that if it pleases G-d that we should be without provisions for Shabbos, it pleases me as well. On Friday afternoon I went to shul to say Shir HaShirim (Song of Songs) and Tehillim.

"When I returned home, my house was glowing with light, and upon entering, I saw the challahs and food on the table. My immediate reaction was that my wife had not been able to withstand the trial of having a Shabbos without candles and food, and must have asked for tzeddakah. This annoyed me, and I looked at her somewhat angrily.

"My wife understood my angry demeanor, and said, 'G-d forbid that I would take anything from anyone after you had told me not to. As I cleaned the house for Shabbos, I saw something shiny in a crevice in the wall, and it was a silver button from a dress I had from our wedding. I sold it and had enough money to buy everything for Shabbos.'

"When I heard that we had been blessed with everything we needed for Shabbos without taking anything from anyone, I could not contain my joy. I was so grateful to G-d for His kindness and that we would be able to have the Shabbos meal, that I took my wife's hands and we danced around the Shabbos table."

The Baal Shem Tov responded, "You should know that when you danced Friday night, the angels in Heaven danced along with you. Your gratitude to G-d and your love for the Shabbos have earned you the blessing of a child, a son who will illuminate the world with his teachings."

Here too the message is clear: a total trust in G-d, with acceptance of His judgment even when it results in hardship, and a boundless love of Shabbos. Although one can set aside one's own needs without too much difficulty, the honor of Shabbos supersedes one's own needs. This kind of faith and devotion constitute a special merit.

It is not unusual in our history that several great scholars and *tzaddikim* were born of simple parentage.

A chassidic master asked the mother of a tzaddik what unusual mitzvos she and her husband had done to merit so wonderful a neshamah. She said, "My husband was not a scholar nor did he do anything unusual in mitzvos. But when he recited the verse at the third Shabbos meal, 'May we merit seeing children and grandchildren who study Torah and do mitzvos,' he would repeat the verse several times with a heartrending tone, and tearfully say, 'Master of the Universe! All I ask is for a child who will do Your will and will bring glory to Your holy Name.' "

The master said, "That is why you were blessed with this neshamah. It is only natural for parents to wish to have children whom they can love and who will bring them nachas. Your husband set his own needs aside, asking only for a child who will bring nachas to G-d, and his sincere prayer was answered."

The Greatest of all Mitzvos

While we are instructed not to grade *mitzvos* as major or minor, there is one glaring exception: Shabbos. The Talmud says that rejection of Shabbos is tantamount to rejection of all Torah and of Judaism itself.

The Torah refers to Shabbos as a "sign" between G-d and Israel (*Exodus* 31:17). The Chofetz Chaim explains that if a storekeeper closes his shop for whatever reason, there is always the possibility that he will reopen it when conditions improve. However, if he removes the sign from the store, this indicates that the closure is permanent. In the same way, rejecting the

Shabbos is removing the "sign," and indicates that one is abandoning the special relationship between G-d and Israel.

Rabbi Chaim of Chernovitz was a chassidic master whose work, *Sidduro Shel Shabbos* (The Order of Shabbos), reflects his unparalleled love for Shabbos. It is said that Rabbi Chaim did not sleep at all on Shabbos, explaining that to be a *shomer Shabbos* requires more than abstaining from work. The word "shomer" means "a guard," and a sentry is forbidden to sleep while on duty. He therefore stayed awake all Shabbos to "guard" it. It is reported that on Shabbos Rabbi Chaim was physically taller than during the weekdays.

While Shabbos is primarily a spiritual day it is customary to serve delicious meals and use one's finest dinnerware. Someone asked the Baal Shem Tov whether it was not inconsistent to indulge in gustatory delights on a day that is meant to be spiritual.

"Not at all," the Baal Shem Tov said. "There was once a king who had to exile his son for behavior unbecoming a prince. The remorseful son lived in anguish, longing to return to the royal palace.

"After a period of time, the prince received a message from his father that he was now welcome to return home. The prince's joy was boundless, and he wished to celebrate in song and dance. He knew, however, that people would think him insane if he abruptly began to sing and dance. He therefore threw a party with abundant food and drink. When the guests were in high spirits, they began to sing and dance, and this gave the prince the opportunity to sing and dance without appearing ostentatious.

"Everyone was dancing, but for different reasons. The guests were happy with drink, whereas the prince, who was sober, was rejoicing, because he was to return to the palace.

"So it is with the Shabbos. The neshamah wishes to exalt in spiritual delights, but it is trapped within a physical body, which may inhibit the neshamah's aspirations. We therefore give the body some physical pleasures, so that it may be happy with its gratification, leaving the neshamah uninhibited in its quest to reach spiritual heights.

"It is, of course, a serious mistake if one thinks that all there is to Shabbos is the food and relaxation. This must be properly understood as only a way to facilitate the spiritual adventures of Shabbos."

The delicacies of Shabbos should nevertheless not be underestimated. One young man who drifted away from Judaism was planning to convert, and his family's entreaties and the rabbi's lectures made no impression on him. A friend of his casually mentioned, "Of course, you will miss the Shabbos *kugel,* roast chicken, and *cholent,*" and this was the catalyst which stimulated the young man to rethink his plans.

In our home, my mother served two *kugels,* one for those who preferred a tangy, peppered *kugel,* and one for those who preferred a sweet *kugel,* although, of course, anyone could have both. There is another custom of two *kugels* that has an interesting origin.

A woman came to the Maggid of Kozhnitz, complaining that her marriage was in jeopardy because her husband did not respect her family traditions. "At our home, the kugel was served with the main course, after the fish and cholent. My husband says that at his home it was otherwise, and claims that by the time the main course is served he is too full to enjoy the kugel. He therefore insists he be served immediately after Kiddush."

The Maggid pretended to be meditating profoundly, then said, "Here is what you must do. Every Shabbos, you must make two kugels, one for after Kiddush and one with the main course. This way, everyone's custom will be observed."

The Maggid then recommended to his chassidim to make two kugels every Shabbos, the second one to be called "The Shalom Bayis Kugel."

Because of its overriding importance, any infraction of Shabbos was taken with utmost seriousness.

Rabbi Yosef Chaim Sonnenfeld was once told that in a certain Jewish home there was cooking on Shabbos. He quickly put on his shtreimel and ran to the house, bursting in with a cry "Gevald! It's Shabbos!"

The stunned residents were embarrassed, but the perpetrator did not hesitate to rebuke the tzaddik. "Rabbi," he said, "is it proper decorum to break into someone's home without knocking on the door?"

"Decorum?" the tzaddik. "When a house is on fire, you do not observe social niceties. I heard there was a fire in your house, and that is why I had to rush in."

One Friday night in the winter, when thick clouds covered the sky, the Shpoler Zeide appeared in the kitchen, and gently urged that the cooking be completed speedily, since the day was short and Shabbos begins early. Many chassidim had come for Shabbos, and there was considerable preparations in progress. The Rabbi's instructions were well heeded, and the kitchen work was completed in time, with the workers saying, "There is still plenty of time until Shabbos."

The Zeide lit the Shabbos candles at the proper time, but inasmuch as the sky was so darkened with clouds and the sun was not visible, the Zeide began worrying that perhaps he had waited too long with candle lighting, and perhaps, G-d forbid, he may have lit the candles when it was already too close to sundown. "Woe is me," he began wailing, "I am afraid that I desecrated the holy Shabbos." Reassurances that he had lit the candles early enough before Shabbos failed to put his mind at ease.

That Friday night, in contrast to the Zeide's usual attitude of unrestrained simchah, he was most solemn. "Oy, Oy," he would repeat. "I may have violated the sacred Shabbos." He turned to his chassidim and with a pleading tone said, "Help me! What can one do if he thinks he may have violated Shabbos?" One chassid said, "Why does the Rebbe even think this way? It was still much before sunset when the Rebbe lit the candles," but the Zeide dismissed this. Another chassid said, "The Talmud says that G-d would not allow a tzaddik to inadvertently commit a sin." This, too, the Rebbe dismissed. "I am not a tzaddik that warrants such Divine protection."

Then the Zeide saw among the chassidim his colleague Rabbi Raphael of Bershad, whose passion for absolute truth is legendary. "Raphael," he said, "you are a true friend who will not mislead me. What can I do if I think I may have violated Shabbos?"

Rabbi Raphael sighed. "What can I say? If one suspects that he has violated Shabbos, one must do teshuvah. But the first teshuvah one must do is to honor the Shabbos by rejoicing with it. We must recognize that it is the day in which G-d rested. It is His day which He made holy, and out of His love for us He gave us this precious gift. When we rejoice with Shabbos we indicate our appreciation of its *holiness, and that it is a bond of love between G-d and Israel. This is the teshuvah for Shabbos."*

The Zeide's face beamed with joy. "You are a true friend, Raphael. The empty reassurances of the chassidim did nothing for me. You showed me a path to restoration."

We have no doubt that the Zeide did indeed light the candles well before sunset. We also believe that he was a true *tzaddik* whom G-d indeed protects from an inadvertent sin. But the importance of this story is in the wise advice of Rabbi Raphael: When concerned that one may have done wrong, do *teshuvah*. Even if one is blameless, *teshuvah* has great merit. Furthermore, as much as one may have remorse for having done wrong, one should rejoice that G-d has given us a way to undo our mistakes: *teshuvah*.

47

More Humble Than Any Person on Earth

There are some things we do not understand and indeed cannot understand. For example, when scientists tell us that a given star or a galaxy is a billion light years distant, these are empty words that mean nothing to us. Light travels at 186,000 miles a second, so that eight light minutes, which is the distance of the earth from the sun, is 93 million miles. How far then is a light hour, a week, a month, or a year? A light year is so distant that it defies our imagination. Inasmuch as we generally deal with inches, feet, or yards, or perhaps a few hundred miles when we travel by car and several thousand miles when we travel by jet, astronomical distances are beyond our grasp. We thus cannot conceive of a light year, let alone a billion light years. It is questionable whether even profound astronomers can really grasp distances that are so far beyond our sense perceptions.

But at least we can understand that we do not understand, and that we must resign ourselves to the inability to comprehend things which are alien to the range of our experience. We would do well to apply the same logic to the spiritual giants of Torah. How foolish of those who try to analyze Biblical or Talmudical personalities. At some point, quantitative differences are so vast that they become qualitative. The Talmud sums this up succinctly: "If the earlier *tzaddikim* are as angels, then by comparison we are humans. If we think of the earlier *tzaddikim* as being mere humans, then by comparison we are mules" (*Shabbos* 112b).

The Torah tells us that Moses was the most humble of all persons on the face of the earth (*Numbers* 12:3); i.e., there never was and there never will be a human being as humble as Moses.

But here we are, just several decades removed from the Chofetz Chaim, about whom we have eyewitness accounts of his total self-effacement. The Chofetz Chaim was the unchallenged *halachic* authority of his generation, revered by everyone, yet did not have the slightest trace of an ego. He was here to serve G-d and to be of help to others, to convey the Torah teachings which he possessed, and this was the purpose for which he was created. Believing that everything on earth was created for a purpose, the lowly ant, too, was created for a purpose in the Divine scheme. "What qualitative difference, then, is there between myself and an ant?" How can someone who believes in G-d and in *hashgachah* (Divine Providence) think of himself to be "somebody"? Inasmuch as we know that the study of Torah and the observance of *mitzvos* is to our own advantage, how can one take credit for doing things for himself? Does a person expect to be praised for eating and sleeping and doing whatever is essential for his own survival?

The Chofetz Chaim dressed in simple clothes, and was indistinguishable from any other layman. He never allowed himself to be served by others, even in his advanced age. People who knew him intimately report that he was deeply distressed when he was praised as being a great *tzaddik*.

"**I**f people think of me as a tzaddik, then it is incumbent upon me to behave as is fit for a tzaddik, else I am bringing disgrace to the concept of a tzaddik. But how can I do that? It is so far beyond my capabilities! I know I have not performed a single mitzvah to its fullest. I do not fully understand a single halachah. All I have done in my writings is to gather the opinions of previous Torah authorities, and make them more accessible to students of Torah. I am just like the shamas (sexton) who takes the books from the shelves and brings them to the student's table. Is that a reason to consider oneself a Torah scholar?"

⸙

The Chofetz Chaim came to Moscow, and as soon as word of his presence spread, many people flocked to greet him. Among them was a prominent citizen, who expressed his regret that no one knew of his coming. "We would have arranged a proper welcome, as is due you."

The Chofetz Chaim shook his head. "My dear friend," he said, "when you wife bakes a kugel for Shabbos, you leave it for Shabbos. You do not eat it on Friday morning. If we are to receive credit for Torah and mitzvos, it is to be in the World to Come, in the Great Shabbos. To accept honor in this world is like consuming the Shabbos kugel on Friday morning."

One Simchas Torah, upon entering the yeshivah to participate in hakafos (joyous circuits with the Torah), the students greeted him by singing the verse "The tzaddik *shall blossom like a date palm." The Chofetz Chaim turned pale, and covered his face, mumbling to himself, "What am I to do? It is Simchas Torah, and out of respect for the Torah I must stay here and suffer humiliation." For him, to be referred to as a tzaddik was nothing but anguish.*

We do not have to go back to early history to find other spiritual giants who were profoundly humble. The elders of Jerusalem told me of Reb Bezalel, who earned his livelihood by delivering milk, and on his route he would recite the Talmud, which he knew by heart!

The great Torah genius, Rabbi Aharon Kotler, was once introduced to this milkman, and soon the two were engaged in a lively dialogue on the most complex portions of the Talmud, a dialogue which continued for several hours. Rabbi Kotler was astonished and asked his friends, "You allow this Torah giant to be your milkman?"

As a young student, Reb Bezalel was known as "the *illui* (prodigy) of Bialistok," and when his boyhood friend, the great ethicist, Rabbi Chaim Shmulevitz, saw him in Jerusalem, dressed in tattered clothes and delivering milk, he burst into tears.

R*eb Bezalel was not a recluse. He associated with people, was cognizant of all that was happening in the world, and lent a helping hand to people in need. Just as the Talmudic author, Rabbi Yochanan, earned a livelihood as a shoemaker, Reb Bezalel was a milkman. Exceedingly great, yet exceedingly humble.*

⟳

R*abbi Shmelke of Nikolsburg arrived in a city where he was greeted by a throng of his followers. Before* meeting the crowd, he asked for a room where he could have a few moments of solitude. One of the chassidim was curious as to what the master was doing in solitude. Putting his ear to the door, he heard the master say, "Welcome to our city, honorable rabbi. It is our privilege to have you here. Thank you for coming, holy tzaddik," and other such expressions of admiration. The chassid later asked Rabbi Shmelke to enlighten him about this strange practice. "It is simple," the Rabbi said. "I anticipated what my chassidim would say to me. I therefore said it to myself first, and it sounded so foolish, that when they later said it to me, it appeared equally ridiculous."

≈)⊂

R abbi Menachem Mendel of Lubavitch traveled to several communities, and took along his young son, Shmuel. The son wrote a letter home, describing the enormous honor and expressions of admiration which his father was receiving in the communities he visited.

Upon return home, Rabbi Menachem Mendel found the letter, and called in his son. "I was suffering," he said. "My blood was being spilled like water, and you enjoyed it?"

The Rabbi went on to explain. "The king wished to get a first-hand view of the lifestyle of his subjects. He disguised himself as an ordinary foot soldier, and had one of his officers accompany him. When the people saw the officer, they stood up and saluted. The officer felt terribly embarrassed that they were according him honor, whereas the king, to whom the honor was due, went unrecognized.

"If people are only aware of the presence of G-d, how can they even notice the presence of a mere mortal? It is terrible to be the recipient of honor when one knows that it should be directed toward G-d."

If these spiritual giants had this degree of humility, how are we to understand that of Moses, which the Torah says was never equaled?

We cannot understand it. The humility of Moses was a quantum leap beyond everyone else's. If we wish to hazard a guess, we might perhaps say that whereas the humility of others caused them to feel distressed when they were honored, Moses was so self-effacing that he did not even feel any distress. The honor he received as the deliverer of his people and their great leader did not even register on him.

The Talmud says of Moses that when he delivered the Divine message, "The voice of G-d was speaking through him," a status which no other prophet attained. This was because Moses' self-effacement was so absolute that he virtually faded before G-d, as though he was not even in existence, and that Divine word that flowed through him was not processed through an intermediary, but was directly from G-d to Israel.

It is only Moses of whom the Torah says that his humility would never be equaled. The implication is that the profound humility of all other tzaddikim is reachable. Yet, our recounting descriptions of our great Torah personalities is not that we should try to equal their great spiritual achievements. These may seem to us to be so far beyond our reach that we may give up in futility. Rather, they represent the ideal.

Perhaps we may not feel distressed when we are praised, but at the very least, we should be able to avoid becoming vain, and regardless of our achievements, not consider ourselves to be superior to others.

And Walk Modestly With G-d

Accompanying the trait of humility is *modesty*, which means that one's achievements should remain a private affair and should not be flaunted. Without doubt there were people of enormous spirituality whose greatness was a well-kept secret. Great Torah personalities became public figures only when this was necessary for the good of the community. For example, the Chazon Ish's enormous Torah stature would have remained unknown had not Rabbi Chaim Ozer revealed his greatness, because he felt that Jewry was in need of his leadership. Similarly, Rabbi Menachem Ziemba ran a hardware store, and no one dreamed that he was a foremost Torah scholar until the Rabbi of Gur ordered him to expound his vast Torah knowledge. Incidents such as these abound, and it is from those that were reluctantly revealed that we can image how many remained concealed. Rabbi Yosef Shmuel, the great-grandfather of the Chasam Sofer, was one who was forced out of the shadows.

R*abbi Yeshayah Horowitz, the author of Shelah, was Rabbi of Frankfurt. When his grandson, who bore the same name, vacated the position, he indicated that his place should be filled only by someone who could resolve three difficult Talmudic problems which his grandfather had left unanswered. The community appointed three of its leading Torah scholars as a search committee, to find someone who could meet these qualifications. The three traveled from city to city, but in their discussions with many Torah scholars, did not find anyone who could resolve the three unanswered questions.*

Upon arrival in Cracow, they were invited to participate in a celebration at which several people gave Torah discourses. One of these was a youngster, who, to their surprise, satisfactorily answered the three questions. Upon remarking on this young man's exceptional erudition, they were told that he was the student of a Talmud instructor, a humble man who was highly thought of in the community, but who was extremely modest and did not assume any position other than that of a tutor.

The three met with the teacher, Rabbi Yosef Shmuel, and told him of their mission, and that they believed he was the proper person to assume the rabbinate of Frankfurt. The teacher told them this was absurd, and that he had no intention of doing anything other than continuing his function as a teacher.

The following day Rabbi Yosef Shmuel took ill, and his condition deteriorated rapidly, to the point where the chevra kadisha (the burial society) was summoned, since it appeared that his end was imminent. At one point he sat up and said, "Master of the Universe! If it is your will that I assume the rabbinate of Frankfurt, I will do so." He then recovered rapidly. This great Torah scholar had preferred to remain in the shadows, and only when he felt his illness was a message that he was remiss in fulfilling the Divine mission, did he consent to allow his spiritual achievements to become known.

This story does not end here. Upon arrival in Frankfurt, he found the Jewish community to be in the throes of depression. It was before Pesach, and there was a blood libel against the Jews. A gentile child had been found murdered, and the local priest, a virulent anti-Semite, had indicted the Jewish community in the crime, citing the false allegation that the Jews needed blood for matzos. The priest gave the Jewish community three days in which to surrender the murderer, otherwise every Jew would be banished from the city with nothing but the clothes on his back, and could be considered lucky if his life was spared.

Rabbi Yosef Shmuel sought to calm the community's anxiety, and said that he would clarify the matter to everyone's satisfaction. On the third day, the case came before the local tribunal, and after the priest delivered his scathing indictment and demanded that the killer be surrendered, Rabbi Yosef Shmuel stated that they did not know who the killer was. However, he was willing to submit to a trial by ordeal, which was generally accepted. He requested that the body of the child be brought, and that everyone in the community pass by and grasp the hand of the dead child. "I am certain that the killer will not be able to release his grasp."

When all the Jews successfully passed the ordeal, Rabbi Yosef Shmuel said, "The killer is not among the Jews. Let the others here pass the ordeal." When it was the priest's *turn to approach the body, he turned pale and began trembling. When he took the child's hand, he was unable to release his grasp and began screaming, "Let me go!" He then admitted that he had killed the child to incite the community to an uprising against the Jews.*

Rabbi Yosef Shmuel served the community faithfully as their rabbi. This stellar personality of unparalleled Torah knowledge and psychological wisdom might have remained among the many who sought to fulfill the prophet's words "Walk modestly with G-d."

Rigorous Honesty

I t goes without saying that spirituality and dishonesty are mutually exclusive. Anyone who is in wrongful possession of the property of others cannot begin to be spiritual.

Ironically, it may be easier for someone who is an outright thief to become spiritual than for someone who abhors theft, yet is in wrongful possession of the property of others. The thief may recognize the unjust nature of his ways, may make full restitution, and do sincere *teshuvah*. The person who thinks himself to be honest may not even consider the possibility that he may be in violation of the commandment "You shall not steal" (*Exodus* 20:13), and hence may never seek to make restitution or do *teshuvah*.

A person may engage in unfair business practices, and rationalize that this is the way business is transacted. It is also possible that a person may inadvertently take advantage of others, and this too is sinful.

In Safed there was a tzaddik, a kabbalist, Rabbi Avraham Galanti, who once came to the Arizal with a request that he reprimand him and help him correct his misdeeds. The Ari refused, saying that he was hardly one who could give mussar to so great a tzaddik, but Rabbi Avraham persisted in his demands. The Ari then studied his face and said, "I see that you have a slight defect and that you are in wrongful possession of others' property."

Rabbi Avraham was shocked, and promptly went home to don sack cloth and accept a fast, with intense soul-searching as to where he might have been dishonest, but to no avail.

Rabbi Avraham operated a textile factory. He called together all his workers and asked, "Am I in arrears to any of you? Have I inadvertently withheld wages from anyone?" The workers responded, "Rabbi, whatever you give us is enough. The Divine blessing is in your money, and whatever we receive always goes far enough to cover our needs."

Rabbi Avraham said, "Then that is the problem. I may have shortchanged you on your wages, but you have never complained. That is why the Ari found me sinful. Henceforth you must be specific and make certain you receive every cent that is due to you.

"But I must make restitution for the past," he said. Rabbi Avraham then placed money on the table and said, "Let anyone come and take as much as they feel is coming to him. Then I wish you to say, 'Whatever Avraham Galanti still owes me, I forgive him with all my heart!'"

Except for one woman who took a few coins, no one touched the money on the table, and all recited the forgiveness formula as requested.

Rabbi Avraham later returned to the Ari who said, "The stain has now been cleansed. It was the small amount of money that was due to that woman that had left its mark on your neshamah."

Let us now reflect on how cautious one must be to avoid retaining that which rightfully belongs to others.

Sometimes we may innocently forget to repay a loan, but unless the debt is forgiven, this constitutes wrongful possession of others' property.

M*y father used to tell a story about our ancestor, the tzaddik of Cherkassy, who once visited the home of a wealthy chassid. After a bit of conversation, he said, "Could you show me your stable?" The chassid took the Rabbi to the stable, and after looking at the horses, the Rabbi said, "I am in need of a horse. Could you spare me that one?"*

The chassid responded, "Rabbi, I will gladly give you any horse you desire, except for that one. That is my best workhorse, and if my wagon is ever stuck in the mud, it is this horse that pulls me out."

They went back into the house, and the Rabbi asked the chassid, "Do you remember Hirsh Baruch, who died a short while ago?"

"Yes, I do," the chassid said. "It is interesting that you mention him. He had borrowed money from me, which he never repaid."

"Do you have a promissory note on that loan?" the Rabbi asked.

"Yes, I have it among my papers," the chassid said, and at the Rabbi's request, he produced the note.

"Will you forgive the loan now?" the Rabbi asked.

The chassid said, "What point is there in not forgiving it? It is no longer collectible," and he proceeded to tear up the note.

The Rabbi suggested they return to the stable, where they found that the workhorse had died. The Rabbi explained, "When Hirsh Baruch came before the Heavenly Tribunal, they decreed that he must make good his unpaid debt to you, and his neshamah then inhabited your workhorse. By forgiving the debt, you have set his neshamah free."

Rabbi Jacob of Lisa wrote in his will to his children, "If you ever have a question in *halachah* that will affect you monetarily, be sure to bring the issue to a *posek*, and never decide the question on your own, regardless of how certain you may be about the *halachah*. Having a personal interest in a *halachic* question disqualifies you to render a decision."

W hen Rabbi Yaakov was a young man, he invested his entire dowry with a merchant, with the intention of being able to devote himself fully to the study of Torah and live from the income of his investment.

Unfortunately, the merchant's business failed. He notified Rabbi Yaakov of this, and returned his money, suggesting that he invest it elsewhere. Rabbi Yaakov discovered that the merchant had declared bankruptcy, and that he was the only one to whom money was returned. He then took the money to Beth Din, to be distributed proportionately among all creditors, which left him with only a pittance. He reasoned that it was unjust to give him preferential treatment at the expense of other creditors.

Honesty in business requires great diligence and devotion to Torah. Too often people assume that what they are doing in business is "kosher."

A shochet once came to Rabbi Yisrael of Salant, and said that he wished to relinquish his position, because he cannot accept the weighty responsibility of ritual slaughter. "If I should err, just think of how many people would unknowingly be eating treifah."

"What will you do for a livelihood?" Rabbi Yisrael asked.

"I plan to go into business," the man said.

Rabbi Yisrael shook his head. "Just think," he said. "Eating unkosher food is indeed a serious sin, but it is a violation of one transgression. In doing business, however, one exposes himself to many transgressions: Do not steal; do not covet; do not cheat; do not deny; do not lie; do not swear falsely; do not take interest; do not withhold wages, etc. Why is it that you are less afraid of inadvertently violating these many commandments, yet you are afraid of an error in ritual slaughter, which involves only a single transgression?"

⁂

The wife of Rabbi Yehoshua Leib Diskin once had a porter deliver a heavy package to her home, and she paid him for the delivery. That night Rabbi Yehoshua Leib noticed the package, and asked her how much she had paid the porter. He calculated that for a package that heavy, the payment was inadequate. He promptly sought the porter and added what he felt was the proper amount.

⁂

A young man reported to the Chofetz Chaim how thrilled he was that he was able to procure tefillin of exceptional quality. The parchments were written by the most respected sofer (scribe), the leather battim (housings) were fashioned by the finest craftsman and met the most stringent specifications, the leather straps were the work of a pious person, etc.

"And how much did you pay for these fine tefillin?" the Chofetz Chaim asked.

"Eighteen rubles," the man answered, which was at that time a huge sum.

"And were you equally diligent that all precautions were taken that these 18 rubles were as perfect as the tefillin? How was the money earned? If money is borrowed and not repaid promptly on the specified date, that constitutes wrongful possession of another's property.

"It is certainly praiseworthy to have perfect tefillin, but they must be bought with perfectly honest money."

Our great Torah authorities showed us that rigorous honesty is the foundation of Torah observance.

50

The Hierarchy of Torah

"To listen, to learn, to teach, to guard, to perform, and to perpetuate." This is how we describe, in our morning prayers, our obligations to Torah. This procession of levels, each building upon the other, can be seen in the life of one of our greatest Torah personalities, Rabbi Moshe Sofer, often referred to by the name of his monumental works, *The Chasam Sofer.*

Born in Frankfurt, the Chasam Sofer was recognized as a child prodigy, and at an early age was taken under the wings of the great Talmudist, Rabbi Nassan Adler, *whose disciple he remained throughout his lifetime, although he also studied under other great scholars. As a young man, he accompanied his teacher to Prague, and stunned the leading Talmudist of the generation, the author of Noda BeYehudah, with his brilliance and encyclopedic knowledge.*

Rabbi Moshe was totally absorbed in Torah study, and when he married the sister of Reb Hirsh Yarvitz, the latter assured him of indefinite support. Reb Hirsh was a wealthy merchant, with interests in lumber and an exclusive contract as supplier of various materials to the government. He was knowledgeable in Torah, and well aware of Rabbi Moshe's enormous erudition. Reb Hirsh was childless, and felt that by supporting the Torah studies of this illustrious young scholar, he was making his contribution to the perpetuation of Judaism.

Rabbi Moshe dedicated himself totally to Torah study, and except for the few hours of sleep which were necessary to maintain his health, his study was without distraction. In those precious years of uninterrupted study, his inquisitive mind absorbed every aspect of Torah, the esoteric as well as the revealed. He maintained an ongoing correspondence with his mentor, and in some of the letters, Rabbi Nassan Adler hinted that great accomplishments awaited him. Rabbi Moshe's fame spread far and wide, and various communities invited him to be their rabbi, but he declined all such offers. A community rabbi would be distracted by the myriad affairs and demands of the community, which would seriously encroach on his Torah study.

Rabbi Moshe's total absorption in Torah rendered him oblivious to some subtle changes that the community noted in the demeanor of their benefactor, Reb Hirsh. An uncharacteristic frugality began to be apparent in Reb Hirsh, and eventually the changes were no longer subtle.

Reb Hirsh's business affairs had begun to fail. He had bought forests at a high price, and the price of lumber fell precipitously. He began to sell off his assets to keep afloat, but never diminished his support of Rabbi Moshe. It was not until one Friday night, when Rabbi Moshe's wife did not wear her bejeweled headpiece, that he found out that she had given it to her brother to sell.

Rabbi Moshe then met with his brother-in-law, who revealed the sad state of affairs, which appeared all but hopeless. As if anticipating Rabbi Moshe's question, Reb Hirsh said, "I want you to know that your dowry remained untouched. When you married my sister, I invested your dowry, and it has since grown to a significant sum."

Rabbi Moshe asked, "Then why did you sell all your assets? You could have used this money to pay your debts."

Reb Hirsh was shocked. "Is that what you think of me, that I would take someone else's money for my own use?"

Rabbi Moshe asked for some time to think things over, and then said to his brother-in-law, "I fear that your financial reversals may be due to my dereliction.

"I have received several offers to assume a position as a rabbi. I declined these because they would divert me from total Torah study, and I could afford to decline them because you were in a position to support me.

"My teacher, Rabbi Nassan Adler, has repeatedly indicated that there were things that awaited my attention, but I was reluctant to accept these hints as a directive that I am to begin functioning as a rabbi rather than to be a full-time scholar.

"There is no more blissful time in a person's life than when he is in his mother's womb, where all his needs are taken care of, and where he develops into a complete human being. There comes a time when this blissful existence must come to an end, and when G-d knows that the infant is sufficiently developed, he is expelled from the

womb into a world which may sometimes be hostile, but even if tolerable or comfortable, can never equal the peace of his intrauterine existence. Nevertheless, his time has come to be in the real world.

"I failed to realize that my master's directives were a Divine message to me."

"When the prophet Jonah refused to fulfill his assignment, a fierce storm threatened to sink the ship he was in. Jonah then said, 'Throw me overboard. I know that the storm is due to my dereliction in obeying G-d's will.'

"I, too, must realize that it is the Divine will that I accept the duties of a rabbi. Your financial reversals, which now make it impossible for you to support me any longer, is the way G-d has chosen to force me to overcome my reluctance, and to accept a rabbinical position.

"Once I have done so, you will prosper again. Take the money of my dowry, and begin your business anew."

Rabbi Moshe then accepted the first of his rabbinical positions. In each community he served he developed a yeshivah, and produced a generation of great Torah scholars. He received halachic questions from all corners of the earth, and his responsa constitutes a treasury of halachic principles. This was the era of the enlightenment, when secular Jews began a movement to deviate from traditional Judaism. Rabbi Moshe fought vigorously to uphold the observance of Torah.

It is not an overstatement that much of the credit for the existence of Torah study and traditional Jewish observance today can be attributed to the untiring efforts of this single individual, who fulfilled all the aspects of the Torah hierarchy: to listen, to learn, to teach, to guard, to perform, and to perpetuate.

Nuggets

The Chofetz Chaim traveled from town to town to sell his book on lashon hara. One time he was forced by bad weather to remain in a village for Shabbos. He entered the beis midrash, where he sat in a corner, studying Torah unobtrusively. No one bothered to notice the stranger.

After services Friday night, one of the worshipers invited the stranger for the Shabbos meal. The Chofetz Chaim whispered to him, "I am the author of the book, Chofetz Chaim."

The man reacted with surprise. "Why did you not tell us who you were earlier?" he asked.

The Chofetz Chaim said, "There was no purpose in my doing so. But now that you have invited me to eat with *you, I felt I had to tell you who I am, so that if your observance of kashrus is not meticulous, you would not invite me.*

"We must take our cues from the Torah," the Chofetz Chaim said. "When Eliezer came to take Rivkah as a wife for Isaac, the Torah states, 'Food was set before him ... then he said, "I am a servant of Abraham" ' (Genesis 24:33-34). Now that they were serving him food, he had to say who he was, so that they would respect his kashrus specifications."

The specifications of the Chofetz Chaim were indeed rigorous.

T he Chofetz Chaim was once at an inn, and asked for a milchig salt shaker. He was given a salt shaker which was parve.

"What does parve mean?" the Chofetz Chaim asked.

"It means it is neither milk nor meat," the innkeeper said.

The Chofetz Chaim smiled. *"Not quite," he said. "In this case, parve means it is both meat and milk. It is handled at meals where each is served, and it is possible that food particles from each meal may stick to it, so that it can be both meat and milk."*

We can easily understand why it was necessary for the Chofetz Chaim to reveal his identity.

R abbi Shmuel Salant was consulted by a man who said, *"My son emigrated to America, and has abandoned his religious observance. He sends me money, but I do not feel it is right to use money that was earned by his working on Shabbos, and I wish to return the money to him."*

Rabbi Shmuel said, "The Midrash tells us that when Jacob left home, Esau sent his son, Elifaz, after him to kill him. When Jacob pleaded for his life, Elifaz said, 'What can I do about my father's instructions?' Jacob then said, 'Here, take everything I have. A poor person is as good as dead, and you can truthfully report to your father that you carried out his will.'"

Rabbi Shmuel continued, "Why did Jacob not try to impress Elifaz that it is forbidden to kill? It is because he saw that Elifaz wished to observe the mitzvah of obeying his father's wishes, and Jacob did not wish to deprive him of that mitzvah.

"It is unfortunate that your son is not observing Torah. However, he has the one mitzvah that he is caring for his father. Is it fair to deprive him of this?"

⇝⇜

Today it is not uncommon for people to put on a second pair of *tefillin* after the morning services, in keeping with the opinion of Rabbeinu Tam, that the sequence of the Torah portions contained in the *tefillin* is somewhat different than that which is accepted as the *halachah*. In the past, however, this was apparently less common, since the *Shulchan Aruch* states that the Rabbeinu Tam *tefillin* should be used only by those who are advanced in their spirituality (*Orach Chaim* 34.3).

The great chassidic master, Rabbi Elimelech of Lizhensk, regularly used Rabbeinu Tam tefillin, and his students were therefore perplexed when he abruptly discontinued this practice for a period of time. When he later resumed the use of Rabbeinu Tam tefillin, he explained to his students:

"One day I was unusually exhausted, having been be-

sieged all day by supplicants with a myriad of problems. I barely had time to eat, because I had not devoted enough time to Torah study that day. I finally went to sleep at 3 A.M., and no sooner had I fallen asleep than I was woken by a loud knocking at the door. A man had come to plead with me to pray for his daughter, who was having a difficult labor, and the midwife was in doubt whether either the mother or infant would survive. I was initially upset, because I was extremely weary after so difficult a day, and here I could not even get the few moments of sleep that I needed so desperately. Nevertheless, I gave the man my blessing, and then began to recite Tehillim (Psalms) to pray for the young woman.

"As I returned to bed, I began thinking, 'If that young woman were my own daughter who was in mortal danger, and someone had alerted me to this so that I would pray for her, would I have been irritated with this person? Of course not! To the contrary, I would have been most grateful to have been notified, so that I could pray for her.' In other words, I was discriminating between my daughter and someone else's daughter. That is hardly being spiritual. I therefore decided that I was not deserving of putting on Rabbeinu Tam tefillin."

Inasmuch as Rabbi Elimelech did resume use of Rabbeinu Tam *tefillin*, we must conclude that subsequently he had advanced spiritually to the point where someone else's child was as dear to him as his own!

When we refer to these spiritual giants, we are obviously talking about people whose character development was of a level of perfection that is beyond our reach. Yet they should serve as models for us, because if we reach for the stars, then we may at least grasp a tiny piece of sky. If we reach only for that which is within our physical grasp, we may come up with only a handful of dust.

Like the Sun at Its Mightiest

To be able to swallow one's pride and remain silent when offended is considered by the Talmud to be one of the most admirable traits a person can have. People who achieve this trait are considered those who truly love G-d, and are "like the sun at its mightiest" (*Shabbos* 88b).

Reacting to an insult by responding in kind intensifies one's resentment toward the offender, and hostile feelings may become deeply ingrained. It is obviously impossible to love someone whom you resent. Yet, the Baal Shem Tov said that love of G-d is achieved through *ahavas Yisrael*, love of other Jews. One must therefore avoid resentment of others if one wishes to truly love G-d.

There are many stories about how *tzaddikim* strove to eradicate every remnant of resentment against others. I recall times when I knew my father had been hurt by someone, and he would say, "I cannot be angry at him. What he said was foolish, and I must feel sorry for him for not having more sense and better judgment. How could I be angry at someone when I feel sorry for him?"

Rabbi Yom Tov Lipman Heller, author of the Commentary *Tosafos Yom Tov on the Mishnah*, was Rabbi of Prague. Collections of the taxes which the government imposed upon the community was in the hands of the most affluent citizens. Then, as now, the wealthy sought exemption from taxation, and inasmuch as there was a fixed amount which the Jewish community had to submit, the burden fell heavily on those who earned less. Rabbi Heller sought to rectify this injustice, and alleviate the burden on the poor by insisting that the wealthy pay their fair share. This aroused the enmity of the latter against him.

O*ne of the wealthy citizens, a man named Raphael, who had once been one of Rabbi Heller's supporters but now turned against him, sought to retaliate against the Rabbi, and tried to use his influence to unseat him from the rabbinate. When this failed, he had someone translate one of Rabbi Heller's writings, and intentionally distort what Rabbi Heller said to constitute revolutionary, anti-government rhetoric. He then submitted this to the authorities, accusing Rabbi Heller of inciting revolution. The government, always sensitive to revolutionary rhetoric and not being great lovers of Jews, promptly arrested Rabbi Heller. Raphael's intention had only been to rid Prague of the principled Rabbi, assuming that the government would depose or deport him, but he had not considered the possibility that an accusation of treason could lead to the death penalty.*

Fortunately, Rabbi Heller's son had been instrumental in saving the child of the French ambassador from a near fatal accident, and had come into the good graces of this French official. He was therefore able to exert political influence to get his father's sentence commuted to a fine, and obtain his release from prison.

Not too long after this, Raphael fell gravely ill. Rabbi Heller wished to visit him, but was concerned that Raphael would misinterpret the visit as the Rabbi's gloating over his misery. The Rabbi was therefore delighted when Raphael sent a messenger requesting the Rabbi to visit him.

Upon entering the sick room, Rabbi Heller found Raphael to be in severe distress. "Holy Rabbi," Raphael wept, "have mercy on me and pray for me. I was guilty in accusing you falsely. I admit my guilt, but even when I sought to depose you, I never thought it would lead to such grave consequences.

"I know that my illness is a Divine punishment for my having harmed you. I am ready to accept death for my sin, but I wish to ask your forgiveness."

Rabbi Heller wept along with Raphael. "I forgive you with my whole heart. Not only do I forgive you now, but even when I was imprisoned I forgave you. I remembered your friendship of yore, and I knew that it was only the yetzer hara that had incited you to act so foolishly. I will pray intensely for your recovery." Rabbi Heller's prayers were not turned away, and Raphael recovered.

Accepting an insult in silence is one of the techniques that can prevent vanity. Inasmuch as the Talmud cites humility as being the finest virtue and vanity as being the most despicable vice, it is little wonder that our *tzaddikim* often turned a deaf ear to those who slighted them. Nevertheless, the extent to which they went to avoid vanity is sometimes beyond belief. Citing these accounts should at least arouse us to appreciate the importance of humility, and how we must avoid vanity at all costs.

Rabbi Yosef of Prague was married to the daughter of the outstanding Torah authority, Rabbi Yechezkel Landau, known for his epochal work, *Noda BeYehudah*. This prominent scholar showed great respect for his son-in-law, yet his daughter would often publicly berate her husband. Often, when he was in the company of prominent citizens, she would enter the room and shout at him, "Who do you think you are, giving advice to people? You are nothing but an ignoramus! Why do you mislead people to think you are wise and learned?" Rabbi Yosef never reacted to her diatribes.

When Rabbi Yosef died, and the community gathered to accord him the final honor, his wife arose and weepingly declared:

"My holy husband! Only you know the truth, and I wish you to testify on my behalf before all the community.

"Before we were married, you told me that you were in mortal fear that your Torah scholarship and position of leadership might cause you to fall into the clutches of the *yetzer hara* and become vain. You then made me promise that when I would see you in the company of other people, I would berate you and humiliate you. Since this was your wish, I reluctantly acquiesced. As G-d is my witness, no one else on earth appreciated your holiness and saintliness as I did."

It would be sufficient if this story ended here, but it continues with the amazing statement that those who stood near Rabbi Yosef saw him nod his head, in testimony to his wife's words.

Shall we believe that a dead man can move his head? As we have noted, the factual accuracy of such stories is not important. We must remember that such stories are not told about you or me. We cannot hear stories such as this without being impressed with how far one must go to avoid being tainted by vanity.

What Life Is All About

A s I mentioned earlier, stories whose authenticity I can vouch for have special value for me. The following story was told to me by my grandmother, who heard it personally from "Baba Beilish," who was an eyewitness to the episode.

Baba Beilish was the daughter of Rabbi Eliezer of Zhikov, who was a son of the great chassidic master, Rabbi Naftali of Ropschitz. She was married to Rabbi Meir Nossan, a son of the *tzaddik* of Sanz. Baba Beilish was widowed at a young age and never remarried. She lived to a ripe old age and related many stories to my grandmother.

We must be aware that our *tzaddikim* had a perspective on life that was quite different than our own. We each have our respective goals, many of which involve personal interests. Our *tzaddikim* had one goal and one goal only, to fulfill the purpose for which they were created, which was to bring greater glory to G-d. Everything in their lives was directed to this purpose. Although we may verbalize this attitude prior to doing a *mitzvah*, by reciting the *brachah* and perhaps also adding a declaration of intent, it is too often only a verbal expression, but lacks the fervor of absolute dedication to G-d. Our *tzaddikim* had that fervor.

B*aba Beilish related that she was present when her father-in-law, the tzaddik of Sanz, came to visit her father, who had fallen gravely ill. She overheard the following conversation.*

Rabbi Eliezer of Zhikov beseeched, "My dear mechutan. Pray for my recovery."

The Sanzer Tzaddik replied, "Why do you wish to remain on this lowly world when the celestial world is so much more beautiful?"

Rabbi Eliezer responded, "It is indeed beautiful, mechutan, but only for those who have merits to enter it."

"I wish that all Jews would have even half the merits that you have accumulated," the Sanzer Tzaddik retorted.

"But," said Rabbi Eliezer, "you must consider that if I die I will be leaving my family destitute."

"And if you recover, do you have any guarantee you can provide for them? Let me assure you that I will care for their needs," the Sanzer Tzaddik promised.

"But mechutan, when I lead the davening on the high holidays, the heavenly angels rejoice. If I die, who will bring joy to the heavenly court?"

To this the Sanzer Tzaddik replied, "So? Then you must indeed live! And I shall pray for your recovery."

Baba Beilish related that the Sanzer Tzaddik later said, "My prayers were accepted, and you will live." Rabbi Eliezer recovered, and lived for an additional six years.

We are quite familiar with the inherent instinct for survival. With the exception of people who are suicidally depressed, the normal drive is to live. But to some people, as the following story illustrates, there were things that were even more important than living.

My great-grandfather, the Rebbe of Hornosteipel, had a devoted attendant, Reb Dan. When the Rebbe was yet a child, he was wont to asceticism, with fasting and denying himself sleep. His grandfather, the Rebbe of Cherkassy, had assigned Reb Dan, who was several years the child's senior, to act as the latter's "big brother," and to make sure that he received adequate food and rest.

One night Reb Dan awoke after midnight, and he saw his young ward sitting on the floor, reciting tikun chatzos, the prayers of mourning for the fallen glory of Jerusalem, and shedding profuse tears for the suffering of the Shechinah, the Divine Presence, which had gone into exile along with the children of Israel.

Reb Dan warned his young ward that it was his duty to report this to the child's grandfather, because he had been charged with the responsibility to see that he received adequate rest. The youngster pleaded with Reb Dan not to expose his secret to his grandfather, whereupon Reb Dan said, "I will keep your secret on one condition. You must promise me that when you become Rebbe, you will take me as your attendant."

"What makes you think I will be Rebbe?" the child asked.

"I can foresee it," Reb Dan answered.

Reb Dan elicited the desired promise, and did not reveal

the secret until the Rebbe's death some 50 years later. Reb Dan served as a faithful and devoted attendant, never leaving the Rebbe's side.

After the Rebbe's burial, the village rabbi, known as "Yankel, the Rabbi," announced that the coveted place of honor, the grave adjacent to that of the Rebbe, was due him inasmuch as he was rabbi of the village. Reb Dan protested, saying that just as he had never separated himself from the Rebbe during his lifetime, he deserved not to be separated from him in death.

The dispute was brought before my grandfather, who by then had moved from Hornosteipel to Kiev. Grandfather's decision was to let the issue be decided by the Almighty, i.e., whichever of the two died first was to be buried next to the Rebbe.

Father said that whenever Yankel, the Rabbi, took ill, Reb Dan would panic. He would insist that they bring the most renowned specialists to treat him, and he would go to the synagogues to urge everyone to pray for Yankel's recovery. The thought that Yankel might predecease him and win the coveted burial place was intolerable. Conversely, if Reb Dan took sick, Yankel carried on in a similar manner.

Father would say, "Look at what some people begrudge and envy. These people had no greed for physical belongings. Their aspiration was to die first so that they would merit being near the Rebbe. They would gladly have given up years of life in order to have the burial place near the Rebbe."

Perhaps human nature has not changed. There was envy then, and there is envy now. Perhaps there is envy among all people. But the object of one's envy indicates how different the capacities of spiritual people are.

54
The Secret Ingredient

This story should be familiar to anyone raised in a traditional Jewish home. While leading a spiritual life requires avoiding overindulging in physical pleasures, there is one outstanding exception: The foods for Shabbos are to be prepared in the finest manner possible, providing gustatory delights. Shabbos is referred to as the "Queen," and it is only proper that one prepare the finest delicacies when one is hosting a royal personage. Similarly, when there is a *seudas mitzvah*, a feast which celebrates performance of a *mitzvah*, such as a *bris* (circumcision) or a *pidyon haben* (redemption of the first born), the foods should reflect the great value which one accords the *mitzvah*.

There are few childhood memories that equal that of the aroma in the home Friday morning. In the days before everything was available as "ready to eat, just defrost" or "take out," all the Shabbos food was prepared at home. The fragrance of freshly baked *challah* is in itself enchanting, as is that of the gefilte fish cooking on the stove. But put those two aromas together, and you have something truly exquisite. Add to these the scent of the baking *kugel,* whether sweet or peppery, and you have a delight which is unparalleled in the finest gourmet restaurants.

There is a certain mystique to this, because if any of these dishes were prepared, say Tuesday, for weekday consumption, it would not be the same. This is substantiated by the Talmud, which states that the emperor once asked Rabbi Yehoshua why the Shabbos foods have a unique aroma, and the rabbi answered, "Because we have a special spice, which is called Shabbos" (*Shabbos* 119a). It is the Shabbos itself which is the magic ingredient. This is also true of *mitzvah* celebrations, wherein the *mitzvah* provides the special flavor.

Toward the end of his life, Rabbi Elimelech of Lizhensk ate very little, and even the entreaties of his friends and relatives had little effect. One time, when his son, Rabbi Elazar, pleaded with him to eat enough to sustain life, Rabbi Elimelech said, "I wish I could eat, but my body rejects all things physical. Ah! One time, during my years of wandering in exile, I lodged at an inn near a certain village, and there I ate a delicious soup. If that were available, I could eat it. But that is so far away!"

Many years later, Rabbi Elazar happened to be in that village, and sought out the inn to which his father had referred. He asked the hostess whether he might have some of her special soup, and she said, "How I wish I could serve you the food that is appropriate for a great tzaddik like yourself. But we are very poor. Very few travelers pass this *way, and we just have enough flour and beans to eat for our meals. I will be glad to make a bean soup for you."*

When Rabbi Elazar tasted the soup, he experienced a spiritual delight, as though he were eating of the offerings of the Altar in the Temple in Jerusalem. He asked the hostess, "Please tell me, what ingredients do you use for this soup?"

The woman began crying. "I am so sorry that it is so meager. I do not have any spices to put in. All I did was cook the beans with water, and then I prayed to G-d: 'Master of the Universe! You have provided me with the mitzvah of preparing a meal for a great tzaddik. If only I had meat, vegetables, and spices, I would prepare a meal for him that would befit him, but I have nothing. But You, Master of the Universe, have everything. You have Gan Eden (Paradise), where there are all the finest scents and flavors. Please put some of these in the soup, so that my holy guest can enjoy his food."

Rabbi Elazar said, "Now I know why my father longed for this soup. This pious woman's sincere prayers were answered, and the soup did indeed have the taste of Gan Eden."

Perhaps we cannot elicit the same taste of *Gan Eden* as this pious woman did, but when our mothers prepared the Shabbos foods, with their silent — and sometimes spoken — prayers that they be befitting for welcoming the Shabbos Queen, they too added a magic ingredient. Little wonder that they had so exquisite a taste!

Forgiveness

E ven a great *tzaddik* may not be able to totally separate
from his humanity. It is related that the *Maggid* of
Mezeritch, who was the chief disciple of and successor
to the Baal Shem Tov, was tormented by his having
once doubted his master. The incident was as follows.

O ne *Shabbos at Shalosh Seudos the Baal Shem Tov*
was expounding the most profound concealed
meanings of the Torah, while in the outer room the simple
folk who were rather unlearned and were unable to grasp
these spiritual concepts were reciting Tehillim. The Maggid

reflected, "How fortunate I am to have been a student of Torah, to be able to understand these lofty celestial teachings of the master. How unfortunate those simple folk are, who are not privileged to understand these teachings. I wonder why the master shows such great favor to these simple folk, who cannot appreciate his teachings."

Abruptly the Baal Shem Tov interrupted his discourse, and instructed his disciples to place their hands on their neighbors' shoulders and close their eyes. The Baal Shem Tov then placed his hands on the shoulders of those adjacent to him, thus completing the circle. The disciples felt themselves being transported to heaven, where they heard voices — that were nothing less than angelic — singing the praise of G-d. One sweet voice said, "My soul thirsts for You, and my flesh pines for You" (Psalms 63:2), and another chanted, "Like a hart that craves a spring of water, that is how my soul craves You, O G-d" (Psalms 42:2). The sweetness and devotion of these songs brought tears to the eyes of the disciples, and the Maggid thought, "If only even once in my lifetime I could chant the Psalms with such devotion, how fortunate I would be."

The Baal Shem Tov then told his disciples to open their eyes and said, "The beautiful chanting that you heard was not of the heavenly angels, but of those simple folk in the outer room who are reciting Psalms with total devotion to G-d." The Maggid said that he was unable to forgive himself for having questioned why the Baal Shem Tov so valued the simple, unlearned folk. For years he was full of remorse for having doubted the master's judgment.

⁊⊱

One night the Maggid had a dream that he was in Gan Eden, and saw that Moses was teaching Torah to some children. When they came to the portion in

Genesis where G-d promised the land of Canaan to the pa-triarch Abraham for his descendants, and Abraham asked G-d, "How can I be certain that I will inherit the land?", the children asked, "How is it possible that the patriarch Abraham had the least doubt of G-d's promise, and asked for a sign as reassurance?" Moses said, "The patriarch Abraham was indeed pure and holy, yet he inhabited a physical human body, and even the purest human can be cast into doubting by his physical body." It was only then that the Maggid was able to forgive himself for having doubted the judgment of the Baal Shem Tov.

Similarly, even the purest and holiest of humans is neverthe-less human, and a person must learn to forgive himself when it is appropriate to do so.

A man once came to a tzaddik and complained that he had not been able to find peace of mind. Many years earlier he had committed a sin, and although he had fasted and prayed for forgiveness, and several Yom Kippurs had passed, he still was unable to divest himself of a feel-ing of guilt.

The tzaddik asked, "Have you forgiven others who of-fended you?"

"Of course," the man answered.

"And your forgiveness was so complete that not a speck of resentment remains with you?" the tzaddik asked.

The man's eyes turned downward, and in a soft under-tone he said, "I cannot truthfully say that."

"That is where the problem lies, my son," the tzaddik said. "You must have an experience of total forgiveness to be able to accept the concept. If you have not been able to feel total forgiveness toward others, you cannot relate

it toward yourself either. You must devote yourself to perfecting your forgiveness of others.

"I now understand a very difficult passage of the Talmud," the tzaddik said. "The Torah states that on Rosh Chodesh, the Jews are to bring a 'sin offering for G-d' (Numbers 28:15).

"The Talmud quotes G-d as saying, 'Bring a sin offering for Me, for My having reduced the size of the moon' (Chullin 60b). How are we to understand this? G-d can do no wrong, and He cannot possibly sin. In what way could He need forgiveness?

"But we frequently find that the Torah refers to G-d in anthropomorphic terms that help us understand His relationship to us, as when it speaks about the 'mercy' of G-d or His 'compassion.' Clearly we cannot ascribe emotions to G-d, but these terms are used so that we can have some notion of how He relates to us.

"So it is with the concept of G-d asking for forgiveness. Forgiveness is a two-way affair. One can only forgive oneself if one forgives others, and conversely, one can only forgive others if one can thoroughly forgive oneself. Inasmuch as G-d wishes us to know that He forgives us when we have done proper teshuvah, He tells us that He has experienced forgiveness Himself, so that we can feel reassured of His forgiveness of our transgressions."

We cannot rationalize our errant behavior on the basis that we are human and therefore prone to sin. We have been given the tools to enable us to withstand the *yetzer hara.* But if in a moment of weakness we have acted foolishly and succumbed to temptation, and we have done sincere *teshuvah,* we should be able to accept Divine forgiveness. Indeed, this is why we say in the prayer *Avinu Malkenu,* "Remember that we are but flesh."

56

A Veritable
Aishes Chayil

Chronicles of our great Torah personalities are lacking in accounts of the many highly spiritual women that contributed so much to Jewish life. This is because their *tznius* (modesty) precluded their being observed by others. The few accounts which we do have were provided by either their husbands and children or by people who worked in their homes.

The chassidic master, Rabbi Sholom of Belz, attributed his scholarship in Torah to his wife's urging him to arise in the wee hours of the morning to learn, even

though he did not retire until after he had c____ the
midnight services. She would awaken h___ ___ay,
"Sholom, I can see a light in the tailor's shop, a____ ee
a light in the bakery. If the tailor and baker c____ o
early to their work, then you must arise early to

≈)≈

O ne time a woman came to ask the Rabbi of
pray for her health. She had developed
swelling of her legs which had not improved with me
treatment. The Rabbi's study was so crowded that she c
not gain entrance, and she went to the Rabbi's wife, ask
her to carry her plea to her husband. The Rebbetzin sa
"Add on an additional candle to the Shabbos lights, and yo
will be healed." Weeks later, the woman told the Rabbi how
she had recovered thanks to the Rebbetzin's instructions.

"What gave you the idea that adding to the Shabbos
lights would bring about healing?" the Rabbi asked his wife.

"Quite simple," she responded. "It states in Tehillim
(Psalms 119:105), 'Your word (of Torah) is a lamp for my
feet.' Since we know that Torah can heal, I reasoned that
adding lights of holiness would bring healing to her feet."

≈)≈

T he tzaddik of Sanz was a student of Rabbi Sholom,
and one time he took his son, Rabbi Baruch, along
with him. As they left, the tzaddik asked Rabbi Baruch,
"What was your impression of the Rabbi and Rebbetzin?"
Rabbi Baruch answered, "They appeared to me as pure
as Adam and Eve in Gan Eden before they sinned, total
holiness." The tzaddik of Sanz remarked, "Ah! You have
a discerning vision."

≈)≈

Rabbi Sholom built his synagogue in Belz, and not only supervised every bit of construction, but also laid some of the bricks himself. He said that one night a saintly person appeared to him and taught him the intricate laws regarding the holiness of a synagogue. "With this knowledge, I only wish that I could build the entire structure myself, from the foundation to the final shingle of the roof." Prior to completion of the synagogue, Rabbi Sholom became blind, and his wife would guide his hands so that he could continue to personally participate in its construction.

⪚⪙

The Rebbetzin predeceased Rabbi Sholom, and he was inconsolable. In the eulogy he referred to her with all the endearing terms found in the Song of Songs: "My dove, my perfect mate, my sister, my partner in building the holy synagogue." When the tzaddik of Sanz came to see Rabbi Sholom after the thirty days of mourning were over, he found him weeping as though it were the first day of the shivah. The tzaddik asked, "My teacher, is it permissible to continue to mourn so bitterly?"

"I am weeping for the greater spirituality I could have achieved if she had lived on. We were one soul, and together we absorbed the spirit of chassidus. Together we built the holy Sanctuary."

Rabbi Sholom paused to catch his breath, then continued. "When I cry for the wife of my youth, I say to G-d, 'If only I had the capability to restore her to life, nothing would stand in my way. But I am a frail human being, so powerless and helpless. But You, O G-d, are all powerful. We are Your chosen people, we are the wife of Your youth. We have been buried by repeated persecutions, and it is *well within Your ability to restore us to life, to the glory of our youth. You can resurrect us, with the Redemption of Mashiach. Why do You not do so?'*

"And G-d said to me, 'If My people were as totally devoted to Me as your wife was to you, I would indeed bring about their redemption promptly.' " And with this, Rabbi Sholom wept even more, but this time not for the loss of his beloved wife, but for the downtrodden state of his people, whose elevation to glory lies in their hands, and they fail to take advantage of it.

57

Nothing New Beneath the Sun

The wise King Solomon said it all: "Whatever has been is what will be, and whatever has been done is what will be done. There is nothing new beneath the sun" (*Ecclesiastes* 1:9). Many people today avoid litigation, often sustaining a loss rather than becoming involved in a costly court case. This was true in ancient times, although for different reasons.

One of the chassidic masters was once confronted by a person who claimed he owed him money, although he had never borrowed from him and never had any transaction with him in any way. This person said he was going to call the tzaddik to a din Torah (judgment in a rabbinic court), and although the claim was frivolous, the tzaddik pawned everything he owned and paid the claim. When asked why he did so, he responded, "The Talmud instructs the judges, 'When the litigants stand before you, consider them both as resha'im (guilty).' (Ethics of the Fathers 1:8). I did not want to be considered a rasha even for a moment."

One Torah scholar gave yet another reason. In the Jewish communities in Europe, the butcher would buy an animal, have it slaughtered by the *shochet,* and then the internal organs would be inspected for lesions. If a lesion were found, the rabbi would be consulted to determine if the animal was kosher. If the animal was found to be *treifah,* this would be a severe financial loss to the butcher, since he would have to sell the meat at a loss.

O*ne time a rabbi was consulted by the shochet because of a questionable lesion that had been discovered in the lungs. The rabbi studied it carefully, and realized that the halachic authorities disagreed as to whether such a lesion was kosher or treifah. The prevailing practice in this community had been to accept the more restrictive opinion, and everyone was therefore surprised when the rabbi ruled the lesion was kosher, according to the more permissive opinion.*

The rabbi explained, "When I come before the Heavenly Tribunal on Judgment Day, the great halachic authority, the Shach, who considered this lesion to be non-kosher, will call me to ask as to why I disregarded his opinion. I will then cite all the other halachic authorities who considered it kosher. I will feel proud that I had an opportunity to engage in a halachic argument with the great Shach. But if I had ruled it treifah, and I would be confronted by the wife and young children of the butcher, who would demand an explanation why I deprived them of food and clothes, I might indeed be able to invoke the opinion of the Shach in my favor, but I would much rather go to trial with the great Shach as the opposing litigant rather than with a tearful mother and her children."

Yet others avoided any litigation for fear that they would be required to take an oath, and the fear of swearing was so great that they were willing to forego any amount of money to be spared taking an oath.

My father told me the story of Rabbi Chajkel, who shared the community leadership with Rabbi Azriel, the dayan. (Many communities had a dayan, or magistrate, whose function was to be the judge or arbitrator in various disputes or litigations.) The two rabbis were close friends, and frequently studied Torah together.

One time Rabbi Azriel was in Rabbi Chajkel's study, when a woman came in and asked Rabbi Chajkel to hold in safekeeping 500 rubles for her. She was leaving town for a few days, and had no one else to whom she could entrust the money.

Later that day, Rabbi Chajkel tried to locate the money but could not find it. He searched all the drawers and cabinets in his study and went through the pockets of all his garments, but to no avail. The money was gone.

With a heavy heart, Rabbi Chajkel went to Rabbi Azriel's home. He asked him whether he had perhaps noticed what he had done with the money which the *woman gave him. Rabbi Azriel said that he had not seen him do anything with the money, and that to the best of his recollection, it had remained on the desk.*

Rabbi Chajkel sighed deeply, "The money is gone, Reb Azriel," he said. "I have searched everywhere. You and I were the only two people present. I know this sounds absurd, Reb Azriel, but this money was entrusted to me, and although you are beyond suspicion, I am obligated by halachah to request that you take an oath that you did not take it."

Rabbi Azriel was shaken. "Take an oath, Reb Chajkel?" he asked. "I should swear? Can you give me just a bit of time to give this some thought?"

"Of course," Rabbi Chajkel answered and left Rabbi Azriel's study.

That evening Rabbi Azriel came to Rabbi Chajkel. "Here are 275 rubles," he said. "That is all I have."

Rabbi Chajkel was upset. He knew that Rabbi Azriel's earnings were very meager, and that he did not own 275 rubles. What was the meaning of this? He knew that Rabbi Azriel was under great pressure to provide a dowry for his daughter who was soon to marry. Could it be that Rabbi Azriel had been unable to resist the temptation, and that confronted with the possible cancellation of the wedding if he failed to provide a dowry, Rabbi Azriel had weakened and taken the money? That was absurd! But how else would he explain Rabbi Azriel's having a sum so large as 275 rubles?

"I cannot compromise," Rabbi Chajkel said. "If I do not have the 500 rubles to return to the woman, I must demand that you swear."

"Give me one more day," Rabbi Azriel pleaded.

The following day, Rabbi Azriel returned and gave Rabbi Chajkel an additional 125 rubles. "This is all I have," he said.

Rabbi Chajkel was stern. He was now convinced that Rabbi Azriel had succumbed to the stress of his daughter's wedding needs and had indeed taken the money. Not, God forbid, with an intent to steal, but just to borrow it for a few weeks until after the wedding, when he would somehow repay it. For how else would the impoverished Rabbi Azriel have gotten 400 rubles in two days?

"500 rubles, Reb Azriel," said Rabbi Chajkel. "Not one kopek less."

"Here is a promissory note to the woman for 100 rubles," said Rabbi Azriel. "I will pay it within 30 days. More I cannot do."

"Good enough," said Rabbi Chajkel. "I shall prevail upon the woman to accept your note."

The next few days, when Rabbi Chajkel met Rabbi Azriel, he looked away. If he saw him coming from afar, he tried to avoid meeting him. He could not make peace with the thought that his trusted chaver (close friend) had yielded to temptation and had taken something belonging to another.

Friday afternoon, Rabbi Chajkel was preparing his study for Shabbos. The Mizrach plaque (a decorative plaque designating which direction was east, so that anyone praying in that room would know which direction to face toward Jerusalem) was hanging crooked, and as he lifted it to hang it straight, the bundle of 500 rubles fell out! Rabbi Chajkel suddenly recalled that he had hidden the money there. He emitted a loud shriek and fell to the ground in a faint.

Rabbi Chajkel's family, hearing the loud cry, came running and revived him. As he came to, he tore at his beard and wept uncontrollably. "What have I done!" he cried. "I falsely accused a tzaddik of a terrible crime! How could I ever have done such a thing! I have sinned against an innocent man and against God!" Nothing his family could say would console him.

In the midst of his weeping and self-flagellation, Rabbi Chajkel said, "I must go to the tzaddik, Reb Azriel. I must ask his forgiveness. He may spit at me and throw me out of his house, the rotten cur that I am! How I have caused him to suffer needlessly!"

Rabbi Chajkel ran to Rabbi Azriel's home. Breathlessly he threw open the door. "Reb Azriel, forgive me!" he cried. "I know I am unworthy of your forgiveness, but as a God-fearing person, I ask you to do as Almighty God does, and forgive the most despicable sinners when they repent their sins!"

Rabbi Azriel's wife came in. "Rabbi Chajkel," she said, "why do you shout? Reb Azriel is not in the house. He has left to shul already."

Rabbi Chajkel ran out and hurried to the shul. A small crowd had already gathered for Minchah. He ran to the pulpit and pounded on the pulpit for attention.

"Hear me, good people," he cried. "Hear me, Reb Azriel the tzaddik. For 20 years I have been your Rabbi, but I do not deserve to be your Rabbi. I have sinned against an innocent man. I have falsely accused a tzaddik of a grave crime. I am not worthy for the earth to support me." The tears flowed freely down his cheeks. He turned and ran to the aron hakodesh (the ark containing the Torah), threw open its doors, and shouted, "Only You, God, can forgive me!"

Rabbi Azriel came up and put his arm around his chaver. "Calm down, Reb Chajkel," he pleaded. "Please, calm yourself. I would gladly forgive you wholeheartedly if there was something which required forgiveness. But what is there to forgive, Reb Chajkel? You have done nothing wrong."

"Nothing wrong?" asked Rabbi Chajkel. "Nothing wrong to accuse my bosom friend, a true tzaddik, of so menial an act? You mock at me, Reb Azriel. Yes, you mock at *me. But I deserve it, and much more. Whatever you wish to do to me, Reb Azriel, I accept, to my great shame."*

"Heaven forbid that I mock at you, Reb Chajkel," said Rabbi Azriel. "You had no other course. There was no one else in the room but you and me, and when you could not locate the money, you had not choice but to conclude that I took it, and to demand that I swear my innocence.

"When I heard that I must swear," Rabbi Azriel continued, "I shuddered. Never in my life have I taken an oath. I therefore took the 250 rubles that I had borrowed for my daughter's wedding, and sold my wife's jewelry for another 25 rubles.

"When you told me that this was not enough," Rabbi Azriel continued, "I sold my library for 125 rubles. I am so grateful, Reb Chajkel, that you took the promissory note for 100 rubles. I am so grateful, for otherwise I do not know what I would have done. I would have been compelled to swear. To swear, even when you know you are swearing the truth, is awesome. You spared me, Reb Chajkel, by accepting my note. I shall never forget this kindness."

For those who truly understand the severity of an oath, no price is too great.

58
Avoiding the Bottomless Pit

The Talmud recognizes the human frailty of insatiability. "A person does not leave this world with even half of his desires being met" (*Koheles Rabbah* 1:32). This is a statement that describes the average person, who is motivated by the acquisitive drive inherent in the human being.

There are, however, people who have achieved a spiritual level where their sole motivation is to fulfill their mission on earth, and money or other material possessions or desires does not interest them. They are truly capable of abiding by the teaching of the sages: "This is the way of Torah: Eat bread with salt, drink water in small measure, and sleep on the ground"

(*Ethics of the Fathers* 6:4). Their needs are few, and even if they can acquire additional earthly goods in a perfectly legitimate way, it does not distract them from their primary mission.

The tzaddik of Apt had originally been rabbi in the community of Kolbasov, and when he was invited to assume the rabbinate of Apt, he requested a much larger salary than the community generally paid the rabbi. However, the community met his demand, and he was welcomed to Apt where he was regarded with the utmost reverence. After several years, he abruptly announced that he was leaving Apt to assume the rabbinate of Yassi, a community which could not provide the salary he was receiving in Apt. The leaders of the community were bewildered. "Why are you leaving us for a position which offers a cut in salary?"

The tzaddik said to them, "Let me tell you why I came to Apt in the first place, and why I demanded a large salary.

"My father, Reb Shmuel, had a brother two years his senior. They were driven from their home at the ages of 10 and 8, respectively, and in their flight they were separated and lost contact with each other. My father grew up in a tiny village and became a teacher in the cheder, barely earning a living wage. His brother, on the other hand, who settled in Apt, went into business and became wealthy.

"My uncle, who was childless, died at a relatively young age, leaving behind a widow. According to Torah law, the widow of a childless man may not remarry if her husband had a surviving brother, unless the latter released her with the ritual of chalitzah. My uncle had told his wife that he had a brother with whom he had lost contact, and the widow was thus in a predicament that she would not be permitted to remarry unless this brother could be located.

"The widow consulted the local rabbi, who sent out letters to the rabbis of all Jewish communities, informing them that a man with this name had died childless, and asking their help in locating his brother, who bore this particular name. The widow was ready to give the brother half of the sizable estate if only she could be released.

"When the letter arrived to my father's village, the local rabbi called him in, inquiring whether he might be the surviving brother. My father recognized his brother's name, and was quite certain that he was indeed the sought-after brother. He told my mother that he must go to Apt to make a positive identification, and that they were in a position to inherit a fortune. My father was penniless, and had to borrow money to make the trip to Apt.

"When my father related all this to my mother, she said, 'Look, you have the rare opportunity of fulfilling the mitzvah of chalitzah, a mitzvah which people wish to avoid because it is associated with tragedy. Furthermore, you will be releasing a woman from bondage. This is a mitzvah which should not be tarnished with personal gain. Go to Apt, and if you are indeed the brother, perform the chalitzah, but do not take a cent from the estate. That which G-d wishes us to have we will have, but a mitzvah should not be performed with any intent other than to fulfill G-d's will. Inasmuch as the desire for wealth is so great, I fear that when confronted with a huge fortune, you may succumb to temptation. Therefore, I wish you to swear, by placing your hand on this siddur, that you will not take any of the money.' My father concurred, and knowing that he had no prospects for repaying the loan, he returned the money he borrowed and set out on the long journey to Apt on foot.

"After some time he arrived at Apt, and after providing the local rabbi with intricate details that established beyond doubt his identity as the missing brother, he performed the chalitzah ritual. The widow then handed my father a purse with money, saying, 'If you wish to receive half the estate, bring your family to Apt.' My father thanked her, and returned the purse to her, saying, 'I took an oath that I would not take even a cent.' The widow, however, said, 'I do not wish to take back this money which is rightfully yours,' and she gave it to the community to be used for local needs.

"At this time, I had not yet been born. My parents' refusal to take the money, so as not to tarnish the mitzvah with any intent of personal gain, merited them with a blessing that they have a child, and I am the child of that mitzvah.

"The money my father refused was therefore my just inheritance, and that is why I specified a large salary from this community. The last payment, however, exhausted the sum my father was to receive. I now wish to move on to another community, where I believe my services are needed, even though I will be taking an appreciable reduction in pay."

Most people would jump at the opportunity to have a promotion with a larger salary, and few, if any, would willingly take a cut in salary when they could earn more. But this would not apply if we were purely motivated by spiritual drives. Perhaps we cannot aspire to the spirituality of the *tzaddik* of Apt, but this should at lease dampen our often insatiable drive for wealth.

Effort Is Essential

There are many differences between Torah knowledge and secular knowledge. In the latter, having the knowledge is all important, and how one acquires the knowledge is irrelevant. It is just the reverse with Torah knowledge, where the factor of overriding importance is the effort one makes in study of Torah rather than the actual accumulation of knowledge.

The Talmud states that prior to the birth of a child, an angel teaches the fetus all of Torah, and then causes him to forget it all prior to emerging into the world. This previous knowledge of Torah serves as a substrate, to facilitate the subsequent acquisition through study. If knowledge of Torah was all that was important, there would be no need for the effort of study, and the angel would allow the child to be born with a wealth of Torah wisdom.

Today, acquisition of Torah knowledge has been made much simpler. We have Torah available to us on audio tapes, which we may listen to while driving our automobiles. We have Torah on CD ROMS and even on videos. These must be seen as helpful adjuncts to Torah study, but cannot take the place of diligent effort. The latter is a vital and integral part of Torah wisdom.

The great Torah scholar, Rabbi Abraham of Sochatchov, was a child prodigy, and the Rabbi of Kotzk once told his father that he was concerned lest the child's intense power of prayer detract from his Torah study.

The Rabbi explained that the young child once had a watch that had stopped working, and he did not know where to have it repaired. He therefore prayed tearfully to Hashem to make the watch work again. When he found his prayers to be effective, he began applying it to his Torah study, and when he came across a difficult passage in the Talmud, instead of exerting himself to gain a better understanding, he would pray to Hashem for enlightenment and he would be shown the meaning of the difficult portion. The Rabbi of Kotzk disapproved of this, saying that Torah knowledge must be acquired by one's own effort rather than by Divine enlightenment.

A similar point was made by Rabbi Aharon of Premishlan, who was a follower of the chassidic master, Rabbi Elimelech of Lizhensk. One of Rabbi Aharon's devotees happened to be in Lizhensk and visited Rabbi Elimelech, who told him, "When you see Rabbi Aharon, tell him that it is inappropriate to be so vain and arrogant."

On his return to Premishlan, the chassid conveyed the message to Rabbi Aharon, who immediately began a soul-searching. "Woe is me," Rabbi Aharon said, "the tzaddik *has discovered my character defects." He then set out to Lizhensk to have Rabbi Elimelech assist him in ridding himself of his vanity.*

Upon arrival in Lizhensk, Rabbi Aharon took up lodging at an inn, intending to spend the Shabbos there, assuming that Rabbi Elimelech would not welcome him. To his surprise, a messenger from Rabbi Elimelech came with an invitation that he spend Shabbos at the master's table.

Friday night, Rabbi Elimelech said, "You are too vain, Rabbi Aharon. It does not befit you to be so vain." This admonition was repeated at the next two meals. After Shabbos was over, Rabbi Aharon asked Rabbi Elimelech to show him in what way he was vain and arrogant.

Rabbi Elimelech said, "The prophet Elijah is sent to tzaddikim to teach them some of the hidden meanings in Torah. Elijah has complained that you have been rejecting him and do not wish to learn from him. How can someone be so vain to reject the prophet Elijah?" Rabbi Elimelech asked.

"So that's it!" Rabbi Aharon said. "I have refused to learn from Elijah in the past, and I will not learn from him in the future. Any Torah knowledge that I acquire is going to be by my own effort, and not as a Divine gift. There is no mitzvah to know Torah, but rather to study Torah. Accepting knowledge from Elijah would eliminate the need to acquire Torah by my own effort, and I insist on doing the latter."

Sometimes we come across a difficult passage of Torah, which challenges our understanding. It is easy to set it aside and go on to something else. We should be aware that mere knowledge of Torah is not sufficient. It is the effort that counts, and when we find ourselves at a loss to understand a portion of Torah, we should redouble our efforts. This is where the study of Torah is a real *mitzvah*.

60

The General
Principle
of Torah

R abbi Akiva said, "Love your neighbor as yourself is the all-encompassing principle of Torah" (*Jerusalem Talmud* 9:4). One of the *mussar* teachers comments that a general principle is one that contains all the detailed items, and no single item can be external to the general principle. Therefore, he argues, every one of the 613 *mitzvos* must be under the general principle of *ahavas Yisrael,* loving a fellow Jew, and the latter must be an integral part of every *mitzvah.* If one has performed any *mitzvah,* but has not thereby improved the quality of his *ahavas Yisrael,* the *mitzvah* is lacking in completion.

This is a somewhat upsetting concept. How often do we do *mitzvos*, with apparently all the trimmings that should make its performance complete, yet we do not feel any increase in our *ahavas Yisrael?* We must come to the inescapable conclusion that we must improve our performance of *mitzvos* so that they do enhance our *ahavas Yisrael.*

We can now understand why our *tzaddikim* were so dedicated to *ahavas Yisrael.* This is not only because it is a *mitzvah* in its own right, but also because it is an integral part of every other *mitzvah.*

The *mitzvah* of sounding the shofar is very special. It is a once-a-year *mitzvah*, which has so many symbolic meanings. The shofar is an arousal call to teshuvah, it is a proclamation of the sovereignty of G-d, and it is a reminder of the total devotion of the patriarch Abraham, who was ready to bring his beloved son Yitzchak as an offering if that was the Divine will. Many people say additional portions of Tehillim before the sounding of the shofar, others read appropriate passages of the Zohar, others immerse themselves in the mikveh, and yet others do all of the above. Rabbi Yeshayah of Kerestier used to seclude himself in his study before the shofar blowing, and one of his chassidim, curious to see how the Rebbe prepared himself for the *mitzvah*, looked through the keyhole. He was surprised to see that the Rebbe was cutting up the cake so that the worshipers could refresh themselves after the long services were over! The Rebbe's concern to satiate the hunger of the worshipers took precedence even over reading from the Zohar. What is the relevance of preparing cake to the *mitzvah* of shofar? The Rebbe was fulfilling the *ahavas Yisrael* component of the *mitzvah*. Sounding the shofar without doing something to make others feel good would be an incomplete *mitzvah*.

Rabbi Yeshayah's hospitality is legendary. The hungry knew that they were always welcome for a meal, and not only were they served to satiation, but the Rebbe and his wife often personally served the food. When Rabbi Yeshayah died, thousands came to his funeral, and he was eulogized by prominent rabbis. At one point the local post-master arose and said, "All of you who have come from far away to pay your respects to Father Shyka (which is how the local non-Jewish residents referred to the Rebbe) have no idea who he really was. I personally handled his mail, and can tell you that he constantly dispensed his money to hundreds of poor families throughout the country."

Rabbi Yeshayah followed in the footsteps of the great tzaddikim. The chassidic master, Rabbi Dovid of Lelov, was famous for his unparalleled ahavas Yisrael, which had manifested itself when he was yet a child. When Dovid was seven, his father — a man of meager means — saved up enough money to buy the child a warm coat for the winter. The first day at cheder (Hebrew school) young Dovid noticed that another child was shabbily dressed and shivering in the cold and he promptly gave his new coat to this child.

When Dovid returned home without the new coat, his mother asked him where he had left it. "I did not leave it any-where," Dovid said. "I gave it to a poor child who had none."

"Quickly run and retrieve the coat before your father comes home," the mother said. "You know how long he has been saving to buy you that coat. When he sees you have given it away, he will become angry and may even whip you."

Dovid responded, "I can bear the pain of a whipping much easier than the pain of seeing another child suffer from the cold."

⊰⊱

As a young man, Rabbi Dovid became a follower of the chassidic master, Rabbi Elimelech of Lizhensk, and he would travel by foot to study under the master. One time, prior to Pesach, Rabbi Dovid followed his usual path through the forest to Lizhensk, carrying with him two peels (bakers' shovels) for baking the Pesach matzah. Although he had followed this path many times previously, Rabbi Dovid became lost in the thick forest. Unable to find his way out, he began to pray tearfully for Divine assistance.

Suddenly a man appeared as if from nowhere, inquiring as to his crying. "This never happened to me before," Rabbi Dovid said. "I know all the paths in this forest, yet I cannot find my way out, and I want to reach the master in time to bring him these utensils for baking the matzos."

"Just follow me," the man said, and as he led the way, the man said, "Let me tell you two bits of wisdom. Firstly, two pieces of wood can never fit tightly together as long as there is roughness on the surfaces that will separate them. They must be planed and sanded to eliminate the roughness, and then they can be joined. Secondly, rather than examine others and take their inventory, it is better to examine yourself and take your own." Soon they were out of the forest, and as abruptly as he appeared, the man disappeared.

Many years later, Rabbi Dovid related this incident, and said, "I am sure that this man was none other than Elijah the Prophet. What he taught me were the foundations for *ahavas Yisrael*. If you feel you are not close to another person, it is probably because there is roughness on your surface that prevents the adhesion. Get rid of your character defects, and you will see you can be joined together. Secondly, one should concentrate on improving one's own character, rather than sitting in judgment of others."

Rabbi Dovid thrived on making people happy. When he came into a town, he would hire a horse and wagon, and when the children came out of *cheder*, he would give them candy, listen to their reciting the *berachah* (blessing), and have the driver take them for a little ride about the town.

Incidentally, one of the most devoted followers of Rabbi Dovid was the famous Dr. Bernard, who had been totally alienated from Torah observance and became a sincere *baal teshuvah*.

Dr. Bernard was called to see a patient in consultation, and found that the patient's condition was terminal. He had nothing to offer in the way of treatment. A year later, he happened to meet this patient, who was robust and healthy. The patient told Dr. Bernard that because he felt his last days were approaching, he went to take leave of his master, Rabbi Dovid. The latter blessed him that he should recover, and since then his health improved. Dr. Bernard then visited Rabbi Dovid and was so completely overcome by the Rebbe's holiness, that he began taking an interest in Judaism and became a totally observant Jew as well as a Talmudic scholar.

Rabbi Dovid's *ahavas Yisrael* was manifested in yet another way, as the following story indicates.

One time, when Rabbi Dovid was making his way on foot to the chassidic master at Lizhensk, he saw a coach drawn by fine horses approaching. On learning that the coach was headed toward Lizhensk, he asked to hitch a ride, and on entering the coach found himself in the presence of a wealthy merchant from Warsaw who was en route to Rabbi Elimelech. The merchant, seeing the young man in tattered clothes, began poking fun at him. When they arrived in Lizhensk, the merchant was surprised to see how warmly Rabbi Elimelech welcomed this young man.

Shortly before the merchant left Lizhensk, Rabbi Dovid said to him, "If you hear a cry for help on your way home, use your good judgment."

Having noted the high regard of Rabbi Elimelech for this young man, the merchant took Rabbi Dovid's words to heart. And indeed, on his way home, he heard a cry for help. Following the direction of the sound, he came upon a horse and coach that were trapped in quicksand. He threw a rope to the man struggling in the quicksand, and attaching the other end to the horse's harness, pulled the sinking man to safety. Upon learning that this man was from Warsaw, the merchant said, "I too am from Warsaw, and you can come home with me."

On arriving at his home, the merchant gave the man dry clothes as well as some food and drink, and allowed him to rest from the exhaustion of his long struggle in the quicksand.

Several days later the merchant received a request to come to a government office, where he found the man he had saved to be a government official, who wished to reward him for having saved his life. "I need no reward," the merchant said. "I am wealthy enough, and I am pleased that I had the privilege of doing a mitzvah in saving someone."

"Then let me have your name and address," the officer said, "so that we may remain in contact." The merchant gladly provided this.

As years went by, the merchant's fortunes took a turn for the worse, and eventually he was impoverished to the point where he joined a troupe of beggars who went from village to village. After a long journey collecting alms, he returned to Warsaw.

One day the merchant passed by a fine coach that had come to a stop, and taking off his hat, he asked for alms. "Come into my coach," the rider said. The merchant, fearing that the officer in the coach wished to penalize him for so-liciting funds, began running away. Soon he was overtaken by the coach, and forced to enter.

"Relax, my dear man," the officer in the coach said. "Can you tell me your name?" When the merchant provided his name, the officer asked "Do you recognize me?"

"How can your lordship expect me to recognize him?" the merchant responded.

"Let me remind you. You may remember that many years ago you saved a person who was sinking in quick-sand. That person is me."

The officer then inquired as to what had befallen the merchant that he had become so impoverished. After hearing the tale of woe, the officer said, "I am now the governor of the area. You are to take this note and discount it at the bank for 2,000 rubles, and try your luck again at business." The merchant did so, and his efforts were blessed with success, eventually restoring him to a status of wealth.

During these years, Rabbi Dovid had become a chassidic master in his own right, and the merchant, who was now once again a prominent citizen, went to visit the new master, whom he did not recognize as the young man in tattered clothes whom he had taunted so many years earlier.

Rabbi Dovid reminded him of the incident and said, "You must know that at that time that you humiliated me, your sin resulted in a harsh Divine judgment, whereby you had forfeited your life. When I spoke with our great master, Rabbi Elimelech, we decided to pray and intervene that your sentence be commuted, and instead of losing your life, you lost your wealth. But no good deed goes un-rewarded. Because you were kind enough to give me a ride to Lizhensk, you were rewarded with being restored to wealth once again."

There Is No
Justifiable Rage

T he ethical works repeatedly stress the importance of
avoiding rage. In his famous letter to his son, Ramban
emphasizes that control of anger is the first step toward
spirituality. Indeed, Rambam states that Moses was denied his fervent wish to enter the Promised Land because he once
reprimanded the Israelites with rage. The Talmud describes the
destructive nature of rage very graphically: "If one is in rage, all
the forces of *Gehinnom* take mastery over him" (*Nedarim* 22a).

Moses' anger was indeed justified by the Israelites' behavior,
but he was punished because he allowed his anger to develop
into rage. Even when justified, the Torah demands that a person
be in control of anger.

In 1848, there was a vicious epidemic of cholera in Vilna. This is when Rabbi Yisrael of Salant, the outstanding ethicist, instructed the Jews of Vilna to drink on Yom Kippur, because dehydration is the mechanism whereby cholera causes death. Concerned that some pious Jews might refuse to break the fast of Yom Kippur, the great sage mounted the pulpit and publicly drank some water, to convince everyone that it was not only permissible but also obligatory to drink in order to preserve one's health and life.

One Friday night during the epidemic, Rabbi Yisrael instructed several of his students who attended the sick to do whatever was necessary for their care, i.e., to chop wood, light the furnace, and boil water for the sick on the Sabbath.

One of the Jews of Vilna came to thank Rabbi Yisrael for having sent his students to attend his grandson, who had recovered from cholera. In the presence of the students, the man said to Rabbi Yisrael, "However, with all due respect, I must be honest with you. Although it is of course permissible to violate the Shabbos when there is a threat to life, I feel that your students took too many liberties, doing some things that could have been avoided. For example, I saw that one young man continued chopping wood even though there was already enough fuel for the fire. They should be instructed to keep their violation of Shabbos to a bare minimum."

Rabbi Yisrael who was never known to have raised his voice, this time shouted at the man. "You boor!" he said. "Who are you to tell me what is permissible and what is not permissible on the Shabbos? I am the one who carries the responsibility for the welfare of the community on my shoulders, and I will be the one who decides what may or may not be done!" The man realized he had spoken out of turn, and immediately apologized to the great sage.

Rabbi Yisrael later explained that he had to protest so vociferously because the man had made his comments in the presence of the students. "Had I not shouted at him, the students who had heard his words might have been somewhat restrictive in attending the sick on Shabbos, and may have inadvertently not done everything that was necessary. I had no choice but to make a dramatic statement in the presence of the students."

Yet, for the remainder of his life, Rabbi Yisrael castigated himself for this show of anger. "I was indeed justified," he said, "but even justified anger should never be permitted to escalate into rage." To the very end of his life, the great sage did not forget this single incident when he raised his voice in reprimand.

Although our great personages were most diligent in the strict observance of all *halachic* requirements, and often had to reprimand others who were lax in their observance, they were cautious to deliver their reprimand in a pleasant manner rather than in rage.

On the afternoon before Pesach, when his chassidim were baking matzos for the Seder, the Rabbi of Vitzhnitz noted that one of his supervisors had shouted at one of the participants for not being more agile in rolling out the matzah dough. "One must never shout," the Rabbi said.

The supervisor defended himself, "But Rabbi, even the minutest trace of chametz is forbidden."

"Of course," said the Rabbi. "But the minutest trace of rage is an even greater transgression than the minutest trace of chametz."

The Talmud relates that it was impossible to provoke the great sage Hillel into rage. Two thousand years later, Rabbi Chaim Ozer of Vilna followed in the footsteps of Hillel.

A young man informed Rabbi Chaim Ozer that his father had applied for the post of rabbi in a nearby community, and that he was certain that if Rabbi Chaim Ozer would endorse his candidacy, he would be selected for the position.

Rabbi Chaim Ozer felt that the candidate lacked the qualifications for the position, but wished to avoid saying this to the son. Instead, he tried to explain to the son that it was his practice not to interfere in the affairs of other communities, and that the elders would certainly make a good judgment.

The son became enraged, and began shouting at Rabbi Chaim Ozer with brazen chutzpah, accusing him of being insensitive to his father's needs, and being derelict in his responsibility to support Torah scholars. Rabbi Chaim Ozer listened to this diatribe very quietly, trying to pacify the young man, whose disrespectful talk was now peppered with insulting terms. Rabbi Chaim Ozer then arose and politely excused himself.

The people who witnessed this scene were furious at the young man's unforgivable audacity, and later said to Rabbi Chaim Ozer, "Even patience and tolerance has its limitations. Why did you not simply silence this upstart?"

Rabbi Chaim Ozer said, "Why do you not understand? This young man was moved by his consideration for his father. How could I become enraged over that?"

We are often provoked to anger by things that we deem to be unjust, particularly when we are personally offended. We may be unaware that although we think our anger is justified, our perception may be faulty.

A chassid once came to his rebbe, complaining that another person had caused him to lose a large sum of money by preempting a deal which he had hoped to make. "He deserves to be punished," he said. "The rebbe must bring down the wrath of G-d upon him."

The rebbe said, "Have you ever noticed small children at play? One child builds a tall building with his blocks, and then another child gleefully topples it. The first child begins to cry and runs to his father to report what the other child did to him, and requesting that his father hit the offending child. Years later he may look back at this juvenile episode and realize how foolish it would have been had his father responded to his request to punish the other child for what was in fact a trivial matter, even though from a child's perspective it appeared to be a major offense.

"What you are reacting to now is what you currently perceive as a major offense. If you will be able to look at this incident from a more mature, spiritual perspective, you will be able to see this as hardly even deserving of notice."

The key word is "justifiable." We must realize that although justice is an intellectual concept, what we think to be just or unjust often depends on our emotions, which then causes us to exercise our intellectual capacities in a way that is compatible with the emotion.

Epilogue:
And Just What
Is Chassidus?

Having related numerous stories about various chassidic masters and *chassidim*, I think I may have answered a question that was not asked at the outset, and it was really not my conscious intent to do so.

Students of Judaism often asked: Just what is *chassidus*? In what way does *chassidus* differ from the observance of Torah that preceded the Baal Shem Tov? Is *chassidus* synonymous with *kabbalah*, the study of the esoteric portion of the Torah? What innovations did the Baal Shem Tov bring about in Judaism?

I have never been able to adequately define *chassidus* to my satisfaction. The chassidic literature is voluminous, but there is no single thread that flows through it. The *Tanya* is a basic chassidic text, but is quite different than other chassidic classics, such as the *Bnei Yissaschar* or the *Be'er Mayim Chaim*.

Chassidus emphasizes love of one's neighbor, but this is hardly a chassidic innovation. *Chassidus* stresses the importance of devotion in prayer, but again cannot claim this as its own. *Chassidus* requires that there be no distinction between what is G-dly and what is non-G-dly, because everything one does must be dedicated to the Divine service. One eats and sleeps and works and does all that is necessary for optimum survival and functioning, so that one can properly serve G-d; hence, everything is ultimately dedicated toward the Divine service. But this concept can be found in Scripture and in the Talmud, and is elaborated upon in the *Path of the Just*, which antedated the Baal Shem Tov. *Chassidus* teaches that a person should always be joyous and accept everything that happens as the Divine will. Even things that are unpleasant or frankly distressful are part of the Divine plan, and since a person's goal should be to merit to see the fulfillment of the Divine plan, one should accept even adversity with joy. Again, this is not a unique chassidic concept. *Chassidus* calls for attaching oneself to a *tzaddik* and being guided by his instructions. This, too, can be found in the Talmud and other ethical writings. *Chassidus* teaches that no Jew can be totally detached from G-d, and that ultimately all Jewish *neshamos* will be reunited with G-d. This is an ancient *kabbalistic* concept. *Chassidus* emphasizes imminent expectation of the Redemption, but this is one of the thirteen principles of faith stated by the Rambam. What is found in the teachings of the Baal Shem Tov and his successors can also be found in Torah writings that preceded *chassidus*. What, if anything, gives *chassidus* its uniqueness?

Perhaps we may better understand *chassidus* by an analogy to the remarks made by Rabbi Chaskel Halberstam, when he eulogized his father, the *tzaddik* of Sanz. He said, "The Talmud states that the world rests on three pillars: Torah, the Divine service, and acts of benevolence. My father was an outstanding

Torah scholar, but no doubt there were other Torah scholars as great as he was. My father was outstanding in his absolute devotion in the service of G-d, but undoubtedly there were others who were equally as great. My father was outstanding in *tzeddakah,* but there were certainly others equally as great. But for all three, Torah, service of G-d, and *gemilas chassadim,* to be found together in one person in the degree of excellence which my father possessed, that was something totally unique."

Yes, *chassidus* contained the features that existed in pre-chassidic Judaism, and we can find them all in Torah literature that preceded the Baal Shem Tov. But for all of these to be brought together in the way that they were, that was the uniqueness of *chassidus.*

But what about those who are not part of the chassidic movement? Did they not synthesize all these spiritual achievements?

Of course they did, and it is a fundamental mistake to dichotomize *chassidim* and non-*chassidim.* It is more than coincidence that the arch-opponent of *chassidism,* the saintly Gaon of Vilna, is always referred to as "the *chassid."*

Throughout Jewish history, Torah leaders have always provided for the needs of their times. History is replete with incidents of two ideas or two discoveries that occurred independently, with the two parties involved having no contact with one another and not being aware of the other's work.

The Baal Shem Tov, Rabbi Moshe Chaim Luzzatto, the Gaon of Vilna, and Rabbi Chaim of Volozhin, lived in the same era. Rabbi Yisrael of Salant not too long after them. For all intents and purposes, their teachings are identical. *Mesillas Yesharim* of Rabbi Moshe Chaim Luzzatto and *Nefesh HaChaim* of Rabbi Chaim of Volozhin can be considered chassidic texts in terms of their content.

There were valid reasons for the opposition to the early chassidic movement, but these have long since faded into history. One would be hard pressed to find major differences between the teachings of *chassidus* and those of *mussar.*